THE BEAVER MEN

Spearheads of Empire

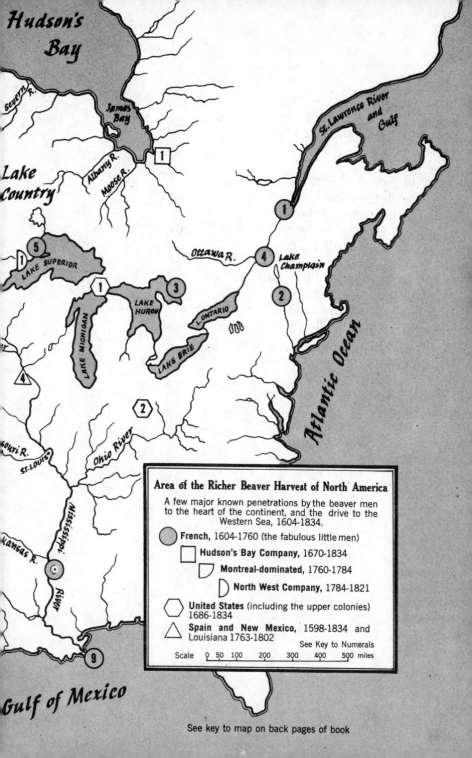

Hudson's Bay

Severn R.

James Bay

Albany R.

Moose R.

Lake Country

Lake Superior

LAKE MICHIGAN

LAKE HURON

Ottawa R.

Lake Champlain

L. ONTARIO

LAKE ERIE

St. Lawrence River and Gulf

Atlantic Ocean

Ohio River

Souri R.

ST. LOUIS

Kansas R.

Mississippi River

Gulf of Mexico

Area of the Richer Beaver Harvest of North America

A few major known penetrations by the beaver men to the heart of the continent, and the drive to the Western Sea, 1604-1834.

⬤ **French, 1604-1760 (the fabulous little men)**

☐ **Hudson's Bay Company, 1670-1834**

◗ **Montreal-dominated, 1760-1784**

◖ **North West Company, 1784-1821**

⬡ **United States** (including the upper colonies) 1686-1834

△ **Spain and New Mexico,** 1598-1834 and Louisiana 1763-1802

See Key to Numerals

Scale 0 50 100 200 300 400 500 miles

See key to map on back pages of book

Books by Mari Sandoz
published by the UNP

The Beaver Men (BB 658)
The Buffalo Hunters (BB 659)
The Cattlemen (BB 660)
The Christmas of the Phonograph Records
Crazy Horse (BB 110)
Hostiles and Friendlies
Love Song to the Plains (BB 349)
Old Jules (BB 100)
Sandhill Sundays and Other Recollections
Son of the Gamblin' Man (BB 626)

THE
BEAVER
MEN

Spearheads of Empire

By **MARI SANDOZ**

UNIVERSITY OF NEBRASKA PRESS • LINCOLN / LONDON

First Bison Book printing: 1978

Most recent printing indicated by first digit below:
1   2   3   4   5   6   7   8   9   10

Library of Congress Cataloging in Publication Data

Sandoz, Mari, 1896–1966.
   The beaver men.

   "Bison book edition."
   Reprint of the ed. published by Hastings House, New York, in American procession series.
   Bibliography: p. 316
   1. The West—History—To 1848.   2. Northwest, Canadian—History.
3. Fur trade—The West.   4. Fur trade—Northwest, Canadian.   I. Title.
[F592.S2   1978]   978   77–14081
ISBN 0–8032–5884–4

Bison Book edition published by arrangement with Hastings House, Publishers, Inc.
Manufactured in the United States of America

CONTENTS

ACKNOWLEDGMENTS   xii

FOREWORD   xiii

BOOK I. *SOFT GOLD*

1. Bearded Men and Summer Fairs   3

2. Castor, Guardian of Hospitality   22

3. Paddle and Portage   45

4. Still Ponds and War Whoops   66

BOOK II. *THE RISE OF THE COMPANY*

1. River to the "Vermillion Sea"   85

2. The Romantic Explorations   103

3. The Gentlemen Adventurers   129

4. A Daring Race of Scots   146

5. The Five Villages—International Prey   168

BOOK III. *THE FIERCER RIVALRIES*

1. Voyageurs of the Plains   185

2. Americans to the Western Sea   198

3. Winter of the Explorers   217

4. Fur Fair and Blackfeet Wall   233

5. Pursuit of the Eternal Remnant   256

6. Romantic Buckskin to the Last *Boisson*   276

7. "Gone" Rendezvous and Foppish Silk   301

NOTES   313

BIBLIOGRAPHY   316

INDEX   323

KEY TO MAP ON PAGES ii–iii   333

ILLUSTRATIONS

Map on pages ii–iii: Area of the Richer Beaver Harvest in North America

Between Pages 144-145

    Giant prehistoric beaver

    Beaver making a stand

    Inset from Moll's "Map of the Dominions of the King of
       Great Britain"

    Hudson's Bay Company beaver token

    La Verendrye's expedition leaving Montreal

    Modifications of the beaver hat

    A trapper and trader of the Old Régime

    Hidatsa village of Upper Missouri (Catlin)

    Ball play of Sioux Indians

    Trapping for beaver

    Beaver plaque in Astor Place subway station

    Pawnee council at Long's Expedition encampment

    Modern trap to catch beaver uninjured

    Summer work of beavers

ACKNOWLEDGMENTS

There is no adequate way to express my gratitude for the information in this book, first to the Indians and old-timers who, with their ancestors, lived much of the story and, second, to all the people who have dedicated their lives to the accumulation of the early records and accounts and to making the material available to the researcher. Among the institutions of outstanding assistance are: Nebraska State Historical Society; Western History Division, Denver Public Library; Colorado State Historical Society; Wyoming State Archives and Historical Department; Library, University of Wyoming; Kansas State Historical Society; Oklahoma Historical Society; Barker Texas History Center, University of Texas; Panhandle Plains Historical Museum; American History and Map Divisions, New York Public Library; New-York Historical Society; War Records and Indian Records, National Archives; and finally the resourceful and tireless Marie Baboyant, Civic Library, Montreal, Canada, and the accommodating staff of W. Kaye Lamb, Archivist, Dominion Archives of Canada, Ottawa.

M. S.

FOREWORD

Now and then, in a passing crowd, I catch a whiff of musky perfume that carries me back to my early childhood and the smell of sweetish, musky castoreum when someone, perhaps father, touched the soft belly pelt of a beaver to my cheek. Later one of my first lessons on the old treadle sewing machine was making beaver sacks from discarded levis, to be filled with sand or earth and fastened to steel traps to drag the captured beaver down, drown him before he could twist his foot off and be lost, left a cripple. The sacks were to help eliminate a family of beavers that had moved in near some of our relatives and were carrying away cabbage and kohlrabi from the fall gardens, sinking the vegetables near their new lodge for winter feed.

By that time the household of Old Jules Sandoz on the upper Niobrara River had heard a great deal about beavers from the Sioux—stories from old Indians and from the descendants of the early fur men among them, men with such names as Lebeau, Bouchay (Boucher), Beauvais, Mousseau, Larvie (Lariviere), Pourier, Salaway, Bissonnett, Charbonneau and so on. While the mixed-bloods still alive were largely from the time of the buffalo robes, Overlanders and gold strikes, most of their French ancestors had pushed westward out of early Montreal following the shrinking beaver along the lakes and across the Great Plains to the mountains. Practically all the old, old stories were concerned with the beaver or his disappearance.

Gradually I became interested in this orderly, inoffensive creature, his fossil ancestors represented by the curved tooth that

xiii

hung on the breast of a Sioux friend of father's—a tooth four, five times as large as those of the beaver skull nailed up outside our house, almost as large as the ones from the fossil beds of the Niobrara country. His great contemporaries, the mammoth and the mastodon, had disappeared but the beaver just became smaller. The glaciers withdrew and the water he needed filled lakes and dried up, the river beds shifted and changed and perhaps vanished. He survived and burgeoned greatly until the white man came with powder and iron.

It was a sobering thought, and made me feel a little sick under the waistband of my calico dress, much as when Old Jules talked of the spiral nebula that he believed fathered the universe. Sobering, also, was his anger about the deforestation, the overgrazing and poor farming that bared the top soil to the roaring spring waters sweeping to the sea, and the consequences he feared —our region a bald and denuded wasteland, all its riches gone the way of the beaver and the buffalo, and the aborigine too, driven to arid reservations.

Gradually I discovered that what the white man did to the Great Plains, good and bad, was largely a repetition of what man of any color did elsewhere, Europe, say, or Asia, from Stone Age to the present. In the older regions, the process had been very gradual, so protracted that much of the record was lost. On the Plains the transition was swift, the tangible records preserved in local repositories or farther away, and amazingly complete, much of what happened still visible on the earth itself, much of the story still within the memory of the great-grandfathers, ready for investigation, ready for anyone who would listen.

To understand something of so-called modern man on the Great Plains, I found myself planning a six-book study to cover the entire period, beginning, chronologically, with the beaver men of the 17th and 18th centuries who gathered much of the riches that fired the appetite for empire in the great courts of Europe and dictated their foreign policy over much of America and Europe too, so long as the beaver lasted. Then there was the story of the Plains Indians, symbolized and crystallized, it seemed to me, in the life of the Sioux war chief Crazy Horse, from 1854, when the white-man forts were little islands in a great sea of buffaloes and Indians, to twenty-three years later, when the buffalo was gone, the Indians on little islands in a wide sea of white-man country. The rebellion against the reservation system was epitomized in the flight of the Northern Cheyennes from the sickness and starvation of Indian Territory in 1878-79.

At this chronological period, at the suggestion of my publisher, I added a book on the buffalo hunters and the great herds that they destroyed. Then there had to be an over-all account of the cattlemen, from Coronado to the present, added to the volume on the settlers—the biography of my father, *Old Jules*.

Now only one book of the series remains to be written, the one that is to illustrate the rise of Plains-rooted power that grasps for wealth anywhere in the world and often molds the nation's foreign policy, reversing the era when the Plains were the prey of empires seeking the power of beaver gold and of a river that was to lead to the Western Sea and the wealth of China.

When the series, now grown to seven volumes, is done, I hope to understand something of the white man's incumbency on the Great Plains from Stone Age Indian to the present, to understand something of what modern man does to such a region, and what it does to him.

M. S.

BOOK I

SOFT GOLD

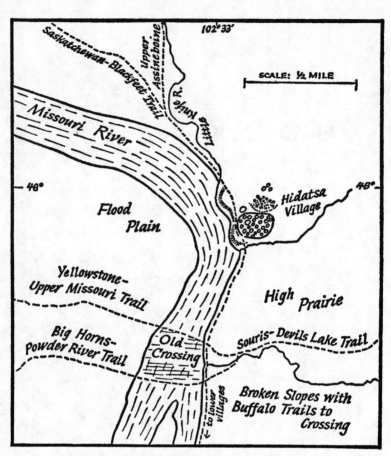

**THE VILLAGE OF THE BEARDED MEN and the
OLD CROSSING OF THE MISSOURI RIVER**

(Based on maps of Missouri River Commission, 1894, and Missouri River
Diversion, U. S. Engineers, 1943. The point to which trails led, which
held the Hidatsa village described by old Indian accounts and by
Verendrye, was washed away in late 1700's).

CHAPTER I

BEARDED MEN* AND
SUMMER FAIRS

THE evening sun lay warm and brooding on the upper Missouri valley and on the little creek that flowed from the eastern coteau, coming quietly through the yellowing timber of the canyon and a little more noisily over several beaver dams, one after the other. The last pond was very smooth, with only an occasional browning leaf to settle to the shadowed surface under the timber of the bank. Farther out three beaver houses stood solid and gray, the largest wide as a little knoll of roots and mud, with two half-grown beavers on the top, idling and combing their shining brownish fur.

Out on the bottoms young Indians, stripped to breechclout and moccasins, knocked a wool-filled ball flying this way and that with clubs, everybody racing after it, perhaps striking it out from between the feet of an opponent with whoops of triumph. Not until the ball came soaring into the water did either of the young beavers look up, or move, and now only to slide down off the house toward the water, waiting there, looking back over their flat tails as the youths plunged into the pond and wrestled for the floating ball, splashing the water high.

On the benchland overlooking the river twists of smoke rose from domed earth houses just visible above the

* From the old Indian stories, told and retold; see notes.

3

palisade of tree trunks set into the ground. Women in short buckskin dresses worked on the worn space outside of the moated wall. Others, bending low under their burdens, came from the fields along the bottoms where clouds of ducks, geese and sandhill cranes were kept flying by boys and girls shouting and swinging branches with strips of painted hide to flap and pop. Women and old men and children bore in the last of the plums and grapes from the canyons while the herb gatherers trailed in from the browning prairie. At a scout's wolf howl, the youths near the beaver pond stopped their game, picked up their robes and bows and scattered to night guard far out on the coteau and in the other directions.

A signal from off west of the Missouri brought men hurrying down to the cluster of round bullboats lying upside down on the bank. Flipping them up and into the water, they paddled across to pick up the hunting party, ten or twelve of the men carrying antelope across their shoulders. As they came up the rise, maidens ran out to welcome them, to sing the antelope song, while in front of the village the smoke of the cooking fires began to spread.

By now the moon had come to stand a moment on the eastern ridge, meeting the sun's reflected path over the ponds where the beavers had ignored all the man-noises. The encroaching shadows of the timber crept out upon the water and a whiskered nose came gently through the surface, followed by a bit of glossy back as the animal moved before a spreading lance of ripples toward the darkest, brushiest bank. Several other beavers broke the water and headed out to cut wood for the winter food—young willow and cottonwood to be sunk below the deepest ice of the frozen time. The heavy animals crawled out upon the bank, darker forms in the dusk. Snuffling, they set to work at bush and tree, with soft sounds of shaking where they gnawed that stopped as they drew back from the slow, noisy fall and then moved to the work again. One of the old beavers started to drag a sapling across the shadowed grass toward the water, tugging and pulling. Suddenly he stopped, his head lifted and turned back toward the creek. An exploding burst of light broke from the blackness there and knocked the beaver forward, the roar of the blast followed by loud plungings all along the ponds, the echo of the shot lost in the cries of alarm and warning up at the village, and in the shouted orders, the running moccasins.

Down at the pond everything was still except the lap of the disturbed water and a soft kicking from the lone beaver left on the bank. Once he lurched forward, slid half-way into the shallow edge of water, and then lay still.

Silent as the darkness about him, a man moved out of the timber to the shadowy bank, listening, looking off toward the village, still in reflected sun-glow. Then he pulled the beaver out upon the grass by the tail as the figure of another hunter came to stand behind him, peering carefully all around under his palm to shut out the brightness left in the sky, and off toward the village. Breechclouted Indians with bows and spears were racing through streaks of light and shade toward the pond, separating as they came, some to one side, some on the other, in a sort of surround. When the stink of the powder smoke struck them, they stopped, shouting their surprise, their alarm, at this unknown scent, and moved more cautiously, the leader motioning the most impetuous back, beside him. As they neared, one of the hunters stepped out into the fading light, stroking his long beard to show his difference from their smoothness, then holding up his left hand, palm forward, in the sign of friendship, his companion, also bearded, but smaller, close behind him.

Seeing these were only men, of man's stature, not some strange, gigantic, thundering relatives of the civet and the skunk, the warriors whooped and leapt forward, spears poised, arrows set to the bow. Calmly the short stranger pointed a long thin pole out before him. There was another of the fiery roaring blasts and the top of the nearest beaver lodge exploded into the air, sticks and dried mud flying over the pale gleam of water, scattering and falling.

The Indians had jumped back, crying out in awe and fear, but the leader shouted his scorn upon them. "Do you not see that they are the thunder-stick men of whom we have all been told?—those with the hairy faces?" he demanded.

"It is known that these men can also bleed from the pale skin, and die!"

The taller of the strangers nodded to what the Indians seemed to be saying, and coming farther from the shadows, he pushed his ragged sleeve up to show the whiteness underneath.

"Ah-h-h!" the leader exclaimed in triumph, and, motioning the warriors back, he pointed toward the village, making the beckoning sign of welcome.

There were growls of protest to this, but plainly guests, and strange ones, had to be thus welcomed, even enemies, no matter how dangerous. The bearded men were taken up through the late evening light, walking between the leaders and the warriors, the two in ragged and mud-caked cloth, unlike anything those around them had ever seen. But they walked like Indians, the tall one ahead, saying something quietly over his shoulder to his companion, both certainly aware of the covetous eyes on the guns, but ready to thrust the barrels quickly toward anyone approaching too close.

The Indian directly behind the white men was carrying the dead beaver by the tail, holding him away, dark blood still dripping a little off the whiskered nose. He was measuring the big hole in the plump flank, a hole bigger than the fist he held against it, and made without arrow or spear, just the hole and the bleeding and torn flesh. Repeatedly he exclaimed at the wonder of it to those behind him, and to those running out to see and then racing back to send alarm spreading through the village, alarm that such mysterious and powerful weapons were to come into the midst of their families. The flat ground outside of the high palisades darkened with Indians standing to look, the women and children out too, but back, and ready to run for the gates.

Yet there must be no show of fear, and so the guests were taken to the council fire and motioned to sit before the headmen gathered in a solemn and formal half circle. The strangers squatted like the Indians, cross-legged, but still holding the guns, standing tall in the crooks of their arms, the powder horns and ball pockets turned forward so no sly, quick fingers could cut them away, nor were the small bundles on the backs of the men laid aside.

When the long-stemmed pipe of red stone had been filled and passed around the scar-breasted men in silence, the bearded ones took the slow pull at it with more ease than some stranger Indians. Afterward the oldest of the chiefs made a welcoming speech, the words no more intelligible than the wind to the guests but the tone mellow on the cheek. It was answered by the taller stranger, already called Long Beard by the Indians for the wonderful face hair that fell far down his breast, the name by which he would be remembered hundreds of years. Everybody pushed forward to hear the alien words. They had seen the beaver stretched out at a fire off behind the council circle, where men and women too, came to examine the mysterious hole in the fat flank, and then looked toward their guests in alarm and horror.

After a while Long Beard tried some sign talk, awkwardly, and a little strange but the old chief seemed to understand some of it and answered slowly, for understanding, through a young sign talker from an eastern people. Yes, the chief said, it was truly as they had been told by visitors returning from the far southwest, for here among them were two of those pale skins with the thunder sticks, except that they did not have the hard shells like the turtle as the southwest men had, shells that must be chopped away to make a good killing. Nor did these men have big dogs to sit upon as part of themselves. They must be of those described to the village sons who made their youth journeys eastward to the People of the Seven Fires and on past the great sweet-water seas with a war party. They were told of bearded men, with no hard shirts or the big-dogs—men with garments that seemed soft to the eye but were perhaps not to be penetrated either, for all the bearded ones seem to have powerful magic.

When the orations to the strangers were done, the two men made some gifts more wonderful than seemed possible to the head chiefs, one kind that the men called *mireor**—

* Old French for *miroir*.

bright, round image-catchers which held the face for the observer as still water does, but much clearer. The round objects could also catch the firelight and send it far, even to the shadowed bluffs across the river. A scout was called over to test the mirrors against the flake of mica he carried on a rawhide string and exclaimed in dismay at the poor light his sliver of stone cast compared to the work of the others. There were also gifts for the young wives of the chiefs, strings of blue beads, and small cakes of vermilion for the face, a red such as the Indians had never seen except in the evening sky and the fall leaves of the sugar trees or the creeper vines. And for these things there were solid walls of admiring faces shining in the firelight, small children held up high to see, to remember, so the story could still be told in their years of age and feebleness.

Afterward the young women brought the food to the headmen and their guests, wooden bowls of bean soup, and big chunks of fresh roasted antelope set on slabs of cottonwood. The bearded guests drew out weapons three times as long as the stone knives of the Indians, gleaming in the firelight and so sharp that the men cut off large mouthfuls with single thrusts and, spearing the pieces, lifted them to be savored on the tongue. The Indians looked up from their meat, the serving women stopped with their gourd dippers in the air in astonishment, wanting to feel the edges of these weapons, murmuring among themselves, and embarrassed at their unseemly conduct before strangers.

"*Le couteau,*" it seems Long Beard tried to explain in French, tapping the cutting tool, and then spoke some Indian words for *knife,* probably Huron or Ottawa that he had picked up on his way west.

The headmen sat unresponsive, understanding one language no better than the others, none as well as the use of the tool. It was a little more difficult, with the awkward signs, to make the Indians understand that these things—the knife, the beads, the vermilion and much more—could be obtained for the skins of the castor, the beaver, like the one with the hole in the flank. Long Beard did not include the guns in his gestures. It was some time, the old stories tell, before the Indians discovered that even those without special medicine could own a thunder stick—that it could be obtained with hides of their beavers—and that there were other dangerous things to be bought with their animal neighbors.

Soon after dawn a runner came in to say that the meat makers, out a full moon's time, were approaching, hurrying because there were signs of a large war party not far away. Even those watching outside of the chief's house where the palefaces slept went out to look, but only for a moment. A hunter appeared on the river bluffs, a dark figure against the eastern sky. He started down the worn trail and others came close behind him, warriors with bows and shields, those in the lead singing the song of a good hunt, followed by a string of women bowed under bundles of dried meat, some leading big dogs carrying packs or drawing their burdens on stick-drags behind them. The hunters were loaded too, proof of a very good buffalo surround. Finally the rear guard of warriors appeared, bows and spears in their hands, always unencumbered by bundles, always ready for instant defense. Off to the sides, some far out, strode the flankers with their large shields, large enough to protect a lone defender for a little while.

Plainly the hunting party was returning in triumphant pride, unaware of the happenings at their village, unaware that in one boom of a gun at a beaver pond the tribe had been thrust into a new age.

A welcoming escort went out the village gate in the old way but it was very small, the faces looking back, afraid something of the bearded ones might be missed. Only the crippled old man in a mountain-lion skin, an honored old hunter wearing the hide of the animal that had wounded him, led out properly, limping fast. His going shamed more of the young men and women, even a few girls and boys, into joining to sing the meat makers home, rejoicing that no one had been injured by stampede or wounded buffalo, no

one reached by enemy arrow, or captured. The young people
lifted the burdens from those who had carried them a far
distance, even through the uneasy night, and bore them
home in erect pride and gratitude.

Somehow even the old women who usually worked to
teach the girls the care of the meat and the thanking ceremonials were half-hearted in these tasks now, busy telling the
hunting party of all that had happened yesterday and to come
today. There had been two visitors here from the village
down the river when the bearded men arrived. They had
hurried out to send home messages of the strangers with the
powerful and magical things. After the village had quieted
for the late sleep, runners brought news of a planned visit;
everybody of the neighboring people not watching for men
with thunder sticks too, or standing off possible raiders, was
coming up for the evening fires.

The headmen had been awakened and called together. There must be a feast for these neighbors coming,
one proudly made for the great honor of the strangers here
among them. It was not good to use up winter meat for this,
and not a proper feast, so there must be a beaver hunt. But
not among the playmates of their children, the friends of anyone wishing to sit at the ponds in communion with these examples of diligence and orderliness. The beaver neighbors
were only to be thinned a little now and then, one or two
taken for the surprise visit of some far chieftain, and then all
done quietly and decently, with a proper thanking ceremony
for their little brothers of the water. The big hunts, which
damaged the beaver villages and frightened all those left behind, must be made on ponds far from any people, friend or
enemy.

The special hunting scouts sent out immediately in
the night were now signaling that there were no enemies
among the ponds up along White Earth River, nobody around
at all. By the time the sun was two fingers high a man with
the beaver skin and toothed mask of his hunting power led a
party up the trail along the river bluffs, the pale-skinned
visitors behind the hunters, behind the beaver-dog men and

those who carried bundles of stakes and large stone hammers hafted to stout ash handles. They turned up the side stream, so rich in the castor that the Frenchmen had stopped at the rim of the valley in astonishment, pushing their old muskrat caps back at the sight of the ponds, like a string of mica disks on a thong trailing down from the north to the Missouri.

The Indians had stopped back out of sight of the stream while the man with the beaver mask made his medicine pleas to the beavers for enough of their brothers to show a proper honoring of their guests, and promised a good thanking ceremony after the feast. Then the hunters started at the lowest pond. The hammer men drove stakes across the spillway of the dam, so close together that only a very young mink could snake through, and then left several Indians with spears and clubs to kill any animal that might try to climb over the dam. Next several young men swam out to the beaver houses and chopped them open with their stone axes, starting dull sounds of diving deep down, and dark shadows fleeing through the water toward the washes, the escape tunnels that ended far under the bank. By then the dogs were barking, wild with excitement. Released, they ran around the pond, whining, smelling out the washes. Where they stopped to sniff and scratch, the Indians stamped on the sod to follow the direction of the tunnel to the entrance at the water's edge. There they drové more stakes, to close the opening and prevent the beaver's escape into the pond while the hunter kicked the growling dogs aside and tore a hole into the tunnel, usually as large around as the circle of two arms, and half-filled with roily water. A gentle rise and fall of the surface showed the beaver's presence by the breathing. Sometimes the Indian plunged his arm into the hole, dragged the fighting animal out by the tail and gave him a swift blow on the spine back of the head to kill him instantly, before the sharp incisors cut into an arm or a leg. Sometimes the hunter drove a stake with one mighty blow of the stone hammer where the dogs pointed and then dug out the impaled beaver to be dispatched swiftly and thrown on the pile with the rest.

Long Beard, seeing this easy killing, ran in excite-

ment from one dead animal to the next, rubbing his hand
over the soft, dense fur that would have been winter-prime
very soon, reluctantly letting them be taken to the river, to
be rafted down to the women waiting at the roasting fires.

By the time the three ponds had been worked and the
beaver dogs weary and full of rewarding meat, fifty-two of the
fat beavers were dead, surely enough for the feast. Long
Beard became talkative with words and hands, making signs
as well as he could. The traders down the St. Lawrence, down
the great stream of the sweet-water seas, would pay with
knives, hatchets and beads and red paint for the skins of these
beavers.

"Even give the thunder sticks—" he added, patting
the gun across his forearm, trying to make the Indians understand, but this thing of the gun they could not believe.
Surely such power must lie in the magic of a man's own
dreaming, perhaps carried in the medicine bundle, perhaps
in the strange horns these men guarded so carefully.

The dark faces around Long Beard were grave and in-
tent to understand, but watchful too. Some must have thought
of overpowering the two strangers, away from the protection
of the chiefs, but there was the sacredness of the guest over
them. Besides, even the hot-headed warriors must have realized that one had to learn the use of these thunder sticks and
perhaps have the dreamer's gift for the magic.

On the way back the hunters saw a cow elk and her
half-grown bull calf coming out of a patch of brush, to stand,
heads raised. No one was eager for the long sneak to get down
wind from them for a bow shot, but the Little Beard stopped,
took aim by steadying his gun against a tree and fired. The
young elk jumped up in front, as though startled, turned to
run and began to fall, going down to his knees and over, some
Indians running to cut the tawny throat, while others stood
in astonishment, the blast of the gun still in their ears.

"It seems far," they made Little Beard understand.
He grinned, his lips turned back red in the black tangle of
his hairy face. It really was no farther than a good arrow's
flight with the iron point they would soon have instead of the

heavy stone, but the effect of the great noise and stink of the gun pleased the fox-faced little Frenchman.

When the hunters reached the village there was a rising heat shimmer in the fall air over the roasting fires. Some women hurried to butcher the young elk, to be cooked for those whose dreaming forbade the meat of the beaver.

Toward evening several buffalo bulls plodded down to Old Crossing along the same trail that had brought the bearded men to the village on the rise. The bulls stopped to drink and then climbed out on the other side, ignored by a party of far hunters with winter meat approaching the river from the west, to camp there for the night at the place that was sacred to all travelers, man and animal, as free and open to them as to the moving sun. Here all creatures could find a wide, shallow and solid-bottomed way to the other side of the Missouri and the country beyond, east or west.

Up at the village the hunters rested and slept a little, to be awakened by the drumming and the song of the visitors coming up around the river bend, the young from the village going out to welcome them to the feasting, to hear of the medicine sticks, perhaps to see one make a great hole in game without the touching, and then let them think of such things pointed against people, the women and children.

At the row of fires the beavers were roasting in their skins, the tails, livers and other choice bits to be offered to the guests and the headmen and war leaders. The sun settled beyond the river during the orations and the quiet eyeing of the strangers and their possessions, the men seated in the place of honor at the chief's fire. During the feast all the beaver bones were carefully gathered into willow baskets and later taken out through the moonlight by a procession following the beaver medicine man and two bearers of flaming pitch-pine torches. At the nearest pond the bones were dropped into the depths just above the dam, where no dogs or wolves or magpies could dishonor them. Then there was dancing around big fires outside of the village wall, and some sly offers of great advantage to the bearded men if they would come to dwell in the lower village, with good earth lodges of their own and power in the tribe through the relatives of handsome young wives.

Long Beard pushed his cap back to look straight into the eyes of the offering chieftains, one after the other, and shook his head, but there were some who said that the smaller man, the one with the fox face in the short bearding, already cast eyes at one of the maidens from down the river.

The stories vary or are silent about the Village of the Bearded Men the next few years. It seems that many beaver pelts were properly cured for market that first winter and carried eastward by a special party of young Indians early in the spring, early enough to catch those in the upper lakes country going to trade with a tribe far east, the Hurons perhaps. The bearded men told the Indians how it was to be done, and warned the leader of something called firewater, the brandy of the French. This was not to be tasted until after they had obtained the knives, hatchets, needles and awls, and the thin iron for lighter, sharper arrow and spear heads. If they bargained well there might be furs enough for some small luxuries and trinkets too, and a little powder and ball for the two thunder sticks here, if this was possible, although the whites seldom traded these things to the Indians.

When the beaver was thickening his fur again the party returned. They came without signals of joy, and with empty hands. Robbers, perhaps the Iroquois, had waylaid them, as happened to many. The next spring another party went out, not openly but as through enemy country. They traded with the Hurons but were cheated, Long Beard complained. The third return was apparently a triumphant one and when the news of it spread along the Missouri the two Beards, in buckskin now like any Indian of the village, had to help stand off the raiders lured by the stories of wonderful new things. These raiders were surely the first in the region preferring to steal the white-man goods to preparing the beaver hides and making the long journey to market, but they were not the last.

If the Indians are right in dating the coming of the bearded men, the coming of powder and iron, to the upper Missouri during the late 1630's or the earliest 1640's, the first fur fair reached by anyone from the Village of the Bearded Men must have been at Montreal. The fair at the mouth of the Richelieu in 1623 is surely too early, although there were men with reason enough to flee to the wilderness in New France long before that, either from such authority as existed (enforceable by 'flogging, legal for generations after this, even for women) or from vengeance, white or red. There were Indians on the Missouri who had been to Montreal long before the news of the massacre of the Hurons and the missionaries in 1649 sifted westward, men shocked by what had been done in what was plainly dangerous country.

The fur fairs of the St. Lawrence region grew out of the marketing carnival of small-town France, a time of noisy trade and robust entertainment that was enlarged and exaggerated in the transplanting to America. Even the environment contributed to this, although in midsummer, the usual fair time, the roar of the saults, the rapids, of the St. Lawrence above Montreal usually quieted a little as the sun leveled off toward noon. The depths of the water darkened under the white leap and break upon the rocks, and under the boiling flow past the stony, tree-tufted islands. Afterward the foam-streaked river smoothed out a little as it rounded the bend to the fur-trade town and rolled past the Atlantic-worn vessels, their salt-stained canvas furled, the anchors down.

The town lay between the rises toward Mount Royal and the river. Along the bottoms, below the buildings, a commons had been set aside for pasturage and trade, which was fur trade. Here every summer for two weeks or more the dust or the mud was stirred by the soft tread of thousands of moccasins on red man's feet and white. There were wide-spaced rows of temporary booths, log and rough board, and always

the last-minute goods borne up by strings of men bent under
their burdens from some newly arrived vessel. They came
along the muddy paths, past hammerings of the tardy and delayed hurrying to set out their goods as merchants had been
doing in the annual fairs around the world for thousands of
years.

But here there was a difference. Here the earliest parties were brown-skinned men with long black braids of hair,
painted faces and silent feet wandering around, looking,
while their few women remained at the camps at the water
front, looking up to the commons, perhaps wondering about
the new goods this summer, and the feasts and entertainment and dancing to come. After a while one of the Indians
among the booths lifted his head, then others around him
stopped too in the Indian concentration of listening, catching
sounds too far to hear, their brown lips parted to trap the
faintest quiver of air. More and more of them turned to look
off northwest, up the noisy St. Lawrence toward the mouth of
the tamer Ottawa. Seeing these listening Indians told even
the rawest immigrant what was coming, led him to join in the
shouting that went up all over the commons, echoing up the
slope and over the farthest palisade that protected the merchant houses and the scattered dwellings of the town.

"They come!" was the shout carried on the light wind.
"They come!"

Yes, of a certainty the furs from the Great Lakes and
beyond—some of the finest beaver of all—were coming, and
before long the head canoe would appear. In the meantime
rafts loaded with baled peltry were pushing out from the
southern shore of the river, from the small village of tame,
missionary Iroquois, and poled past the scattered islands toward Montreal. There were canoes from the other side too,
and long slender ones from down river, the lines of men at
each side digging their paddles deep, the whole party like a
string of millipedes struggling against the power of even the
lowish summer current and then turning in toward the Montreal shore where bits of foam from the rapids above still ran
in thin lacy threads.

Finally a loud whoop swept over the commons and along the river as the wind brought bits of a far rising song that told the listeners the portage around the wildest saults of the St. Lawrence had been completed and that the crafts were once more afloat, the men fighting the lesser rapids. In a short time the first of these stout, heavily loaded western canoes shot around the bend, a brown figure squatting in the painted prow, the man painted too, with beads swinging on his shiny, gnarled breast, bright brass bands around the upper arms and rings on the fingers that held the feathered lance erect before his paddlers, gaudy too, but struggling hard against the river's thrust. Behind this first canoe came more, as painted and gay, strings of them reaching back out of sight, each as long and loaded as the first, so loaded that it seemed they must all slip under the rolling current. The voyageurs, lean-armed from perhaps a thousand miles of water and portage worked frantically with their paddles, tipping, thrusting, backing, the force of the stream driving them on, the drops from the paddles glistening as the canoes slid between the outcroppings of rock and spraying foam, guided with skill and noisy, joyous concentration.

Other parties followed, Indian or coureur de bois. Shouting, singing, quarreling for space, the canoes turned in at the landing just outside of town until they looked like rows of insect eggs in the neatness of some of nature's creatures. The men poured out upon the muddy bank, tipis of bark and skin went up, and fires began to twist their smoke into the air. Perhaps a great, wide-hulled vessel, belated somewhere, drew in from the far sea, the sails bleached and billowing as they faltered and came down. Eager merchants at the landing strode back and forth, peering under their wide-brimmed beaver hats, arms folded behind them, silver-buckled shoes clumping on the rocky pier, now and then one shouting across the narrowing strip of water to the boats coming in.

Even after the local merchants and those from as far as Quebec and France were ready, and most of the fur men there, no word of business could be spoken until after the proper ceremonies—an official welcome extended to all from the upper stretch of the commons. Finally the little parade of dignitaries came marching down the slope, eight or ten soldiers and two priests escorting the governor in plumed hat and satin coat and breeches in the lead. The governor settled himself in the gilded armchair, his gold-hilted sword across his knees, with the rest of the welcoming company in formal array behind him. Then the Indian chiefs came up, one behind the other according to rank, and seated themselves on the ground, the headmen in the center, the others to one side or the other in a large arc wide as a drawn bow. Now there was the invocation from one of the priests, the lighted pipe went around the Indian chieftains, and the welcoming speech of the governor was translated into Iroquois and Algonquin as he spoke, with perhaps none to explain it all to those of Siouan stock, like those from the Village of the Bearded Men.

In reply one chief after another rose, wrapped the robe or blanket of his high position about him, over one shoulder and under the opposite arm, and spoke with the soft murmurings of the Algonquin, the emphasis of the Iroquois or the Athapascan or perhaps in the gutturals of the Sioux, all orators among people where oration was the power that moved men.

While the bales of furs down at the landings were examined and perhaps evaluated, with credit sticks issued by most buyers, the trading started on the commons. The first requests were always for guns, powder and lead and, as usual, denied. There was some smuggling of those items, but certainly not the opening day of the fair, very public, with gentlemen escorting plumed and bewigged ladies among the picturesque groups, and priests and sometimes gray nuns there too, curious and pleased with the scene. On display at the booths were all the items of the Indian trade, including knives, axes, awls, hoop and sheet iron for arrow and spear points, netting for fish and for beaver, cooking kettles, good red cloth, paint, vermilion, beads and other finery, brass wire for rings, ribbons and gilded trinkets, mirrors by the thousand, and many other offerings.

One item was always in demand—French brandy, particularly by the eastern tribes, many long trapped by alcohol as no beaver was ever ensnared by net or trap or stake-closed wash. Whole tribes like the Montagnais from down around Quebec were sharply reduced, almost destroyed. During this first day of the fair brandy barter would be less open than later, but it was there because alcohol not only brought a high price in beaver for itself but made the purchaser, Indian or mixed-blood, reckless and foolish in all his other trades, sometimes the white man too.

At first the Indians, mostly men but including some women even from the far western tribes, weighed the values carefully, standing in dignity and deliberation, perhaps to savor the pleasure. By evening there was less reserve around the great fires kindled along the avenues of the booths, with feasting on roasted venison, fowl and fish, vegetables too, and ending with the sweets the Indians liked, dark sugars perhaps and *la melasse*. Afterward there was dancing, and the drums too, and singing, and the music of fiddles and flutes, far toward morning. Now and then a voice was lifted in anger or hilarity above the usual Indian tone; perhaps the boisterous one was a Frenchman, one of the coureurs de bois—the bush lopers—or of the many mixed-bloods, with the ambiguity of two cultures and the discipline of neither.

By the second trading day there was plain sign of brandy and high wines, some fermented in the St. Lawrence country from the great yields of wild grapes and other fruits and berries. By the second afternoon the people of Montreal usually took to their homes up along the rise, locked the palisade gates where these had been erected, at least barred the doors and shuttered the windows close, particularly at the large houses belonging to traders dealing in brandy. Yet some of the Indians had come a thousand miles for this heat that raced through the body, for the visions and dreamings it brought while awake, surely something sacred. But in the laughter of the alcohol or its anger and fighting violence before the sickness and the stupor, many ran through the avenues of the commons and up among the houses, brandishing war clubs and knives, singing, shouting, whooping, perhaps stripping off their last garment, the breechclout, in most tribes not to be removed publicly except in deliberate and deadly insult and scorn. Any nuns around covered their shocked faces, and the priests tried to rescue their Christianized charges, to quiet them in spite of insult and worse.

It was grieving too that some Frenchmen, particularly the bush lopers, were as wild in their drinking and fighting, and as ready to strip off their clothing in the heat of the alcohol as any brown-skinned heathen from beyond the lakes. The missionaries, Sulpicians and Jesuits, tried to control at least their countrymen during these wild days when their years of work with the Indians seemed a hopeless waste. They protested the sale of alcohol but the income by which the missions were maintained came from the profits of the fur trade augmented by the foolishness that the liquor brought, even though the town usually fell into chaos all the fair time and for days later.

By the time the fur rendezvous of Montreal had become well established, there were always young men from the far western tribes with some of the more experienced trading groups, as those from the Village of the Bearded Men had come. Usually such young men had been to the lake country in their journey years, that time after the budding warrior had honored his family with a bold exploit or two and before he settled down to larger war duties and a family. It was considered very important that any man rising in the tribe should know something of other places, other peoples. Even so the paddling around the tops of the lakes seemed very long and strange to the youths from the walking country, youths like those Long Beard sent with beaver to Montreal. They could scarcely believe that the world could be so large, and contain all the wonderful things that the whites below the rapids possessed. Usually the newcomers had never seen drunkenness, never tasted firewater, and when they asked why no warrior or policing society kept order, controlled the unseemly conduct, they were told that it would interfere with trade.

Ah-h-h, the trade, they said, not understanding. The

great summer trading fairs of the Indians, from the valley of the Annapolis westward, north and south, were carefully managed.

But then there was no comprehending these pale-faced men here, although some were as smooth-cheeked as any Indian, with not even the down of the skin on chin or jaw, and with curling hair falling over the shoulders, many dressed to gleam and glitter like sun on the rapids, the colors like the drawn bow in the sky after rain. There were women too, among these pale-skinned people, and the stories of these told at the home villages seemed less strange. With their smooth faces and their soft voices, soft as an Indian woman's in the lodge, they seemed less alien, more akin than any of their men.

But perhaps strangest of all to the far Indians were the great winged ships, and the vast mounds of beaver pelts on the piers, great bales and mountains, surely so many that most of the beaver in the world must be dead.

CHAPTER II

CASTOR, GUARDIAN
OF HOSPITALITY

THE beaver is perhaps the world's most orderly and responsible creature, although some authorities say the
Greeks named him castor* for *gastro*, the stomach, which
suggests a self-centered glutton. Plainly the beaver was adaptable. Herbivorous, without defense of hoof, horn, tusk or
carapace, and without speed or guile, the beaver in America
managed to remain practically unchanged, except in size,
from the *castoroides* of the early Pleistocene age until long
after the glacial ice was forgotten. He was a contemporary of
the greatest terrestrial mammals of the earth's history: the
giant, wide-horned bison; the mastodons and mammoths; the
great ground sloths, of which *megatherium* stood twenty
feet tall when he reared up on his hind legs; the saber-tooth
tiger that fed on these bulky creatures; and an early cousin
of the condor, the *teratornis*, with a twelve-foot wing spread,
who cleaned up after the kills.

Castoroides was a giant of his kind too, leaving his remains from central Newfoundland to California, from Alaska
to Florida and Texas—with part of a femur discovered near
the Arctic Circle; a practically complete skeleton seven feet
long, and not fully grown, in Indiana; and an incisor eleven

---

* In Greek mythology Castor, one of the twin sons of Leda, was, according
to one legend, the protector of travelers and the guardian of hospitality.

and a half inches long in Ohio. The more spectacular Ice Age creatures vanished during the later period of the repeated advance and retreat of the continental glaciers which had perhaps initially stimulated the gigantic growth. Not even the mammoth, who managed to grow a thick coat of wool against the cold, survived, probably because the vegetation became scarce. During this time the beaver accommodated his size to the feed but his life changed little otherwise, perhaps because it had served him so well against every predator except man. Unfortunately, with the retreat of the glaciers, man increased so rapidly in Europe that attempts to protect the castor from extinction became necessary. By 1103 a German charter conferred the right to hunt the beaver with other hunting and fishing privileges. In 1182 Pope Lucius III gave a monastary the beaver rights within its bounds and by the 16th century castor reserves were being set up, notably in France and Poland, and still the European beaver was soon extinct except in remote Scandinavia and toward northern Siberia.

In America early man lived in such amity beside the beaver in his pond that there were many millions of the animal when the Europeans came, giant beaver too, at least in legend and tall tale spread all the way from the Eskimo country southward. The Micmac Indians of Nova Scotia claimed to recognize the site of an ancient beaver dam so vast that it had flooded the Annapolis valley, and told stories of beaver teeth six inches wide. Farther west there were legends of immense beaver teeth used to hollow out log canoes. It seems that Nanahbozho or Manabozho (whose legendary exploits were appropriated by Longfellow for his *Hiawatha,* the name of a 16th-century leader of the Iroquois) once chased a giant beaver in Lake Superior, a nice tender one just right for the great man's breakfast. The wily beaver fled toward the falls and to Lake Michigan, where the pursuer flung a stone thirty feet in diameter. He missed the beaver but finally caught up with him in the Ottawa River and dashed his head against the rocky bank, leaving a great rusty-red spot pointed out to the early fur traders.

BEAVER AND ASPEN REGIONS OF NORTH AMERICA

In 1600 the beaver ranged over all the territory enclosed in the heavy black line. The aspen (shaded area), the most widely distributed tree in America, is the favorite food of the beaver, with the cottonwood, found over practically all the remainder of the region, a close second. The less common poplars are also favored, with birches and various other lowland trees and shrubs sometimes utilized. The fur hunters exterminated the beaver over much of the original region but restocking is bringing many new dams to old sites.

Many legends identify the beaver very closely with man. Like some Plains tribes, who attribute their origins to their great benefactor, the buffalo, usually through a buffalo woman, several eastern peoples considered the beaver their tribal ancestor. One of the eight Iroquois divisions called themselves the Beaver People and an Algonquin group near Lake Huron claimed descent from the carcass of the Father of Beavers, the first one of all. Charles Leland identifies Quahbeet, whose tail clappings made the thunder, as the giant beaver of the Algonquins.

These eastern stories give the reader little inkling of how much they may have been altered in the interpretation or the recording, or through contact with Christian teachings, augmented by the Indian's strong desire for approval or advantage.* The imaginative, metaphorical qualities of any poetic people can suffer a great deal of unconscious violence from linguistically inadequate and literal-minded interpreters and recorders.

The early missionary accounts give various creation stories, one from the eastern Indians who believed that in the beginning the world was entirely covered by water and peopled by beavers, musquash and otters, all gigantic. The great beavers dived down and brought up mud from which the Manitou built the earth. The mountain ranges, the waterfalls and the caves were all from mud provided by the giant beavers. The detached boulders so common in some glaciated regions were missiles thrown by enraged spirits trying to stop the work. Some believed that the early animals could speak and that those who used wicked words were killed by Manitou and man was brought forth from their spirits, a typical bit of Indian satire too often wasted on the recorders.

---

* The author found considerable discrepancy between the accounts of members of the same tribe, Sioux or Cheyenne, for instance; even within the same band between long-time agency dwellers and those who had remained out on the buffalo plains well into maturity. Tinges of Christian doctrine and mythology crept into the reservation versions of the basic religious beliefs such as tribal origins, creation myths and culture heroes. Crazy Horse, betrayed by his own people and killed by the conquerors, has become closely identified with Christ.

Apparently the Manitou, to apply the Algonquin name for a hazy sort of sporadic creator, reached out his hand and smoothed the giant beasts gently, reducing them gradually in size and ability to speak and making them more and more subject to man, although he came from the wicked-mouthed ones. The creatures and their spirits retained some power to affect man, some sort of affinity. Even far out on the buffalo plains a sacred bone of the roasted beaver was some-times placed on a medicine, a holy, shrine within the village circle or, as with the Hidatsas, in the medicine house out-side as an offering to all those who had died that the Indian might be fed. The remains of a beaver feast were usually dropped into deep water, as at the Village of the Bearded Men, to keep scavengers of any kind from dishonoring the bones. If this was not done, the beaver would become shy and avoid the hunter and the nets and traps.

The legend-making was not all in the prehistoric past. A Saulteau, a Chippewa, came to see Alexander Henry, the Younger. After lighting his pipe and smoking a while he said he had been to a small river a few years ago, out in a canoe shooting beaver. Through the dusk he noticed a very large animal coming toward him and assuming it was a moose, he raised his gun but it was a Mitche Amicks, a giant beaver, passing very close. Henry heard many stories of this giant among the Saulteaux but wrote "I cannot put any faith in it." Or, probably, in the other Chippewa accounts of immense beavers in Lake Superior, one as large as an island two and a half miles long and half a mile wide, with rumors of a thirty-mile island that was plainly once a beaver.

Many, including the British scientist Charles Fother-gill, seemed certain that these legends were based on fact but the romancers of the 18th and 19th centuries offered tales as fantastic as any Indian legend for truth. There was the fabu-lous nonsense of the *Avantures du Sr. C. Le Beau,* pub-lished in 1738, in which the author claims he saw a dozen beavers on hind legs gnawing down a tree twelve feet in cir-cumference, fifty others cutting up one already down, more beavers off through the timber selecting new trees while two whiskered old-timers sat on their tails directing the work and keeping any reckless youth out of the fall line of the trees. Le Beau insisted that beavers always sent the trees crashing toward the water but others pointed out that timber along streams usually leans that way and naturally falls in that direction, but who wanted facts when the fancy was so beguiling?

In 1824, almost a hundred years after Le Beau, Beltrami, in his *La decouverte des sources du Mississippi,* credited his guides with tales of beavers divided into small bands or tribes, each with a chief and a territory. Any strange beaver caught trespassing was brought before the chief, who meted out the punishment: first offense *ad correctionem,* second, the offender was deprived of his tail "which is the greatest misfortune that can happen to a beaver, for this tail is their cart, upon which they transport, wherever it is desired, mortar, stones, provisions, etc. . . ." A whole tribe of mutilated beavers might organize an avenging attack, winner to take the territory and the pond of the loser.

Naturally such fabulous castors should be provided with a fitting society of fauna and all Le Beau and others had to do was go back to Arnoldus Montanus of 1671 for a picture of the "Wonders of the New World," including an animal resembling a horse but with cloven hoofs, a tail like a wild hog, a shaggy mane and a horn in the center of the forehead—a unicorn. It sounds a little like the Pliocene *synthetoceras,* except that he had the horn on his nose, with a nice, more ordinary pair on top of his head, and lived in North America in an age that ended a million years ago.

But the actuality of the beaver was to prove larger, more fabulous than the most outrageous exaggeration. The accidental felting of fur and wool was known to prehistoric peoples of every continent, but Clement I, Pope about 88 to 97 A.D., is credited with discovering the felting qualities of lamb's wool and became the patron saint of the Hatters' Guild. In Ireland and other Roman Catholic countries festivals to St. Clement are still celebrated November 23.

Beaver fur was long known for its superior felting

qualities. A single particle under the microscope shows scales that overlap, and looks a little like a juniper leaf. Pressed together with steam or hot water the fur became felted cloth. So the castor soon disappeared from Europe and the American beaver became the soft gold of the French—the English, and the Dutch too, for a while, and even the Spaniards, when they could give up the hunt for a more glittering Quivera, and then finally of the Americans.

No physical barriers, not even the wild Atlantic of the 16th century, could be expected to shield innocents of any commercial value from the peculiar avarices of the worldly forever, although the religious conflicts of Europe did help protect the beaver and the Indian of the beaver regions through the century. In 1517 Martin Luther had denounced the sale of indulgences by the Church and so added another conflict to the eternal struggle for power among the rulers of Europe, with new massacres, new refinements of torture. It is true that Cortés began the conquest of Mexico in 1519 but north of the Spaniards most of America was saved from much of the inventions and the enlightenments of the white man for over a hundred years after the Cabots came and departed. Cartier did find iron and French weapons among the Indians he passed in 1534 in his search for a passage to China. The search was blocked by the saults of the still unnamed St. Lawrence—the great rapids above the Indian village called Hochelaga, an Algonquin word he was told meant Beaver Meadows, a prophetic name for the future city at the foot of Mount Royal, the future queen of the beaver trade.

Cartier spent the winter at the river and although he was from St. Malo, much farther north than the St. Lawrence, the weather was rigorous beyond anything these Frenchmen had experienced. They were so ravaged by scurvy that this became known as the disease of the country, meaning the white man's disease there. Cartier's crew might have

learned something from the health of the Indians around
them, something from their dietary habits, but man learns
hard, consciously superior man hardest of all.

Since Cartier there had been other explorers seeking a
passage to the Indies, and more out for gold, both hard gold
and in the shape of furs and fish, many of the fishermen from
the Spanish peninsula, particularly Basques. In 1555, the
Spanish historian Gomara called the river the San Lorenzo,
evidence that Cartier's name of St. Lawrence for a small
bay had already spread to the gulf, and of Spanish familiarity with the region. In 1578 there were 350 vessels fishing at the Grand Banks off Newfoundland—English, French,
Spanish and Portuguese. With the steady drift into fur trading accelerated, trinkets and iron tools and weapons were
spreading far inland. Three years later the profits from one
French ship to the St. Lawrence proved so great, with beaver
blooming into fashion in Paris, that the river soon teemed
with traders. But no one wanted to settle and colonization
became important to hold the French claims. A real attempt
was made in 1598. Prisoners under death sentence willing to
go to New France as colonists were pardoned. They never
reached the mainland.

After the Edict of Nantes, guaranteeing the rights of
the Huguenots and establishing religious freedom, Pierre
Chauvin applied to the king for a monopoly of the St. Lawrence fur trade for twelve years. Chauvin had been sending
three, four trade vessels to America each season for some
time and although he was a Huguenot, he had served the
king well as captain in the royal navy. Henry IV, hoping to
restore the torn and impoverished French empire, added
one condition: Chauvin must take fifty colonists to America
each year until there were 500 located there. In return the
king agreed to bar all others from trade on the river.

The first expedition sailed in 1600, with some colonists, although not the promised fifty. They reached Tadoussac, far below the rapids that had stopped Cartier. Bales of
fur—marten, otter and fox but largely beaver, greeted the
arrival of the great ships while more canoes kept coming in,

slipping down the dark-walled Saguenay River and the broad St. Lawrence, and crossing over from the fur-rich Iroquois country to the south.

All across the continent beavers slept in the sun on their houses, or cut the glassy surface of the ponds with their whiskered noses as they swam and played and worked, but to the east a great fur-trade era had opened, and the race of three nations to build empires on beaver hides.

When Chauvin's expedition returned to France, sixteen colonists stayed behind to gather furs and, it was hoped, establish permanent homes. But Tadoussac, on tidewater, was so foggy, barren and cold that probably all the white men would have died that winter if the Indians had not fed them. When the next summer's trade was done, they went home, all those who survived, to spread their stories of hardship and to make colonization even more difficult. But the sight of the fine bales of beaver rolling out upon the wharf for the hatters brought increasing protests against Chauvin's monopoly, particularly with no colonization. Finally the king authorized two other vessels to enter the fur river, and more crept in illegally. The second attempt to recruit colonists, even from paupers and convicts, also failed.

Chauvin died in 1602. The next year the dead man's partner took Samuel de Champlain along, and sent him up the St. Lawrence to locate more furs, the start of a 250-year pursuit. But the beaver of the lower river was dwindling. Besides, Champlain was to seek out a passage to China. The Montagnais, much like other tribes later, described the great dangers out there toward the setting sun, the cruelty of the Indians, the impassable rapids and the destroying cold, hoping to retain their profitable position as middlemen for the upriver tribes. Champlain was not discouraged. He found the village site of Hochelaga deserted and went on to try the saults, but in spite of his scorn for earlier explorers he was stopped by them too. He did try to work his sailed pinnace up between the islands at Mount Royal but got no farther than the first swift and rock-filled water. He changed to a skiff and five hardy oarsmen who fought the plunging flood but the men were forced to shore. Champlain walked up a league or so to consider the rapids. In plumed hat, full-gathered knee breeches and silver-buckled shoes, his mustache smartly upturned, he talked to all the Indians he could find, by interpreter and by sign, accumulating stories of the western sea and other remarkable and fabulous places to be mapped.

In 1604 Champlain started a fur post at Quebec. The following summers there were still Spanish vessels in the river and plotters hoping to kill Champlain and hand Quebec over to the Basques. Four of the men were put into chains, the head of the leader raised on a pike to the highest point of the new fort, visible far along the river, a warning to over-ambition in white man and red.

The dearth of colonists continued and those who came were largely impoverished laborers or plain beggars and criminals. Most of them had to be fed by the traders to get them through the winters. Some must have made alliances with the Indians, a few marrying into the tribes and becoming members of the woman's family in the matrilinear way, perhaps never to return to the colony, leaving no record of their ends or their blood. Some gathered fur for the trade and became known as coureurs de bois, bush lopers, also generally unnamed. Early accounts of any region usually concern themselves with important men and out-and-out scoundrels.

Champlain was interested in the new country and its animals and people beyond commercial profit. He took notes on the Indians around Quebec, how they lived—almost entirely on eels they caught from the 15th of September to the middle of October and then beaver until January. He described the snowshoes they made for winter travel when the stream lay hard as the white man's iron against paddle and canoe. It seemed to him that the relation of the sexes among

the Indians was rather casual before marriage but afterward
they were chaste. Each Indian prayed in his heart, in his
own way and as he wished, he noted, which was surely one of
the few sympathetic appraisals of Indian religion to come out
of early New France.

In 1609 Champlain went with the Algonquins, the
Hurons and Montagnais up the river later called the Richelieu, his shallop in the long string of canoes paddling southward. As they penetrated deeper and deeper into Iroquois
country, the Indians began to desert but Champlain pushed
on, excited by all the beaver and the beaver sign. Finally,
at the rapids he had to take to a canoe too, and still went on
although there were only fifty-seven of the three hundred Indians left with him and his two Frenchmen. At a lake that he
named Champlain they were finally confronted by a small
Iroquois war party. Champlain's allies hesitated before the
challenge of these enemies, in their tough body armor of
plaited withes, three men, the imposing plumes of chieftain-
ship blowing on their heads, standing tall and firm as rock
before their warriors.

Champlain hid his two companions, divided his allies into two little lines and then came up between in as glorious a stride as he could manage, his arquebus, loaded with
four balls, shining in his hands. The Iroquois exclaimed in
astonishment at a white man fighting among Indians, and
drew their bows. Champlain laid his bearded cheek to the
stock of his gun and fired. With the spit of flame and blue
smoke, the thundering roar, two of the chiefs fell, and one of
the warriors, wounded so he died later. The Indian allies
whooped in wonder and excitement at this power in the
white man's weapon, and charged. A shot from one of the
hidden Frenchmen helped break the Iroquois line. They
fled, leaving everything behind, and were pursued into the
timber where more were killed and ten, twelve prisoners
taken. While the white men stripped the dead, their allies
mutilated the bodies and later began to torture one of the
prisoners with fire brands, burning him little by little, Champlain wrote, and added:

"Then they tore out his nails, and put the fire on the ends of his fingers and on his privy member. Afterward they flayed the top of his head and dripped on top of it a kind of gum all hot; then they pierced his arms near the wrists, and with sticks pulled out sinews, and tore them out by force; and when they saw that they could not get them they cut them. This poor wretch uttered strange cries, and I pitied him when I saw him treated this way; and yet he showed such endurance that one would have said, at times he did not feel any pain."

The Indians urged Champlain to help burn the prisoner but he explained "We kill them at once," apparently forgetting much of recent European, French, history, with the massacre and burning of whole communities and the refined instruments of prolonged torture used. He offered to kill the prisoner with a musket ball. The Indians refused but when Champlain started away he was called back to shoot. Not content with the man dead, the Indians opened his belly, threw the entrails into the lake and took the scalp, as they had of all the others killed in the fight. They cut off the head, the arms and legs, and scattered them. They tore out the heart, chopped it into pieces and thrust bits of it upon the dead man's brother and other companions among the prisoners to eat. The bound Iroquois took the bleeding flesh into their mouths but could not be compelled to swallow the heart of a brother.

Back at the St. Lawrence, the Algonquins went home, and the Hurons too, with protestations of enduring friendship and pleas that Champlain join them in future fights. The French returned to Quebec with the Montagnais. Champlain, jubilant, talked the victory over with the five, six young men he was training in the fur trade, particularly, perhaps, with the seventeen-year-old Etienne Brule, who had a special fondness for Indian life and a quick tongue for their languages. Apparently Champlain was unaware that his active and armed presence in a tribal attack on the Iroquois had turned the most powerful confederation of Indians in

North America into allies of the coming Dutch and English and made these Indians the bitter enemies of the French, an enmity to last 150 years and bring torture and death by knife and firebrand to missionaries, fur men and whole settlements.

Samuel de Champlain was pleased with the riches of fur taken from the Iroquois and hoped to get more. In 1610 the pretense of monopoly in the fur trade was dropped and competing vessels followed him up the St. Lawrence and began to outbid him. The Hurons, of Iroquoian stock and afraid of an avenging attack for last year's foray, didn't come down the river but got their goods through the Algonquins, paying the expected tribute.

The Indians who did come urged Champlain to keep his promise to lead them against their enemy again. He sailed a bark to the same river as last year and joined 400 Indians in an overland attack on an Iroquois fort. He and his five companions were armored in the corselets of pikemen, heavy and cumbersome. The ground was largely marshy, or a tangle of underbrush and timber, with clouds of mosquitoes rising everywhere to the tender white flesh.

The Algonquins and Montagnais hurried ahead and tried to force the enemy barricades before Champlain came up, but were repulsed, some of the boldest of the Montagnais killed and wounded. When the Frenchmen finally arrived, the defeated Indians broke into confident and threatening shouts of war. Once more they charged, painted and whooping, against the roughly circular fort of thick tree trunks set snugly together in the Iroquoian way. This time they attacked under a volley of musket balls, but still they were driven back. As Champlain fired his first shot into the barricade he was struck by a sharp stone-headed arrow in the neck above the armored corselet. He jerked the arrow free and ordered a hot attack of powder and ball. The Iroquois, alarmed by the roar of the guns, the thick, stinking smoke and particularly by the penetration of the lead, were keeping out of sight but resisting vigorously. When the ammunition was almost gone Champlain planned a breeching of the palisades by Indians creeping up behind their shields with ropes to pull a section of logs away.

Help came from the bark, more eager Frenchmen hurrying up with well-supplied arms. Under the protection of the guns an opening was torn in the wall, a small one, but twenty or thirty Indians managed to force their way in, and some of the French too, their swords hacking right and left. The Iroquois tried to flee but were cut down around the barricades. The white men gathered up the booty, getting little but the beaver robes from the bodies. The Indians took the scalps and their prisoners some distance and then set fire to the fort. When the great timbers blazed up, they threw the dead into the flames and danced and whooped around the great burning pile, some of the French among them.

The Indians had kept one body and cut it into quarters to take along to "eat in revenge" they said. On the way home they stopped now and then to torture the prisoners but saved some for the wives and daughters, to avenge their loved ones lost in the Iroquois fighting.

Champlain's picture of the massacre and burning was not unlike one he had recorded of an incident in his voyage to the West Indies earlier, one he had apparently abhorred. The second story of Frenchmen involved in the massacre of the Iroquois was told and signaled far over the Indian country, to be paid for in long, long coin before the tribe was finally conquered. Champlain had helped set the pattern for the expropriation of half a continent, helped sanction the white man's use of every brutality with self-righteousness long after both the Indian country and the beaver were gone.

By 1611 there was much competition for the beaver. Prices were up and the earlier trade regions of the St. Lawrence were practically depleted, many of the dams unrepaired and dry, the houses dead, the bleaching beaver bones a crackling tangle underfoot along the banks and at the old skinning camps. Many, many more beavers had been killed than could be eaten and now none came to feed the hungry. Increasingly the Indians hung around the trading sites, some for the protection of the white man's guns, some for other reasons, becoming beggars, perhaps robbers of far canoes, miserable middlemen in the exchange of maidens for practically anything, chiefly alcohol. Once many Indians refused brandy for their furs but these were gone to far villages or had learned the craving for the firewater that brought visions and thawed the damp bleakness, the frozen cold and hopelessness for a little while. Some of the Montagnais no longer troubled to dry enough food, particularly eels, to carry them through the winter and had to be fed by the traders as the Indians once fed the few wintering white men among them.

To get beaver the trade must push westward. Champlain built a post at Mount Royal, on the bottoms where Indians once tilled the earth. The meadow spots stood deep in grass, the low rises were red with wild strawberries, the brush and timber full of wild plums, cherries and nuts, the hanging vines heavy with grapes. There was good fishing, with deer, caribou, lynx and bear back from the water, and the precious beaver plentiful—at least off north and south, and in the west.

Champlain obtained all the information he could from his young employees living among the Indians, particularly Etienne Brule, who had spent the winter westward from the Ottawa River to learn Indian languages and ways, explore the great seas beyond, if possible, and seek out mines, but always to turn the beaver harvest toward his employer. There were many trader ships in the river now, even up around Mount Royal, but the Indians taunted these competitors, accusing them of making war only on the beaver, with no wish to help as Champlain had, in the fights against the Iroquois, coming with their own guns now, Dutch guns, and with a fierceness none had ever seen in the warring before.

Champlain protested against the competition of the outside traders, mostly Huguenots, and although he got his start through one of them, he had now become a fervent

Catholic. But he had something of greater importance on his mind. A coureur de bois named Vignau had come from the Indians claiming he had followed the Ottawa River to its source in a great lake and northward to the salt sea, where a wrecked English ship lay. Champlain set out in two canoes with Vignau as guide to what might be a passage to China. After arduous distances and portages, Champlain discovered that Vignau had never been in the regions he claimed. Disappointed, but not empty-handed, the trader returned with eighty canoes of fur.

The story of the wrecked English ship in a bay to the north fitted into the wild rumors about an explorer named Hudson. For years the Dutch and the English had been busy along the Atlantic seaboard, not only in the fur trade but also seeking a passage to India. Apparently both nations had sent out the mysterious sea captain, Henry Hudson, to probe the northern regions. Little had been heard of the man before the spring of 1607 when he appeared in the employ of the Muscovy Company, an English trading concern organized fifty-four years earlier with Russian ties and including another Henry Hudson. During the captain's earlier voyages to America he had explored Delaware Bay and the Hudson River for the Dutch. The spring of 1610 he sailed under British auspices and wintered on the great bay of the north, where his mutinous crew, starving and ill, set Hudson, his son and several very sick sailors adrift in a boat. The great waste of water that was to bear the explorer's name became his tomb as well as his monument. Vessels sailing by order of the Prince of Wales and the Russian company came searching for Hudson in 1612 but all that resulted from this was the British claim to the vast region drained by the bay, putting them on two sides of New France, above and below.

Perhaps someone saw these holdings as the jaws of a trap to squeeze the French out. Colonization of the St. Lawrence country was stressed once more. The year 1614 was unprofitable; the Indians followed the warpath instead of the beaver. In the spring Champlain returned with heightened zeal. He brought four gray-garbed Recollet friars to work with the natives and to minister to the colonists, still largely to come.

The pattern of the fur business was changing. Indians, particularly the Hurons, carried away large stocks of goods for trade with the tribes farther west, still rich in beaver. Huron territory, around Georgian Bay, was never really game country and now they sent out few hunting parties, depending on the profit in the commerce learned from Champlain's young men, mostly from Brule, married into the tribe. They spread their influence and their domination southward and far west, beyond the lakes, competing with the Iroquois and their Dutch suppliers. They worked to keep any far tribes from reaching Montreal without paying tribute even if the parties were too strong to give up their furs.

Brule, usually dressed and painted like an Indian now, a black-bearded one, guided his employer up the handsome Ottawa River, truly an excellent route to the vast beaver regions of the upper lakes and beyond. From Georgian Bay Champlain turned south on the old Iroquois trail toward Lake Ontario and joined the Hurons on a mismanaged expedition against an Onondaga fort south of the lake. Knowing the fear of the so-called French Indians for all the Iroquois Confederation, and their tendency to slip away before an encounter, Champlain had sent Brule to bring the Susquehannocks up from along the river of their name. They didn't arrive in time, perhaps because the chiefs knew how to keep out of other people's fights. At the fort the Hurons didn't make the disciplined, white-man attack Champlain had planned. He was wounded and had to spend the winter with the Indians and never led them into battle against the Iroquois again.

It was apparently three years before Etienne Brule came to meet the still angry Champlain at Three Rivers, displaying his mangled hands to prove that he had been captured and tortured by the Iroquois. Whether Champlain accepted this explanation for the delay or not, he did leave future explorations to Brule and settled down to develop New France, not an easy undertaking. Many of the traders, Catholic and Huguenot, realized that if the missionaries gathered the Indians into settlements around chapels, to confine themselves to agriculture and handcrafts there, profit from Indian furs was done. Champlain still complained against his Huguenot connections, stressing their failure to bring in colonists, perhaps because all settlers must be Catholic. Some merchants feared that colonists too, would injure the trade by displacing the Indians and destroying the fur bearers, mainly the beaver, proved so very vulnerable. Champlain's persistent criticism of his financial backers helped bring his replacement but an appeal to the king restored him to command of most of the trade in New France, and the spring of 1620 he brought his family to Quebec, to stay.

Still trade decayed—through the squabbles among the posts of the St. Lawrence and competition from the English and the Dutch, denounced as heretics by the missionaries, who also preached and wrote against the coureurs de bois as sinful and a degrading influence on the Indians. Unfortunately the bush loper merely went deeper into the woods and the heretics burgeoned, helped, often now, by trade from those sinful bush lopers. Plainly what the commerce of New France needed was new blood, new men primarily traders rather than factionists. An eleven-year monopoly was granted to the experienced De Caën brothers. They were ordered to maintain six missionaries and to bring six Catholic families of at least three members each to New France every year. Champlain was their paid lieutenant, with ten assistants for colonization and trade. In 1621 the new company sent the first ships but without colonists. Apparently nobody fitting the qualifications wanted to come.

These were years of inland exploration, much of it unintentional, by unknowns who disappeared into the west, perhaps never returned, although the furs of their initiative might appear at the trading sites. Brule, with Grenoble and some Hurons, paddled westward, past great sweet-water seas and raging rapids, apparently as far as the western end of Superior, finding an almost continuous screen of islands along the northern shore, protection from the prevailing northwest winds, with enough to blow the mosquitoes away. Below Superior there seemed to be short portages to the great southward streams.

Brule had seen much exciting country and brought back a large ingot of copper and stories to raise new hopes of great mineral wealth in addition to the vast virgin beaver reaches, with no beaver bones bleaching in dishonor. It was an excellent return for the 100 pistoles, approximately $400 a year, that Champlain paid him, at least for a time, largely to turn the Indian fur his way.

Champlain had other interpreters out and in 1622 new tribes came, even some Iroquois with thirty-five loaded canoes for trade and peace. They were welcomed but the next year a party of Algonquins took two Iroquois captives. This and other aggressions led to a renewal of the war that Champlain belatedly tried to stop.

The gathering at the mouth of the Richelieu in 1623 drew sixty canoes of Hurons and Algonquins and some western Indians who complained against those tribes. They always exacted toll for passage through their country, sometimes robbing the parties or turning them back entirely. This was well known. Even the missionaries who coaxed some small southern bands to bring their furs in received Huron threats. When the brandy was opened and the drunkenness and brawling started, missionary protest to both Indian and trader was less than the passing wind.

"They cackle like the mission hens," a bush loper who had felt the sting of missionary criticism wrote.

The company of traders headed by the De Caëns and with Champlain's experience and his young men, like Brule, made a profit for themselves and the crown during the first six years. In 1626 they bought 22,000 skins at $2 each, the best season so far, enough to depress the beaver market in France and to pay a company dividend of forty percent. With that kind of profit in his hide, the beaver could not expect to remain above the struggle for power and gain, or to escape being a pawn in the war of political and religious advantage.

In 1627 Cardinal Richelieu launched a new attack against the Huguenot nobles and, ignoring the five years that remained in the De Caën patent, he established the Company of New France (100 Associates) with himself as the head. The new company was granted the whole St. Lawrence valley, including the trade monopoly, large governmental powers, permission to trade guns to Christian Indians and an agreement to bring in large groups of colonists and foster the missions, all an integral part of the plan to manage New France by church and state.

Unfortunately the company encountered trouble with the first expedition, which sailed in 1628 and was captured by the British. The next year a French fleet appeared in the St. Lawrence to protect New France from the Kertk (Kirk) brothers, who were commissioned by England to conquer it. Champlain sent Etienne Brule and three companions down by canoe to pilot the French to Quebec, but the Kertks had already captured or destroyed all the ships except one and controlled the river. Champlain's men fell into their hands and probably under compulsion (how could he resist when the French fleet succumbed?) Brule piloted the English to Quebec. Champlain surrendered and was treated much as an honored guest.

When New France was restored to Louis XIII and Richelieu in 1632 the De Caëns received a one-year monopoly to recoup the losses from the broken contract. Then the business was returned to the Company of New France, now verging on bankruptcy, with Champlain as governor. He could have had Brule captured and hanged for treason. Certainly he realized that his best representative had been compelled to guide the British (who didn't need much help, not after thousands of vessels had found the way). Perhaps he hesitated to antágonize the Hurons, who considered Brule, or any other man married into the tribe, a Huron. Anyway Brule was far out among the Indians and ignored, in spite of Jesuit complaint that he set a bad example and was a stumbling block to Christianizing the Indians, which was prob-

ably true. He was paid to further the fur harvest, not to mis-
sionize Indians. Besides he was on friendly terms with the
earlier Recollets.

According to rumor Brule drank heavily, and if true,
as much could be said of many other bush lopers and of many
traders and merchants, whether French brandy or Dutch rum
was favored. The Recollet, Brother Sagard, who had apparently learned Huron language and ways from Brule, called
him "much addicted to women." As Champlain's man he had
made trade contacts all the way from the Montagnais
through several Algonquin and Huron divisions and other
tribes, southward and west to Superior. To succeed in Indian
trade it was advisable and often necessary to take a wife in
each tribe. The practice was common from coast to coast
and lasted as long as there were Indians free of reservations.
Everywhere the Indian woman had to have a hunter and
protector, and as the women usually outlived the men, especially in the more violent hunter-warrior tribes, polygamy
was natural.

Rumors began to sift down the river to Quebec,
largely through the Algonquins, that Etienne Brule was dead,
that during June 1633 the Hurons tortured, killed and ate
him. The story came second- and third-hand, with the usual
lurid touches of cannibal accounts, whether of the Hurons of
Georgian Bay or in Marco Polo or suggested in the Old
Testament. Brule was a Huron husband and judging by the
prevalence of the name, he fathered children in the tribe.
Besides there are many discrepancies in the stories. In his
1633 journal in *Jesuit Relations* Father La Jeune wrote:

> "On the last day of June, the French Interpreter who
> had been a long time among these sorcerers, and who
> but recently came from them, came to see us with three
> Savages who were his guests; we gave them something to
> eat; they recognized Father Brebeuf at once, having
> passed a winter with him among the Hurons."

While this might have been Nicolet, Champlain's expert with the Algonquins, not the Hurons, it seems more

probably Brule, supposedly tortured and eaten before this. There is no real evidence that the Hurons or any other tribe, short of desperate starvation, ever ate a fellow tribesman, whether by blood or by marriage.

There was a new trading situation to consider, a very bad one. The Algonquins were forcing the middleman Hurons to sell their furs to them, had just taken over 500 canoe loads, furs that would go to the English. Possibly this was what the Algonquins were trying to hide behind the big smoke about Brule, hoping to prejudice the whites against the Hurons, who would surely come complaining, come for help with guns and powder.

Perhaps Brule had slipped down to Quebec, as seems likely from Father La Jeune's journal, to feel out his standing with Champlain, due to take over after the De Caën extension expired in early July. The results may have caused Brule to flee, leaving the story of his death behind to cover his retreat and save the face of his family's people. More probably the Hurons said they had "eaten" him, meaning disposed of him, used him up. Deposed chieftains were said to have been "eaten," meaning thrown from their high position, used up.

There are many stories of white men suddenly appearing among the Sioux beyond the upper lakes during those years, all the way from the Winnebagos westward, and among the Cheyennes and other tribes. Brule may have been one of the two men who came to the Old Crossing of the Missouri between 1630 and 1640, to the place later called the Village of the Bearded Men but this seems improbable. The two men were apparently less wilderness wise than Brule must have been and without his craving for liquor, unless this, too, was a canard. Perhaps the bearded men of the upper Missouri fermented corn and dried fruits for alcohol that first winter.

Gradually more of the Huron story reached Quebec. Under the date of July 25, 1633, Father Le Jeune mentions that the Huron site was already abandoned, the Indians saying "we separated, and broke up our village on the death of the Frenchman who was killed in our country." The next year smallpox struck the village. Men, women and children sickened and died until practically half of the people lay on the ground. Finally those still able to rise fired their long houses and fled. As they ran and paddled away with their pathetic bundles, trying to carry the sick children along, some thought that a woman's shape appeared in the smoke of the sky. Rumors said it was Brule's sister, seeking revenge.

Later in the year the barefoot Father Brebeuf arrived at the village. He had served there and grieved that only one cabin was left standing. All the rest were in ashes and ruins.

In 1633 Champlain was faced with the powerful competition of the British and the Dutch, draining away most of the beaver left in the St. Lawrence valley through the Iroquois and bush lopers, and taking much that came from the west through the Algonquin control of the Ottawa River, the route to and from Montreal. Realizing that he must find new trade regions, perhaps new routes, Champlain sent Jean Nicolet out. The young explorer didn't get as far west as Brule went yet he reached Green Bay, swung down through the Illinois country and back to Quebec in 1635, bringing stories of a great river that flowed to a faraway sea.

But any profit from these findings would go to others. Champlain died the next Christmas day.

CHAPTER III

PADDLE AND PORTAGE

ALTHOUGH the Indians were prominent in the harvest of the beaver, and without much remorse, none could believe in his actual destruction. Old men of the villages grieved, saying that the beaver tribe had been angered by the disrespectful treatment and had deserted their ponds, leaving them dead and fruitless as pockets of snow water. When the missionaries came with their talk of a heaven and the eternal soul of man—of man only—the Indians were confused. They could not believe that a creature as excellent as the beaver—useful, diligent, provident, foresighted and responsible, sober, peaceful and amenable to authority (all the qualities that the missionaries recommended to their charges) —had no soul to live in the white man's heaven.

When the Europeans swarmed in at the eastern seaboard and up the waterways, they found the castor ready food for the hungry traveler, without the bear's truculence, the deer's shyness, the wolf and the wolverine's tooth and claw. All the white men knew the castor, at least by hearsay; the meat was recognized as palatable and filling as far back as cave man, who left the bones in his midden heaps, and probably long before that. The favorite early method of cooking in Europe was apparently the same as the American Indian's, whether in Nova Scotia, along the Soleduck of the

Pacific or in the villages of the great western river, the Missouri—roasting in the skin. The meat was tender and usually very sweet, something like pork. In the 17th century the tail was said to be like the choicest bacon in flavor and appearance, which suggests that bacon was something different than now. Beaver tail is largely muscle, not fat. Cooked, it is light silvery gray inside, like fine fresh pork, with the texture of tongue but generally firmer, and was rightly considered the finest delicacy of the forest and Plains waterways.

Often beaver meat was dried, roasted, and then pounded with wild fruit and packed hot into animal bladders dipped in the tallow of some ruminant—the true pemmican, by the Algonquin word, of the American Indian, whatever the meat, the *wasna* of the Sioux. Pemmican kept well and was concentrated enough for long journeys, particularly those by young men of good family who went out to see the world of other tribes before settling down, and for war parties, when hunting and fires could not be permitted.

During starvation times, such as during the isolation of a blizzard or an unusual stretch of winter, beaver skins were chewed, either roasted or raw, to survive. In the wilderness of New France, where meat was the staff of life and often the only food obtainable for months, the missionaries were forced to make some compromises. The beaver was pronounced a valuable addition to the fast and Lenten dietry on the assumption that the animal lived on fish and so was fish by identification if not in fact. This was plainly a subterfuge of necessity. Even the most naïve Parisian must have understood the meaning of those great orange-yellow wood gnawers of the beaver. The otter and mink would have been better examples of fish eaters but were as unpalatable as such feeders usually are.

The beaver was the commissary of most of the Indians north of the gulf line and east of the buffalo plains. Great tribes lived on him. In addition to food, his furred skin provided the bed robes and much of the clothing, the great coats, the mittens, the winter moccasins. Beaver hide tanned into light but tough and strong leather, and was used for short dresses, summer shirts, stockings, leggings and breech-clouts; waist and shoulder belts; quivers, pipe and fire bags as well as many other containers for various uses, and provided stout and pliant thongs for every need.

As the American beaver flooded the markets of Europe and Asia too, the castoreum, two large glands in front of the rectum of both sexes, once more became an important item of trade. It has a sweetish, musky smell and is still used as a fixative for perfumes. The French found some Algonquins mixing dried castoreum with their tobacco and kinnikinnick for the soothing fragrance from their pipes. Bits of it were often scattered with sweetgrass among the garments, regalia and sleeping robes of the long houses as it was added to the mints and sages scenting the robes and parfleches farther west. The Indians valued castoreum as a medication but perhaps less than the pale-faced newcomers did. The supply from the European beaver had practically vanished and with it the demand for medicinal uses, but back before 400 B.C. Hippocrates suggested castoreum as a valuable curative. Later the romantic nature-faker, Pliny, wrote that the castor's life was spared on the surrender of his valuable pouches of castoreum, as though the beaver could take them out and hand them over.

For generations castoreum* was the accepted cure for such ailments as earache, deafness and dropsical abscesses, and a most powerful remedy for gout, headache, colic and other pains, including toothache, and, applied externally, an alleviator of tumors in the liver. At various times castoreum was offered as a palliative for sciatica, as an excellent stomachic, and to stop hiccoughs, induce sleep and prevent sleepiness, strengthen sight and if snuffed up the nose, to produce sneezing and clear the brain. It was considered helpful in madness, particularly if the victim was taken to the quiet ponds for his recuperation. Several of the early families of

---

* Crude castoreum, dried, looks like withered furless paws. It was sold in drug stores and pharmacies into the 20th century. Rough Canadian castoreum brought $8 to $10 a pound in 1890, six pairs to the pound. The Russian was more valuable, perhaps because so much scarcer.

New France tried this for unfortunate relatives, apparently without reporting the results. Castoreum was also offered for the destruction of fleas, administered as an antidote for "the sting of spiders and scorpions and tarantulas" and the bite of the rattlesnake and water moccasin, to alleviate the bad effects of opium, and to ward off the dreaded pestilence.

Occasionally it was admitted that, as with other medicines which might fail under adverse circumstance, and even become injurious, so too castoreum could fail. Still the honored doctors of Augsbourg introduced castoreum into thirty of the best compositions of their pharmacopoeia; Bacon praised it for the brain, and there were reports that a girl who had lost her memory in a malignant fever recovered it through castoreum. It was said that Solomon had used it for his prodigious memory—one was to wear a hat of beaver skin, rub the head and the spine each month with beaver oil and take castoreum to the weight of a gold piece twice a year.

The fabulously plentiful beaver from America had brought a new surge of interest in the medicinal, and mystical, qualities of castoreum and the castor as a whole. In 1685 a treatise on the medico-chemical uses of the beaver suggested various of its parts as specifics for most human ills. Castor blood was administered to an epileptic beggar boy and freed him of his attacks for six days. When he never returned after the second dose it was assumed that he had been cured. Matted beaver hair stopped some hemorrhages and proved effective after a surgeon had applied styptics without success. The belief that beaver teeth hung around the necks of children eased the teething was probably based on the ancient faith in the example; powdered, the incisors were recommended for pleurisy and to prevent epilepsy in children. According to Watts' *Dictionary of Chemistry*, beaver skin was efficacious in colic, madness and spasms, and cured both bed sores and consumption in children; the fat, useful in all maladies of the nerves and in epilepsy, prevented apoplexy and lethargy, stopped spasms and convulsions and was of great help in giddiness, toothache and asthma. Some of the coureurs de bois carried fish bladders of ointment made by the Indians from beaver fat to heal scratches, burns, sores and insect and animal bites and to prevent frost bite of the face above the bearding. A coat of grease on the feet, the hands and the entire body kept the cold off, particularly during long exposure to the icy waters of winter.

Tanned beaver hides had symbolic value in the adjustment of disputes among Indians. A present of handsome skins, perhaps painted or quilled on the leather side, served to bind treaties. Some tribes and groups had medicine (holy) bags or packets called beaver bundles, supposedly carrying special supernatural powers. Various Algonquin divisions, including the western Blackfeet groups, and some of the Cheyennes valued them highly, not only for prosperous hunts but for tribal health and luck.

During the years of English claim to New France, mid-1629 into 1632, many of the coureurs de bois pushed farther into the wilderness, and even the employees of the well-respected Champlain, men like Brule and Nicolet, had trouble getting trade goods and marketing the few furs they managed to gather. In France the hatters were compelled to go to the enemy English and the Dutch for their beaver, and pay the price demanded. When the French returned to the trade the Indians complained that the British had paid more for the plew. Further, they wanted more brandy now that the rum was gone, and at rum prices. In reply they were told that the English had enslaved them with alcohol, the French conveniently overlooking all the brandy and high wines their own traders had brought in during the last thirty years, and the long degradation of the Montagnais, whole divisions of the Hurons and Algonquins, even the small group of mission Iroquois tolled up close.

Champlain also deplored what he called the English depletion of the beaver although he had seen this happening

for twenty-five years and had sent not only Brule but perhaps
a dozen other young men west at various times to search out
new trapping grounds as well as mines and that western
route to China. In 1634 Jean Nicolet had been welcomed
out beyond Green Bay by a great community feasting in
which at least six score roasted beavers were eaten. Pleased
by this wealth of the castor, he demonstrated his brace of
pistols, new to his hosts. He fired them simultaneously, it
seems, with a tremendous roaring and blue smoke. The Indians called them "Thunder-in-His-Hands" and told him
stories of the great river that flowed to the sea.

But the news of so much beaver and a possible western passage came too late for Champlain, and the changes
that his death brought in the newly re-established Company
of 100 Associates affected the farthest regions. Champlain
had concerned himself more with mines, military conquest
and trade than the colonization whose neglect had brought
such bitter denunciaton of the earlier traders, both from his
tongue and his pen. Now the company lost even Champlain's
minute zeal for settlement, and by 1636 Father Le Jeune was
complaining that the Hundred Associates "do not care how
they get Beaver so they pass through their hands."

The company did bring in some impoverished noble-
men who received large grants of land as seigneurs with
peasants and workers—their habitants—ostensibly to build
solid communities including merchants and small traders, the
bourgeois. But the habitants soon learned of the Indian
trade and slipping away from their rude homes, took up the
irresponsible, improvident, clever and adaptable life of the
bush loper. The land-poor seigneurs soon discovered the
profit in fur and encouraged even the more staid habitants
to go into trade, supplying them with goods, while they began to live like feudal lords, even carrying on wars of a kind
with rival seigneuries up and down the river.

There was a serious effort to concentrate the fur trade
into the hands of a small group who were to have one-third
of the profit. They set up trading houses where all the furs
bought from Indians, bourgeois and coureurs de bois were

received and shipped abroad under conditions and prices set by the company. The missionaries, particularly, complained about the colonists who did not remain in the settlements to fulfill their duties as husbands and fathers but went far out into the wilderness and did not return, men who usually married into some distant heathen tribe and fathered more heathens. By now practically every people west of the lakes had legends of early white men suddenly appearing among them, from the Winnebagos to the far Shoshonis, Kiowas and beyond. Those without them felt neglected. The Mandans told Maximilian that long, long ago they had a new chief who searched out these white men:

> 'A saying was then current among these people (the Mandans) that on the other side of the great water or the sea, there lived white men, who possessed wampum shells. Bodies of fifteen or twenty men were frequently sent thither, but they were all killed. Whereupon the chief said, "I will send my boat thither, with eight men; this is the right number." And the boat went, arrived at the right place, and brought to the white men the red mouse hair (beaver hair) which they highly valued. They were well received, feasted in the dwellings, and material for smoking given them. Each received buffalo skins filled with wampum shells, and the boat returned quickly. The boat then went, for a second time, with eleven men . . .'

Perhaps these early ventures were undertaken while the Iroquois preyed so heavily on the fur trail to the St. Lawrence and whole parties were killed. There is no mention of iron; probably the Mandans had obtained this earlier from trading Indians and possibly the knowledge, at least, of powder and firearms. Perhaps from the Village of the Bearded Men, their neighbors.

These years, particularly the confused 1630's, were a time of hearsay and rumor. Endless stories of Indian atrocities reached Quebec, not only about such events as the burning of Brule but of priests headed west being deserted, left

tied to trees by their Huron escorts, as Father Le Jeune re-
lates, only to discover that the latter rumor, at least, was
without foundation. The new decade opened more auspi-
ciously. In 1641 Fathers Raimbault and Joques followed the
already worn trail of the coureur de bois to Lake Superior.
Next year Maisonneuve, one of the Hundred Associates,
brought some substantial families to the mountained island
below the sault and founded Montreal as a solid community
instead of a mere trading station, on and off, most of the
twenty-nine years since Champlain built a small temporary
post there. Maisonneuve's settlement brought the center of
the fur trade up to the mouth of the Ottawa River, smooth
and broad-bosomed to her own far rapids—the gateway for
trade with the upper lakes and the country beyond, trade
that included kegs of brandy hidden in the canoe loads,
hidden from the Indians along the route.

A few of the Algonquins and Hurons still tried to
avoid the burning water and petitioned the government to
ban all sale or gift of it to Indians in their region. The petition was easily granted—intoxicants, like guns, were not to
reach Indian hands—and as easily ignored, although the
missionaries tried to protect their little nests of converts from
the evil. Unfortunately, without the tolerance for alcohol
developed by the white man through uncountable generations of imbibing ancestors, the American Indian north of
the pulque regions of the southwest was very susceptible.
With his traditional and frequent recourse to visions through
long fastings, torturous ordeals and trances in his religious
rites and for personal guidance, it was difficult to make him
understand the missionary's objection to this short-cut to
more fantastic visions than he had ever imagined.

In spite of all the earlier protests, the new management of the Associates increased the price of trade goods and
cut the value of beaver, of the plew. The Indians complained again, and sneaked their furs to the Dutch and to the
Iroquois traders for the English. More and more of the bush
lopers dropped their contacts with the official warehouses
and obtained their goods from smugglers. With the shrink-

ing trade, the company let its stock run down, until a small group within the organization took command and in five years earned a profit of 300,000 livres. This sprouted envy; management was shifted to another faction, which lost money. In 1645 the Hurons went down the river with eighty canoes, much of the fur obtained from Indians far west of the lakes, two men from out there along this year, so the stories say, from the Village of the Bearded Men. The party paddled clear to Quebec and even there couldn't get the supplies they wanted and so they went elsewhere. It was spring before the Indians from the Missouri returned to their homes, carrying, probably, English powder, lead and knives, also iron for spear points, and certainly great stories of what they had seen.

By now Richelieu was dead too, and it was plain that the fine plans he made with Champlain for the company were little more than a fox fire in the snow. Finally the monopoly was leased to the eight principal traders of New France, called the Company of the Habitans. Now the Associates were relieved of all pretense to support the missions and the government, or even to fight the Iroquois, no longer necessary with a new peace recently arranged. A tax of one-fourth the value was laid on the fur business to cover those expenses. One way or another the Habitans were to help keep up the old responsibilities, including colonization, it seems. The bush lopers were expected to buy their goods from the Habitans, at prices that left no profit.

"It is the tax," the Habitans explained.

"Naturally. One plew in four to the priests and the governor, two to the Habitans, one to the trapper, for me, nothing," the coureur de bois replied, and went out to where traders from the south waited behind every other bush or bend.

In Europe the Thirty Years War closed at last and the market for beaver began to rise, with some price adjustment, but by 1648 many coureurs de bois were ruined—those who didn't buy their furs with brandy and rum, or never sought outside markets. The Dutch still paid better and many trad-

ers, even women like the Aulmus sisters, were accused of
sending their furs to them. This aroused the anger of the
French company, and the horror of the missionaries, who
called it furthering heretics, although some of the mission
hirelings also took advantage of the better prices from the
Dutch and English, while even Father Le Jeune had to explain some furs sent south.

In all of New France the first really successful missions
were those of Huronia, as the region stretching southeast-
ward from Georgian Bay was called. Perhaps the depletion of
all game in their country helped drive the Hurons to guns,
legal only for Christian Indians. They needed firearms and
all the white man's magic of cross, holy figures and rites
against their fierce Iroquoian enemy. The magic worked: the
two years of peace restored the Hurons to a profitable trade
with the Indians of the west. Then suddenly the Iroquois took
over the business. The Hurons resisted but almost nothing
seeped through and French fur trade fell off seriously. Early
the next July—1648—the Iroquois struck in earnest, destroying two missions and the villages around them, killing and
carrying off hundreds of Indians, with practically no resist-
ance. All the escaping stragglers could do was flee to neighboring tribes, who accepted them, realizing that the venge-
ful enemy might strike them next.

The easy destruction of the missions and their villages
should have shocked both the Indians and the missionaries
into a little thought. Traditionally the Hurons had lived in
fortified communities of from two hundred to many thousands each, with an active body of young warriors for protection, and aggression, as they grew corn and squash to sup-
plement the hunting and fishing. An open-handed people,
with whole villages where any stranger was welcomed with
food and housing for as long as he wished to remain, they
were not always property-conscious, not in the white man's
way, and were called thieves when they took as freely as they
gave. Friendly, humorous and competitive, they were enthu-

siasts for games. Loose hair flying, they played ice hockey with its curved sticks and light wooden ball, and the rough, wild game that the French called la crosse, the game the coureur de bois often joined.

It was in fact the penetration of the bush lopers and their marriages into the tribe that made the coming of the missions possible. The young Frenchmen taught the missionaries the language, helped them win tolerance from the Indians, and often supplied the missions with meat, perhaps even the Indians settled around them, living, for the first time, without fortification and apparently without initiative. But the coureurs de bois were traders and rather generally observed that universal rule for traders anywhere: keep out of the wars of the natives. In this way some of those bush-loping Frenchmen grew wealthy enough to become bourgeoise, perhaps even merchants in the Company of the Habitans. Often they went south, deep into Iroquois country, to bid against the Dutch for the rich harvest of furs, and then returned without much difficulty anywhere. In 1648 twenty-six of them brought out such hides as could be gathered right under the war whoops and fire brands of the attacking Iroquois, and without serious trouble.

Such immunity during the bloody raid increased the anger against the coureur de bois, both among the missionaries and in the government.

The Hurons had depended on the magic of the missionaries instead of the stout fortifications of the past. Surely the experienced Father Brebeuf should have understood this but perhaps he and the rest were afraid of disturbing the new faith of the Hurons. Besides, much of the softening of the once great warrior tribe could be blamed on the white man's alcohol and disease, especially the decimating smallpox.

The raid of 1648 had been so easy that early the next year the Iroquois struck again. Armed with Dutch guns, the warriors marched 600 frozen miles to surprise and destroy the Mission of Ste. Marie and the majority of the Huron villages still standing, and to punish the tribes that accepted the refugees last year. The surviving Hurons scattered; some fled to the shadow of the cannons at Quebec, the rest were driven westward, beyond the lakes.

Before the smoke and stench of the raids died there was news of the appalling torture and death of Fathers Brebeuf and L'Allemant. In 1678 the story was published by Christophe Regnaut, Coadjutor Brother of the Jesuits "as told by several Christian savages worthy of belief, who had been constantly present from the time the good Father (Brebeuf) was taken until his death."

This account says the missionaries were stripped naked, tied to posts, their hands bound, the nails torn from the fingers, their backs beaten. While Father Brebeuf prayed, a captured, fallen-away Huron convert poured boiling water on him. Six red hot axes, strung on a large withe of green wood, were hung around the neck of the good father and a belt thick with pitch and resin was twisted around his waist and set afire, roasting his body while the priest prayed and preached. Finally, apparently to silence him, the torturers cut off his lips, tore strips of flesh from his thighs and arms and put them to roast, to be eaten before his eyes. Then the weakened man was forced to sit on the ground while one of the Indians cut the skin from his skull and another opened his chest, tore out the heart and roasted and ate it.

Some of the Huron captives escaped with the story of the attack, surely hoping for a French revenge expedition that was never to materialize, for international reasons that the Indians could not understand. In the meantime Brother Regnaut had gone out to rescue the bodies. No one seems to have noticed that this attack was almost exactly forty years after Champlain injected the appalling surprise and magic of his arquebus into the attack on the Iroquois deep in their own country—forty years since the captives taken there were tortured and killed by the Hurons and their allies before the eyes of the white man. His account of the treatment the prisoners received is astonishingly like that reported for Fathers Brebeuf and L'Allemant in Regnaut's story, except the red-hot axes, a more modern touch, and probably the withe

would have been burned through. Stories of native torturings
tend to be much the same, whatever the people, the region
or the century, arousing a suspicion of at least unoriginality
in the narrators. Perhaps, however, patterns of torture are
deep-rooted in man and took on little variety until the later,
more refined, means provided by iron and its civilization,
as in the Inquisition running strong in Europe and Spanish
America in the 1600's.

Of all the Huron country, it seems that only the bush
lopers were spared the torch, the blasting guns. The Iroquois
moved against other tribes trading with the French, and
threatened Quebec, the very resting place of Champlain. The
remnant of Algonquins along the Ottawa, like the Hurons,
escaped north and west as far as the head lakes. In 1653-54
the Iroquois drove them on to the Mississippi River, to the
country of the powerful Sioux, who welcomed the fleeing
Indians, and were repaid with treachery. Roused to fury by
this, the Sioux whipped them northward, the warring still
active when Radisson and Groseilliers arrived, the first coureurs de bois recorded by name to reach the upper Mississippi
region. There they discovered that warriors who had been on
far raids had brought back a prisoner from the Bearded People of the west. It was said they were much tawnier than the
raiding Indians and that they lived in great cabins and had
long knives like those that Radisson and his companion carried.

For several years after the attack of 1649 the fur harvest from the Huron and upper Algonquin country was practically dead, the warehouses of New France empty. It was
said that for a whole year not one Indian-made plew reached
the Montreal trade. Once more the peaceful beaver began to
flourish; the ponds were well-kept and living, new houses
were built, old deserted ones repaired. Playful young kittens
sunned themselves on the tops, perhaps pushing each other
into the pools, quiet and blue as fallen October sky.

But by 1654 the trade was reviving, spearheaded by

the enterprising Radisson and Groseilliers. Medard Chouart, Sieur des Groseilliers, later known as Mr. Gooseberry, had become a lay helper around the Jesuit missions when
about twenty. He learned both Algonquin and Huron and in
1653 married the sister of Pierre Radisson. Young Pierre had
arrived in New France two years earlier. Still some under
twenty, it seems he had been over much of Europe and wrote
English well. In 1652 he was captured by the Iroquois, escaped
to the Dutch and was taken to Europe. In 1654 he returned
and with Groseilliers started a series of western penetrations, one to the displaced Hurons and Ottawas in the upper
Mississippi region, and finally spent a winter with the Sioux.
One of his expeditions was typical of the wilder bush lopers—without permission from the governor. For this the two
men suffered heavy fines and a twenty-five percent duty on
the value of a very fine haul of furs, some evidently of that
finest of American beaver, the dark silky ones from south of
Lake Superior.

Radisson's account of his voyages is not completely
clear, perhaps because he had reason to keep the extent of
his penetration and the sources of his excellent trade a secret.
He claimed that his first trip lasted three years and that he
went so far south that no snow fell, no ice froze, and apparently even reached the gulf. When he returned from one of
his trips, in 1660, he brought 300 Indians along and a wealth
of fur estimated at around 200,000 livres, enough to glut any
one market, so he divided his canoes into lots, for Montreal,
Three Rivers and Quebec. The handsome harvest drew a
swarm of fur-hungry traders to spy out his sources, and to toll
more young men from the humdrum life of the St. Lawrence settlements into the western woods and the prairies,
with more tawny young Indians to be born.

By this time contraband trade was a serious drain on
the profits of the authorized merchants. In 1659 De Laval arrived in New France as vicar apostolic. He believed that the
state must act in the interest of, and on orders from the
church, and so Easter Sunday he declared the death penalty
for anyone furnishing liquor to Indians. He had sufficient

power to force the recall of the new governor, who was un-
sympathetic with his extreme measure but not enough to
stop the liquor traffic, no matter what the threatened penalty.

In 1661 nine traders went down to the rendezvous
with the Ottawas, Algonquins who had fled west. They carried bad news. Last year Father Menard, eight helpers and a
supply of trade goods intended to support his work had gone
out with them. It seems that although there were at least
fifteen Frenchmen living at the Ottawa village by then, the
Indians treated the missionary with neglect and brutality.
He started to the Hurons on upper Black River and was lost
on the way. His companions tried to carry on for a year but,
being poor traders, the beaver they collected did not pay
expenses.

Usually the Jesuits did not engage in the trade themselves but had coureurs de bois like Louis Jolliet, known as
donnes or engagés, do it for them. There was considerable
opposition to Jesuit trade, their competitors saying that it
was contrary to royal orders and their own vows, but evidently these commercial activities were rather widespread
among the missionaries, at least for a time. A Jesuit reported
that 260 pounds of beaver hide were found by searchers in
the room of an Ursuline nun.

The Jesuits, in addition to the wide-spread authority
they assumed over the Indians, were free to go anywhere,
any time, and free from all trade restrictions. The coureurs
de bois, severely regulated by law if not by practice, complained loudly, condemning the wealth of the Order, which,
they said, was used for selfish ends. In return there was angry
denunciation of the whole way of life of the bush loper and
his debasing alcohol, an inducement not completely avoided
by the traders for the missions.

The gap between the two white groups in the far
wilderness of New France was widening. Some blamed the
missionaries for drawing the Hurons from their fortifications
and no one denied that sometimes the Indian traded a whole
season's catch in one day for drink if a liquor-carrying bush
loper got to him before he reached the company warehouses.

He could buy no brandy direct from the company, at least not under the eyes of the authorities. Even so, there was the always appalling drunkenness of the rendezvous, the fur fair, at Montreal, and much of it Indian drunkenness.

These were still dangerous times, not eased by the increasing raids of the French Indians down upon the spreading English settlements, with retributions by the Iroquois. There was also a growing lawlessness against Frenchmen from their own uprooted tribes, inflamed by alcohol and the greed of its appetite, some said, but perhaps also aggravated by a festering anger at the loss of their homes, their livelihood. In 1661 Father Le Jeune wrote that eighty Frenchmen had been massacred, often with fiendish tortures, many from the clergy. This violence threatened the collapse of the missions among the remote tribes and with them the whole French empire in America.

The Company of the Habitans was dissolved, the old Hundred Associates, suspected of trade in brandy, surrendered their patent, and a new combine, the Company of the West Indies, or The West, was organized in 1664, with reestablishment of a monopoly urged by Colbert, the finance minister of Louis XIV. Canada became a royal colony, with a governor general and, after 1665, an intendant. These two, with the bishop and a council of five, ruled the colony and managed the fur trade, the only business of Canada. Under the new plan permits for trade were limited to twenty-five, called congés or fermes. The fermiers were extended credit or furnished goods and were to sell their peltry to the issuing merchant. Without overseers in the Indian country they traded with the Iroquois reaching well west of the lakes now, and the English direct, all at double the French price, tax free.

The Dutch who honored the beaver by putting him on the New Amsterdam coat of arms were dispossessed by the British, who now held all the territory north and south of Canada, like huge rodent jaws ready to snap down on the western movement of the French, cut off the whole unprotected colony like a green sapling.

Some of the wilderness French went over to the English, others dealt wherever the profits were best. The coureur de bois who tried to abide by Quebec's regulations might grow fat from beaver meat but not from the pelt. He had to paddle and portage for months from Montreal to the retreating beaver country and so had to carry a large cargo to pay for the trip. Poorer men were reduced to working as voyageurs for some fermier or smuggler, others simply moved on, sending the furs back by Indians or the tawny mixed-bloods more and more common over the west. Young men became bush lopers or prairie trampers almost as soon as they could carry guns. Green from the settlements or from France, many knew nothing about fur or its care and yet started to make beaver, killing the friendly half-grown, taking worthless summer hides and coaxing the uninitiated Indians into the same foolishness. The French government tried to establish grades of beaver, with the summer hides declared the property of the king "bought without examination" and carelessly stacked in warehouses to be eaten by moths and other vermin.

Out west as elsewhere the Indian had to be coaxed at first, bribed to take more beaver than he and his family and friends needed for food and their own fur and leather uses, and be taught not to roast the animal in the valuable skin. By now the tribes far beyond the Missouri were saving the hides for the goods that reached them from the sunrise country somewhere and from the southwest: knives, kettles, beads and at least iron for arrow and spear points if not a gun or two and powder and ball—worn sometimes, but often fresh from the white trader.

Talon, the intendant of Canada, saw the colony's wavering population scatter, not only the lopers without legal ties but many of the fermiers never coming back, defrauding their creditors. He decided that the men going west should be compelled to marry French girls before departing for the Indian country, tie themselves to wives and coming families. But where were the girls to be the brides, and the men who would certainly return to them? There were

Frenchmen far out in the wilderness whose growing sons and daughters in the settlements did not remember them, perhaps had never seen them at all.

But some of the traders who took the far journey to the Sioux and the Assiniboins and other tribes of strange and unknown names sent back fleets of canoes heavily loaded with fine mature hides, and under Talon's push and energy, the production of peltry was increased from an annual of 550,000 livres in 1667 to over a million and a half in five years. Now the beaver had reason to flee to far places or to turn on his predator, but the mild, gentle creature of the soft pelt could do neither. Nor did the old tricks of diving deep or fleeing to the washes in the banks save him. Once more carcasses lay frozen and naked at the skinning places, the sweet flesh left to feed the wolves, the wolverines and finally small carnivores and worms, the bones to bleach in obscene, blaming white. Suddenly, under Colbert's influence, French beaver hats became the rage all over Europe and French deerskin shoes. Once more there was a good market and then once more the warehouses of the St. Lawrence were full, and over full. France restricted the purchases, the prices fell, first at Quebec and then westward to the farthest hunter. Traders and merchants, those who made one trip west a year, were caught with vast stores of furs at the old prices and slipped toward failure. Talon tried to cut down on the beaver harvest. He set up a factory for shoes and hats, and a tannery at the St. Lawrence, but France permitted no importation of goods from the colonies, and so the ventures failed.

The displaced Ottawas were making new acquaintances and finding increasing use for the calumet, the sacred pipe, which they believed had been given by the sun to the Panys, the Pawnees, located along the Niobrara and the Arkansas rivers, the gift communicated from village to village clear to the Ottawas. They spoke of the attachment of the prairie tribes to their sacred object, so honored that a pledge given over the pipe was never betrayed.

It was true that there was constant communication up and down the open plains: raiding war parties; hunters stalking the buffaloes, more and more by horse; the far gatherings for the big summer ceremonials and barter; the general visiting, often from the river of the Yellow Stone to the Rio Brava, the Rio Grande of the Spaniards. Before the Spanish hope of pillaging the legendary golden Quivira had died entirely, there were rumors of French penetration into the upper regions of the southward-flowing streams claimed by New Spain. There were rumors also of a Pawnee captive brought to Santa Fe in 1650, an arrogant, talkative young warrior who taunted the iron-shirted soldiers, saying he had seen bearded whites called Frenchmen on the upper Missouri River, well-entrenched with the Indians of the earthen villages.

The Spaniards had heard such stories before but were not given to swift moves except on rumors of gold, which had already drawn them far along the river of the Big Horns. Apparently they did send men to spy out these French eventually and perhaps three or four got as far as the Sioux of Minnesota and left a Spanish name there as father of a son born. If true, these might have been of the expedition that discovered the Picuris, a group of Taos Indians, who, early in the 17th century, wearied of the Spanish yoke and fled northeast some 150 leagues and built a pueblo assumed to have been El Quartelejo.* They grew corn and other crops there, with irrigation canals and hunting grounds, but were finally coaxed back. Governor De Peñalosa of Santa Fe, in his defense before the Inquisition, offered an expedition he claimed he led about 1662 to these wandering Taos Indians, bringing them back, but he was expropriated anyway, humiliated and driven out.

The pueblo uprising of 1680 destroyed most of the records of Santa Fe and the New Mexican region but there is an account of an expedition under Garza in 1663 whose extent seems unexplained. Although the Indians of Texas, particularly the Apaches and some of the Comanches, didn't

* Supposedly the pueblo ruins in Scott County State Park, Kansas.

need urging for raids across the Rio Grande, the drouths of
the middle 17th century drove them with hunger. In 1660
war parties struck the frontier Mexican settlements, looting,
burning and whipping herds of cattle back to the hungry. In
October 1663 the frontier towns sent out an expedition of
100 men, with 800 horses and eighty loads of flour and other
provisions under command of Sergt. Maj. Juan de la Garza.
They crossed the river near Eagle Pass, attacked the enemy
Indians gathered in a rancheria, killed 100 Indians, and captured 125 men, women and children. Six months later the
soldier-farmers returned to Monterrey and sent many of the
prisoners as slaves to the mines.

But if the expedition was actually gone six months,
where was it? What driving purpose would keep such men
from the work of their haciendas from October into April,
long after planting time? Could these men with their 800
horses and the eighty loads of provisions be the basis for the
references of Spaniards north as far as the Platte, the Belle
Fourche, the Bighorn, even the small group said to have entered Minnesota? Perhaps it was this expedition that inspired the ousted De Peñalosa to produce the narrative of his
doubtful expedition in 1662, to the "River Mischipi and
Quivira," the account purported to be by Father Freytas,
who was Peñalosa's confessor at Santa Fe, but usually labeled
a forgery written by the ex-governor himself during his stay
around Paris in the 1670's. In the meantime he was suggesting that he attack New Spain with the help of Louis XIV,
take over much of the region, at least New Mexico.

But by then a new power had entered the northern
regions, a new fur regime. Radisson and Groseilliers had
turned from the French to the English, where Radisson
helped organize what was to be the political as well as the
financial power of much of the Canadian northwest and
Oregon, and to penetrate at times as deep as the Platte and
across the Colorado. This new group was the Hudson's Bay
Company, chartered May 2, 1670, with practically absolute
power over their domain, for which they were to pay "His
Majesty two Elks and two Black Beavers" whenever he hap-

pened to enter the country,* as a gesture of allegiance, and a proper one it seemed from the Company of Gentleman Adventurers, as the organizers called themselves.

* Queen Elizabeth II was given a fine beaver coat on her first visit to Canada as queen.

CHAPTER IV

STILL PONDS AND
WAR WHOOPS

THE men who pushed their ever lengthening strings of canoes westward, sweating, singing, cursing against the power of the rapids, the bite of the portage straps, were unaware that in 1665 the early casualties in the race for empire in America already lay behind them. The Italians had had their chance, through the Columbus whom Genoa had not cared to back; the Swedes and Dutch, with actual footholds, were gone; the Germans, bled by the Thirty Years War, were a nest of quarreling princelings, but the rest of Europe was grasping with the left hand for the American earth while the right seemed occupied maneuvering men and ideas for power and territory at home. Perhaps the hands were reversed. It was true that although Spain had let her west-turned eyes be blinded by the glitter of the gold that could be wrested from man, she clutched at all the region draining southward. She had looked toward the fur riches of the mountains and the plains long before the pueblo uprising and would again.

North of Spain the traders of France and England, particularly of the former, because her Canada existed only for the furs, had been moving like a pestilence over the land, the blue-flowering chicory of the Frenchman's coffee gone wild behind him the only gain. Now the ambitious and magnificent Louis XIV, with his competitive missionaries, the earlier Recollets and the Jesuits becoming as energetic in exploration and publicity as in soul saving, was opposed in America not only by the English colonists but north by the new Hudson's Bay Company, with unequalled extra-governmental powers that were to last almost exactly 200 years.

The incentive for this international struggle was financial—to a large extent the skin of a lowly rodent, the gnawer called the American or Canadian beaver. True, this rodent was large, exceeded in size by only the rough-haired, piglike South American capybara. The adult beaver of the wilds was said to weigh from around forty pounds up to sixty, rarely seventy, with a record very fat one of a hundred pounds or a bit over. If these figures are true, the beaver, like some other creatures once nearly exterminated, has never regained his full wild stature under protection. His usual length in the 18th century was forty to forty-five inches, exclusive of twelve or fifteen inches of tail. More recent measurements put the length at thirty to thirty-five inches, plus the ten-inch tail. The fur, lighter brown in the south, darker in the north, has a dense under-coat, with long guard hair on the upper parts, glistening guard hair, often with a blue or purplish iridescence. The finest of the dark strain, called beaver-black by the old Sioux, came from a stretch south along Lake Superior or from near Hudson's Bay.

Long before the bleacher's art touched the felting for the handsome plumed hats of the court of Louis, an occasional plew pale as mist along the Missouri bluffs showed up in the catch of the white trappers. These albinos, usually sacred to the Indians but sought by the traders, might occur anywhere yet seemed more common in the Yellowstone country and near Little Slave Lake, where nine pure white hides were reported in one parcel.

Rodents are considered of low general intelligence but the beaver has an amazing instinct for building dams and waterways. The first requirement for a new colony is always a sufficient body of comparatively still water of some depth below the freeze line, which the beaver usually forms by damming a small stream. Anyone in beaver country during the summer may run into a whiskery scout or two sniffing out a possible new site. Sometimes Indians scattered green cotton-wood, poplar or aspen bark with castoreum in a beaver-drawing ceremony to toll the wanderer to a promising creek near the village. With the location selected, other beavers appeared. Bush willow, alder or other brush was cut down and dragged along the ground, big end clamped in the power-ful jaws, the hind feet thrusting hard in the pull to the place for the dam. Here the brush was dropped, butt ends upstream, the bushy, branchy tops anchored with mud, gravel or per-haps stones and left to catch silt from the rising water. More layers of brush and mud and often rock were piled on top until the wall was high enough to build up the required depth of water. The dam would leak at first, as is the nature of earth dams, in spite of careful plastering with mud.

The beaver carries stones and earth held against the chin with his handlike forefeet or uses his tail. The tail of the castor is oval, a little like an oval stone-baked Indian corn cake but almost black, about six inches or so in width and ten long—thicker in the middle and toward the root, with a hard, scaly surface. The tail is completely mobile, and can be turned in any direction, and well under—to carry mud and sticks clasped tightly against the belly but not to haul loads like a sled. It serves as a brace when standing to cut down a tree, the beaver working alone, not with a dozen around one trunk as in Le Beau's "marvelous vision." In the water the tail is the rudder, a scull for speed and an instrument to give alarm with a loud slap on the surface as the beaver dives.

Dams vary with the site and the material available. They may be built from one willow clump to another across some flat bottoms that are to be flooded. Some of the walls are all mud and sod, particularly where there is no real cur-rent. Much of this material may be simply dug up from the bottom, to deepen the pond as well as dam it. Such mud walls need some protection from the wash of rain and playful ani-mals, particularly the sliding otter, the beaver's one real en-emy in water. This is usually accomplished by slanting long poles or thin brush along the outside wall of the dam as well as inside. Some of the walls are largely stone. An old one southwest of the Village of the Bearded Men, beyond Kill-deer Mountains, was made of the black stone that the white man called coal, dragged from a nearby bluff.

Beaver dams vary in form too—straight, concave or convex—and in length. The longest usually mentioned was in the great beaver region of the Jefferson River near Three Forks, measuring a full 2140 feet, and apparently of more than one vintage, the top plainly much newer than the lower portion, perhaps a repairing after a long decay. Sometimes there are several dams on one stream, as at the creek near Old Crossing of the upper Missouri. The walls may be four, five feet high, perpendicular measure; a few reached eight or even an exceptional eleven feet. Before the white man came, ponds were seldom abandoned except for water failure or food exhaustion, and when new water came or new brush and timber grew up the beavers might return to repair and re-build. Or others may have moved in.

Beaver dams are always planned with sufficient depth of water to protect the entrances to the lodges as well as any burrows or washes in the banks, deep enough for swimming under the thickest winter ice and for retreat from an enemy in the lowest summer flow. Sometimes extra ponds are built to float wood to the main one, or a dam may be erected above the inhabited pond to control floods and to store water for dry seasons. Perhaps a second dam is built below the first to back water against it, protect it from unusual pressure of flood or winter ice. Sometimes canals are dug to transport large logs for considerable distances, with one water level or two. In the mountains beavers sometimes ditch around rocks and rapids to shoot their logs down, while in drier regions feeder streams may be turned in above the pond for needed water.

When a dam is finished and the water level good, the houses or lodges are built. Some of these have been set against a bank and, rarely, entirely on the shore. Occasionally beavers live in burrows, and most ponds have refuge washes or underground tunnels into the bank.

Beaver houses are usually built like low beehives, on a

solid foundation, either on a shallow spot in the pond or on one built up. Sticks are laid across the base haphazardly with perhaps a little more care on higher. The spaces are filled with mud, little or none in the center portion so there will be ventilation between the sticks. The entrances are usually gnawed out later, starting well below the thickest possible ice, and leading to the main room. Some houses have two floors or at least a sort of dripping place below the living and sleeping quarters to keep them snug and dry. The houses are always clean, with no dunging and no smell of urine.

Beaver houses vary considerably in size. John Colter, in his reported escape from the Blackfeet, was said to have hidden in a large one. Although there have been lodges of forty feet and more, outside diameter, the one on Lost Creek, pictured in Warren's *The Beaver,* is only sixteen and a half feet at the widest but with a forty-two-inch entrance, large enough for him to crawl through. The main living room was fifteen inches high and not over six feet across yet with eight tunnel entrances offering escape from the two floors to the bottom of the pond. Hearne speaks of a large house on an island, with nearly a dozen "apartments" as he called them, but only two or three were connected by passageways. He says his Indians took thirty-seven beavers from it, and some got away.

Beavers, with low respiratory and circulation rates, need less air than some other animals but the lodges are well ventilated. They are usually started small and built up with time and the growing family. Sometimes two or even three are joined, or, spreading, just come together, as the large one Hearne reported was probably formed. Most ponds support three or four houses although some have sustained six or even eight, particularly in the earlier and more plentiful days. Often good-sized poles are dragged to the top, perhaps to discourage otter slides, although there may be small slick spaces for the young beavers. Piles of sticks, barked, are often discarded on the roof, like bare bones thrown away.

A man with a small, sharp hatchet cuts wood no faster than the beaver with his large incisors, the chips falling around the busy, murmuring animal, the chaff clinging to his furry cheeks and chest as he works. These teeth are sharp as scissors and grow very rapidly all the beaver's lifetime, to replace the wear nature anticipates. If one incisor is broken off, the tooth it met in gnawing will not be worn down but keep growing at the normal rate and reach enormous length, so long the animal may be unable to close his mouth and so creeps off to die somewhere, of starvation.

As soon as the spring high water is gone, beavers begin to prepare for winter. The dams and houses are to be repaired, perhaps replaced, and food is gathered for the long frozen months. The favorites are the poplars, particularly aspen and the cottonwoods that send their fluffy whiteness to cling like thin summer snow to the tangle of brush at the dams and houses, and tickle the sprouting whiskers of the young beavers sleeping in the sun.

The American castor can thrive on many woods, and harvests willow, alder, box elder, some birch—preferably the yellow, wild cherry, pin cherry, viburnum or witch hopple, black and white ash, silver and bird's eye maple and so on. But the aspens and cottonwoods are preferred. The food supply, green brush and small trees, is dragged into deep water during the summer and submerged, with mud or stones to hold it down, the bark kept green and soft for winter.

In the summer beavers vary their diet to include raspberry bushes, various roots and grasses, berries, mushrooms, sedges, wild roses, cow parsnips, service berries and thistles. Indian corn patches were often invaded, and great piles of it cut and dragged into the ponds, stalk and corn together. Guards watched during the forming time, and dogs were often caged in the patches, not to harm the beavers but to keep them away, and still the bolder ones would stay, to sniff around, sneak off with a little. When the harvest was done, both in the milk stage for boiling and drying, and when ripe, a few ears might be left on the bank of the ponds as a sort of gift. The beaver was usually so tame and so pleased that he hurried out to carry the corn away, perhaps looking back to the gift makers, often children, once or twice as he went.

Beavers even gnawed the bark of the douglas tree and other conifers, mainly pine, but such a diet, prolonged, spoiled the flavor of the meat for both the Indians and the white men.

The beaver family is normally two adults with their young, both kits and yearlings, all living together. Some Lake Superior trappers estimated seven to the lodge; later in the Rocky Mountain region the conclusion was eight. The beaver is usually monogamous for life, with the sexes about equal in number. The young remain in the home until fully grown and then set up another house, often in the same pond. The rutting season is apparently in late winter, January through February, depending upon the latitude, when the beaver lives largely under the ice. The young are born in April and May, helpless and, most trappers agree, blind or at least with the eyes closed for a brief period. The usual litter seems to be four or five but may vary from one to eight, or exceptionally, more, too many for the four teats of the mother. As with most animals, the male seems to leave the house about the time the young are due, living in a burrow or wash and returning when the kits are a few weeks old. In good weather the young come out of the house well before a month. They seem to wean themselves at about six weeks and start on bark and tender shoots. If the house is cut open, a beaver seven days old can be handled like any other kitten, with no apparent fear or attempt to escape. At three weeks or older they dive away, fleeing like the adults.

The cry of the young beaver is often compared to a baby's, some say like the muffled whine of a very young baby. Alarmed, small beavers may give the shrill cry of a lost and frightened child. A little older, they hiss in menace or utter a querulous "churr." In the house they make a purring, rhythmic sound. The adult has a sort of love or comfort ditty, a rhythmic murmur and sigh, very appealing to hear over a twilight pond.

Beavers have a regular training pattern for the young. Until the snow melts and the ice goes out, the kits stay close to the warm nest. As soon as they can toddle they are

brought out to swim and to play on the banks on warm evenings, learning to search out tender sprouts and buds. As the
weather moderates they are led up the river or creek to other
ponds and perhaps beyond. At night their bed is some nook
or hollow of soft grass, pleasant for a little scuffling in the
moonlight but always at the bank for a swift dive into the
water at the first scent of wolf, coyote or wolverine. There is
little dread of hunters even by the old during the summer.

Toward fall, when the first thin needles of ice begin to
push out from the edges of the still ponds at night, the young
are started back. To survive they must grow cunning, for not
only animal predators but some Indians and the white men
who lived among them liked kitten meat. It is now time to
repair the dam and lodges. The adults gnaw down great trees
to fall with a thundering, the young cut off the smaller
branches to be dragged away. The dam is strengthened, the
houses are patched, with new mud to dry on the tops. Inside
there is new bedding of fine grass, twigs and chips. The burrows and washes are repaired, perhaps increased. More winter
food is dragged in and sunken deep near the lodges. During
warm spells in the winter the castors do sometimes forage out,
perhaps for water lily roots, but they prepare for a solid
freeze-over.

Adult beavers can submerge four or five minutes, easily
swim half a mile or more under water and have been known
to survive up to a quarter of an hour in sunken traps, probably from breather holes or captured bubbles. In these bubbles, the Indians said, "air is made"—a keen observation of
results without understanding the cause—the exchange of car-
bon dioxide in the trapped air bubble expelled from the lungs
of the beaver for oxygen from the water and the ice, and
capable of continued reuse.

"You got to break the bubble," old trappers used to
say. "You got to break the bubble under the ice or the
beaver won't drown."

Often toward spring the food supply dwindles and the
old beavers push out to make holes in the ice and drag in
trees. It is dangerous, for predators are hungry too, and in the

early days trappers were waiting, seeking the fine plew primed by the cold.

But with spring the young are born and the cycle is repeated.

The white man, in his curious egotism, seems always to assume that what he does not know does not exist. That extensive trading fairs had brought Indians from far regions, often enemy regions, together annually in peaceful barter and amusement all over America for thousands of years seems never to have occurred to the invading Europeans. After the journey of Jolliet and Marquette down the Mississippi much is made of European goods found among the Indians at the mouth of the Arkansas. Although this was probably Spanish, the goods could have come down the Mississippi from the French, by way of the Iroquois, and be French or English, or from any of half a dozen available Indian trading fairs—on the Kaskaskia, near Lake Okoboji, out on Horse Creek of the North Platte, up the Arkansas near the later Ferdinandina, or down in Texas.

In 1678 Duluth, only two, three years in Canada, but soon to be called the king of the coureurs de bois, became interested in the beaver out west and the stories of the great sea beyond. That year he started from the post at Michilimackinac, between Lake Huron and Michigan, to the Sioux country, with perhaps twenty bush lopers, men more inclined to commerce than exploration. At the headwaters of the Mississippi Duluth set up trade, his place a sort of free area where enemy tribes could bring their furs in peace and carry their purchases away, many to the buffalo plains and beyond.

Duluth rescued the Franciscan Recollet, Louis Hennepin, who had been with La Salle and who, with a companion, had walked his energetic if frail figure into captivity among the Sioux. Duluth heard of the two white prisoners and thinking them English poachers on French-claimed territory, he paddled 160 miles and with three companions stalked into the midst of perhaps a thousand Sioux warriors and got the two men restored to freedom and their gray robes. As a reward, Father Hennepin glossed over the rescue and belittled the work of his rescuer as he did La Salle's, taking much of the credit for the latter's explorations upon himself.

Duluth worked for peace between the Sioux and the neighboring tribes, especially the Chippewas, and became known as a successful but stern, even a hard man. Some laid this to his war wounding and apparent laming in Condé's dubious victory over William of Orange at Seneff in 1674. But it seems that Daniel Greysolon, Sieur Du Lhut, was just, a virtue valued highly by the American Indian. After they killed two Frenchmen in the woods in Duluth's territory, and took their furs, one of the killers came strutting around the fort, apparently making the usual threat to "eat the Frenchmen" that the literal-minded considered a prediction, or the accomplishment, of cannibalism. He would burn the fort and its twelve defenders to ashes, loud in his brags, perhaps, out of experience with other whites, feeling secure.

Duluth went out, arrested him and had the other man pursued to the far western tribes. The two were treated not as prisoners of war but as murderers, tried and found guilty. In the face of 400 angry Indians Duluth, with his slender force of forty-two Frenchmen, had the murderers executed. There were no reprisals; the stolen property was turned in, and the incident closed. The Indians recognized bravery when they saw it. Duluth was hard as stone but he never cheated them, never lied to them, and his justice was dealt out to white skin as to red.

It was a more fortunate example to set before the proud and ferocious western tribes than the unprovoked participation of Champlain and his arquebus in the attack on the fiery Iroquois, and helped set the pattern for an easier relationship for a long time, until the United States government started making treaties and breaking them.

Duluth, with his brother Charles, took over much of the Cree trade that had been draining off to the Hudson's

Bay Company, but his other task was not entirely neglected. In 1679 he dispatched two men with a Sioux war party headed west, probably as far as the coteau at Big Stone Lake. They gathered stories of the waters that must flow to the western sea, of great ships there and settlements of white men, as well as others of the bearded ones to the south and the west. The beaver, however, was here, within reach of Duluth's traders, Indian and white. While marketing a fine cargo of furs he was arrested for unauthorized commerce, his furs confiscated, the lamed veteran compelled to defend himself, perhaps his life, apparently unaware of the drastic steps taken against the coureur de bois while he was out in the wilderness.

When Frontenac came as governor of Canada in 1672 he faced several serious problems in addition to the threat of the English on both sides; he must punish the raider Iroquois and sustain the colony's trade and a real expansion somehow, even with the legal but largely ignored limit of twenty-five trading permits. He subdued the Iroquois and pushed the fur business, to his own profit, his enemies charged. Many of the merchants were against Frontenac largely because he tried to keep both liquor and guns from the Indian trade and worked to check the shameful disorders of the annual fur fair at Montreal. The Jesuits opposed him because he said they were more concerned with conversion of beaver than of souls, and that they moved their activities on westward as soon as a region was cleaned out of furs.

Confident, knowing that the king was behind him, Laval, now Quebec's first bishop, made no reply to these charges, not in public personalities but used political pressure and reiteration of church policy instead. To build up New France the young men must be compelled to stay at home, marry and increase. They must not run out into the woods infringing on the profits of royalty (and, by implication, of the local government and the Church) in the only business of the colony—the fur trade—while debauching the Indians with alcohol and examples of loose living, and meanwhile endangering their own souls.

Finance Minister Colbert realized that without the fur trade Canada was hardly worth the annoyance and that yielding to the cleric would drive the Indians to the heretic English, lose both the profit on the furs and the savages' favorable disposition toward the bishop's "one pure and true religion." Astutely Colbert referred the problem to the important men of the colony in what was called the Brandy Parliament, the first even mildly representative gathering in New France. October 26, 1678, about twenty of the most important seigneurs and merchants met with the Sovereign Council at a long table headed by Frontenac seated under crossed white and gold banners. They were a handsome group of men, generally young for their importance, most of them clean-shaven, cheeks too healthy and browned for the court of Louis XIV, but with the fashionably long curls of their perukes falling over velvet or satin or fine cloth shoulders, lace at their wrists, their fingers mostly white and soft except those of the explorer La Salle and the former engagé turned explorer, Jolliet. Altogether the twenty were very different from the hairy-faced, deerskin-britched men who gathered the furs in the wilderness, made the profits that maintained these men in their luxury, sustained them in New France at all.

There was a great deal of emotional talk. Jolliet argued that the eagerness for brandy drove the natives to kill each other and run into debt and that they would prefer to trade where there was no liquor. La Salle pointed out that when no brandy was available at Montreal the Indians took their furs all the way to Albany on the Hudson River for rum. It was alcohol or no trade.

Many there must have realized that the real antagonism between these two men was not alcohol or even trade so much as the ambition in wilderness penetration and the competition of the missionary orders backing them, the Jesuits behind Jolliet, La Salle with an older brother a Sulpician. In the end fifteen of the twenty men around the table voted for the brandy trade as it stood.

Laval protested to Colbert and suggested that the Frenchmen be kept in the settlements, the Indians compelled to come to the well-established posts with their beaver. In this way he could control both.

But who was to enforce these measures?

One attempt was through the king. April 1679 he ordered that bush lopers trading without permits be whipped and branded for the first offense, sent to the galleys for life on the second, the same penalty doled out to soldiers trading in furs, officers found guilty to be broken in rank.

Two years later the intendant estimated that 800 men, forty per cent of the adult male French of Canada, were out in the bush. While the number may have been exaggerated, certainly some had been out for years with perhaps Indian children and grandchildren growing old, as age went in the wilderness. In the meantime Governor Frontenac tried to moderate the king's severe orders. The threat of such punishment merely sent more men farther away, drove more soldiers to desertion.

The king finally granted amnesty to all the coureurs de bois who returned from the woods promptly and agreed to obey the law in the future. The intendant approved, and proposed such pardons for all but two men, one of them Duluth, with a trade permit from Frontenac, himself, so low had the prestige of the governor fallen. It was in these circumstances that Duluth found himself under arrest, his rich cargo taken from him. He managed to get permission to make a defense, was released and his confiscated property restored. Angry enemies of Frontenac said he even permitted Duluth to send beaver to the English at Albany, for double the Canadian price. The ambitious intendant charged that Frontenac's friends had spread rumors of a pestilence at Montreal to scare the fur canoes away so his bush lopers could pick up the peltry at sacrifice prices. There had been no pestilence except one of alcohol. Eighteen or twenty Indians had died at the village of Lachine, above the falls, from too much brandy.

There were even complaints that Frontenac received a percentage in beaver from the bush lopers, when everybody around Montreal realized that this was a long-accepted if irregular practice, and obviously helped to keep the official salaries at a minimum that was far below the most ordinary living expenses. Even Champlain had accepted gifts of fine plews from Indians and bush lopers not on his pay roll.

So Frontenac was recalled in 1682. The day he left the Jesuits were openly triumphant as they moved among the gay crowd celebrating the governor's departure, the gray-gowned Recollets there too, perhaps a little less exultant than the blackrobes. Frontenac walked, proud and erect, through the people pressing up to see, unattended by the men who might have been in step beside him to testify their allegiance, but La Salle, Duluth, Nicholas Perrot, Cadillac and Tonty were far away. This was the year his friend La Salle reached the gulf by way of the Mississippi and claimed all the region drained by the great stream and all its tributaries for France, naming it Louisiana, for his king. The explorer set down an accurate description of the Missouri River and the next year wrote of Frenchmen living among the Missouri tribes. Many thought, even then, that La Salle did more to further the growth of France in America than anyone else, unless it was Champlain. This was France in the new world as Frontenac envisoned it, bold, daring, expanding.

It must have been some satisfaction to the saddened Frontenac to see the stupidity of the men who succeeded him, men who aroused no respect among the Iroquois, not even among the Christian Indians sitting close around Montreal and the missions. The first, La Barre, was welcomed by the Jesuits and especially by the great merchants, to some of whom he gave La Salle's Fort Frontenac after he seized it. Soon, however, the new governor was issuing his own trading permits and found himself accused of sending beaver to Albany too. After a while he decided to lead a great expedition against the increasingly aggressive Iroquois, one to include many bush lopers and mixed-bloods from the west. But at Niagara three chiefs of the tribe stopped him, promising bloody reprisal by all the Iroquois and their English allies unless he retreated. La Barre ordered his force back, with complete loss of face.

November 1686 England's new king, James II, and Louis XIV signed a treaty to restore peace and maintain the status quo in America. James gave orders to avoid violence but Louis insisted that the Iroquois were really French Indians and must be brought under subjection. The next summer Denonville, governor in La Barre's place, undertook the subjugation. With 1500 regulars, militia and Indians he crossed Lake Ontario to Irondequoit Bay, where he was met by the war canoes of Durantaye, Duluth, Perrot, De Troyes, Tonty of the iron hand and other adventurers with their western Indians bright in little but paint, 1500 altogether, making a force of 3000. The regulars were in shining breast-plates and plumed headgear, the nobility of Canada with the curls of their perukes tumbling over the armored shoulders and catching on branch and brush until put away in their cases. Under their command were the Canadian militia, the Christian Indians and the others, some with heads crowned in deer or elk or bison horns,* some, probably those of the far plains, with animal tails, surely buffalo, flapping at their buttocks as they danced for war.

The expedition started from the lake the middle of July and twelve days later was back at the shore. Some Seneca villages whose dwellers had withdrawn were laid waste; little more. The hopeful buzzards were left sitting in trees, their wings spread as after a soaking rain.

Two years later, in 1689, the infuriated Iroquois had their reprisal ready. They destroyed the Niagara post and advanced toward Lachine, six miles above the recently palisaded Montreal. The warriors reached the settlement in a wild night of rain, hail and crashing thunder, the storm and the roar of the rapids drowning the war whoops as the Iroquois struck.

---

* Apparently several Indians and a mixed-blood from the upper Missouri villages were along. Among the Teton Sioux was a man called Man, the Enemy Is Afraid of His Dog, of the family later called Man, Afraid of His Horse. He brought back a piece of bone or ivory with a tree and a man carved on it, a piece he picked up at the main village burned, probably Seneca.

Charlevoix says the 1500 warriors surrounded the homes, struck down the occupants, apparently as they came from their beds. When the morning grayed, 200 lay dead and 120 had been carried off. They were taken across the river, where for several weeks friends and relatives could see the nightly fires blaze up and realize that their loved ones were being tortured there, the treatment probably much like that inflicted upon the captives in the presence of Champlain eighty years before. Back in 1609 the victims were Iroquois taken with the help of the new and appalling magic of the white man's thunder stick but now the tribe possessed better guns, and many of them. This was not Iroquois retribution upon Hurons and a few helpless missionaries but upon a French community, the captives not only men but French women and children crying out.

Morning was in full light before the commander of the troops in the little fort at Montreal knew of the attack. He hurried to Lachine with a good fraction of his available soldiers and took up the bloody trail, ordering his men to follow, but he was overruled by the governor. The troops must be held strictly to the defensive, ready to protect Montreal and the other settlements from attack, although the Indians were drunken with victory and captured brandy, and dancing into weariness and stupor. Nothing short of mutiny, it was reported, would have altered the situation, and so the troops could only look toward the night fires of the enemy while the prestige of France in America fell lower and lower. It seems that for over two months the Iroquois kept the populace along the river in terror. Then, in October, they left, taking along the ninety captives still alive, prisoners much of this time practically in sight of their people. There would be revenge, much instigation of French Indian raids against the English settlements, the dead and the captured many times the casualties of Lachine, and with violence spreading for years, far into the region south of the lakes.

·   ·   ·

There seemed only one man capable of punishing the Iroquois, able to restore some security to the fur trade, and to push the attacks on the English colonies. Louis XIV sent Frontenac back to Montreal. His friend La Salle was dead, in the southern region to be called Texas, finally murdered after the failure of an earlier attempt by Nicholas Perrot, instigated, the explorer had thought, by the Jesuits. The seigneury of La Salle, named Lachine because it seemed an outpost for his explorations to China, was pillaged. There were even controversies over La Salle's American explorations, particularly over the discovery of the Mississippi, whether by Marquette with Jolliet, whose map and notes were reported lost in an upset canoe, or by La Salle. It was a curious controversy, when the river had been seen at both ends and most probably all through the midsection by white men long, long ago. True, most of the early discoverers were mere bush lopers whose business was to make profit for the merchants, with no one to publicize their ventures, to make proud achievements of them. Then there was De Soto, the real explorer of the Mississippi in 1541, whose bones lay quietly buried in its spreading brown waters.

Frontenac returned to Canada with the same proud step that had carried him away. There were smiles for him now from merchants and even the clergy, smiles and welcoming words and the hope that he could undo some of the evil brought on during the seven years since his departure in a public celebration.

But most of the beaver men were far away, in new beaver regions. Some of the hides would eventually reach Montreal and the failing market but more would go elsewhere, some over the long cold rivers to Hudson's Bay and the gentlemen there.

BOOK II

THE RISE OF THE COMPANY

CHAPTER I

RIVER TO THE
"VERMILLION* SEA"

THE new century came to the fur-trade regions under a
dark cloud. Since his restoration as governor of New
France, Frontenac had once more harried the Iroquois so they
requested peace. He put the colony back on a high producing level—very high—but with both France and England
bankrupt enough to face peace after seven years of warring,
there was little money for fashionable furs and fine hats.
News, however, traveled slowly to the traders in the fur-fat
reaches beyond the lakes, particularly to those in illicit trade.
Besides, there was the merchandise already carried those far
leagues. This must be paid for, and discouraging the Indians
from their trapping would only send them to the encroaching
English.

The coureurs de bois kept gathering beaver, and although the king closed three of the most important western
posts, including Michilimackinac, the harvest was still so vast
that by 1700 European markets were glutted and the ware-

* Apparently meaning the western sea to the Canadian French well into the
18th century, from the name the Spaniards gave to the sea they thought lay
between California and the mainland until Ulloa sailed up to the mouth of
the Colorado in 1539, proving Baja California a peninsula. Although Drake
turned up the Pacific coast perhaps as far as the present Washington in his
voyage 1577-80, a Hudson's Bay Company map labeled 1748 still pictured
California an island.

houses and temporary storages so full of skins ready for shipment that at Montreal three-fourths of the furs were burned.
It was a difficult decision, and a more difficult burning, with
so much of the beaver baled hard and bound, but with energy
the fires finally rose, to spread an almost unbelievable stench
and gloom of dark greasy smoke over the town and its handsome rounded little mountain, and over all the clean-flowing
river too, far back to the most remote of its sources, and beyond, to waters flowing to other seas, under other and purer
winds.

In Paris the *Conseil d'Etat* decreed that the 107,587
livres of skins fished from the wreck of the ship *La Manon*
be burned to avoid further injury to the glutted market. Next
year Canada was given permission to place guards at the sea-
ports to check on the beaver entering France in an effort to
protect her markets against English or smugglers, and in 1703
all who concealed beaver plews were to be fined five livres.
The steady complaint against the established tax of one-fourth
the value of exported beaver brought a decrease of sorts, followed by a further release by decree, from annual payment
to the crown. But there was nothing to be gained from another
decree—that of fashion, which dictated much narrower hat
brims, demanding less felt, less of the over-plentiful beaver.

Frontenac had died late in 1698 and was greatly
mourned by many Canadians. The new governor busied himself writing a seventy-page denunciation of the brandy traffic,
charging that the forts had become places from which soldiers
were sent to other posts with wares and brandy for the com-
mandants illegally trading in fur, places with public taverns
for trade in alcohol with Indians, and where gambling was
encouraged, fast days forgotten and Indian women taught that
their bodies were even more welcome than beaver skins in
exchange for merchandise.

At seventy-six Frontenac had made a last powerful invasion of the Iroquois country and although the Indians fled
before his force until winter stopped him, the long houses, the

fields and crops were destroyed. The Iroquois made peace with the Canadians and traded with both sides but remained hostile to the French Indians and attacked their commerce so seriously that in 1702 Father Carheil urged the complete destruction of the Five Nations as a way to protect western trade —destruction of the Iroquois men, women and children. So important was commerce to the black robe.

The turn into the 18th century was a time of further tumult in the upper country. The governor of Canada had sent Tonty with troops to Michilimackinac to bring in the bush lopers. He returned with only twenty, saying that eighty-four decided to go to an establishment on the Mississippi and that thirty had already descended in ten canoes loaded with plews they owed to the merchants of the St. Lawrence. Iberville, who had been sent to the Louisiana of La Salle in 1698 to start a colony, put these furs on his ship at Biloxi and gave the thirty men 1200 to 1500 pounds of powder, while others furnished further merchandise. Since then ten additional canoes of beaver went there, and more were preparing for the easy downriver journey. To the governor of Canada this could only seem wholesale robbery of property belonging to his merchants, his colony, and stirred a growing jealousy of Louisiana, the lush country with the snowless years. Some argued that the king should have these Mississippi rebels sent to the galleys for life. But there would be many. A letter from Iberville's Biloxi in 1701 mentioned sixty coureurs de bois there at the time. Besides, it was necessary to settle the Mississippi country against England and Spain. Either could seize the river with small craft, draw away the richest trade left to France and challenge the claim La Salle established to the vast Louisiana, challenge the whole western empire of France in America.

The forts starting up in the Ohio country were important against the English colonies but there must be a string of these along the Mississippi too, and westward—up the Red and the Arkansas against the Spaniards and along the Missouri and northward against the English of Hudson's Bay; perhaps against Spain up the Missouri too. There were many rumors of Spaniards far up, among them stories of the expeditions before 1650 seeking out the ancient mines at the head of Running Water, the Niobrara River, and possibly building the fortified little post in the Big Horn Basin.

As the beaver grew scarcer in the east and the vise of English territory and power closed down upon Canada, exploration and exploitation of western lands became the established policy at Quebec. Back in 1688 a report purportedly from a voyageur named De Noyan had described a way across the continent from Superior to Lake Winnipeg and from there by an easy route to the Pacific, with Indians offering to lead the way to the Sea of the West. This account helped inspire various maps with fanciful pathways across the west. Lugtenberg's, in 1700, showed a long river reaching from the fabled Straits of Anian* to Lake Superior. Soon De L'Isle, also a map maker, put the source of the Mississippi in a lake from which a "Grand Riviere" flowed westward to a sea. The real publicity, however, for the dream of a western passage to the Vermillion Sea and the China trade came from an adventurer, Lahontan, who had traveled extensively in the heart of America. In a book published in Holland in 1703, he claimed that while ascending the Mississippi he discovered a sluggish stream flowing in from the west, up which he and his companions paddled pleasantly for weeks in 1688, until they neared the source of this "Long River" and there learned of another stream flowing west into the Pacific where Spaniards lived. Although very probably intended as satire on the society of his time, including marriage and the church, for years Lahontan's account was accepted as literal truth, and French maps showed the source of this "Long River" in a region a little like the headwaters of the Missouri.

There were disturbing rumors in Santa Fe too, of course. In 1703 it was reported that twenty Canadians left the

---

* Believed by Spanish authorities of the late 16th century to lie somewhere north of the pueblos and opening into the Pacific.

Illinois country for New Mexico and in 1706 Ulibarri found evidence of French traders in Spanish territory and heard of a white man and woman who had been killed. Since La Salle's Fort St. Louis was discovered on Garcita Creek, Texas, there was concern about the French on the lower Mississippi and now those from Louisiana were openly looking westward for a passage to the Pacific, certain that the Spaniards had a well-traveled trail across to the sea, across trade territory. As early as 1700 Iberville expressed the belief that the overland distance to the strait at California could not be substantial.

But the great river of the plains would not be overlooked. In July of 1700 Father Marest of Kaskaskia wrote Iberville that he had been told the Missouri was as long and as large as the Mississippi and well peopled, including the Kansas and Pani tribes, who carried on commerce with the Spaniards. Marest had seen the Spanish horses himself.

Nothing much was done on any recommendations, not even the many suggestions for trade and Indian management from Iberville, because France was at war with England again, one mostly fought in America, it seems. In 1706 Iberville died and his brother Bienville took his place. Two years later Nicolas de la Salle wrote of the importance of exploring the Missouri, said to be the most beautiful country in the world. He had questioned slaves of the Indian nations up that stream and learned that iron of the same quality and color as piastres had been discovered and that Spaniards frequented the region with mules. Sensing the urgency, he suggested an expedition of 100 men and 40,000 livres of merchandise, munitions and food to discover the source of the Missouri. There should be an engineer along, to map the river. In 1710 he wrote that Ensign Darac and two soldiers had been sent by Bienville to ascend the Missouri, ostensibly to make presents to the Indians to gain their friendship but that they went actually to trade for pelts and slaves to sell in the Islands. He urged that the minister in Paris refuse to pay their salaries.

LeSueur took Duluth's place in the western trade when the old veteran retired because of his lameness, maintained trading posts along the Minnesota River, and in 1697 agreed to explore the copper and lead mines known to be in the upper Mississippi region. These mines had been worked by prehistoric Indians and probably ever since for malleable and easily reduced metals. LeSueur, holding one of the two permits from the king to go to these mines, left much grumbling and protest behind him. Why should this mere voyageur lead fifty men at his own expense all those long 700-800 leagues from Quebec when six helpers were all he could need in the mines? Plainly his intentions were trade, and for beaver, specifically forbidden in his orders; he had already sent two loaded boats with a capable bush loper ahead to winter at Michilimackinac, in time for the spring trade, long before LeSueur could reach the beaver country himself.

In 1700, with twenty-eight men he paddled from the gulf up the Mississippi to be met above the mouth of the Missouri by three voyageurs come to join him. Apparently from them LeSueur heard stories of the Sioux of the West, who had more than a thousand cabins of buffalo skins laced together, used no canoes, did not farm or gather the wild oats (rice) but kept to the prairies between the upper Mississippi and the Missouri rivers and lived entirely from the hunt. There were many stories about these Indians from bush lopers who had traded with them for years and had seen some of these western Sioux down at Montreal, their strings of canoes filled with fine beaver and handsomely tanned and quilled buffalo robes. A few had even been with those who accompanied Denonville in his attack on the Seneca villages long ago.

Unfortunately the last few years the Plains Sioux seemed to favor trade with the English, their attitude made clear when seven Frenchmen came in to LeSueur's post in the upper Mississippi country, saying they had been plundered and stripped naked by them. Not long afterward some of the Indians actually appeared at the gates, bringing over 400 beaver robes, each made of nine skins sewed together—

fine winter hides, tanned soft as velvet. They stayed for a week, trading and telling stories of their country, of cherries that grew in clusters like French grapes, and *atoquas,* a fruit like strawberries but larger and square, and artichokes growing along the river bottoms. They described the many varieties of trees in their prairie country, some of the poplars five times the length of two outstretched arms in circumference. They tapped maple and box elder for syrup and sugar. But their plains were very cold in the winters, so cold the trees popped like gunshots, and the bears grew large as coach horses. But they hunted them, the Sioux said; they used the flesh and traded the skins to the Canadians.

There was a serious penetration of Englishmen into the plains country of the Sioux, not only colonial traders but men known to them, often mixed-bloods like the grandson of one of the bearded men who came to the village on the Missouri almost sixty years ago. These northern men tolled the Indians up the old, old trails to the rivers that flowed northeastward to the salt waters of Hudson's Bay, where great warehouses stood full of goods, it was said.

The three vessels of the first expedition sent to America by the Hudson's Bay Company carried 200 fowling pieces; 400 powder horns "with proportional quantity of shott"; 200 brass kettles in sizes from two to sixteen gallons; twelve gross of French knives; two gross of amber beads and about 500-600 hatchets. The trade was good and Radisson set the standard in prices to be paid: ten good beaver, meaning adult, winter-prime northern hides properly stretched and cured, paid for one gun; one good beaver bought either a half pound of powder, four pounds of shot, one hatchet, eight jackknives, half a pound of beads, a good coat or a pound of tobacco. Yet with the bright prospects of those early years Radisson, one of the chief organizers of that Company of Gentleman Adventurers, soon deserted it. Perhaps it was the attractive French promises but he claimed that he had been slighted, his experienced advice ignored. This defection started a sad period of changing from side to side for Radisson, shadowing the success of his earlier years as a

shrewd trader, an exceptional organizer, a bold and intrepid
explorer. Perhaps of him too, it can be said that great men
are those with the luck to die in time.

Ninety French bush lopers captured some posts on
Hudson's Bay and didn't give them up until expelled after
William came to the English throne. But in spite of war or
peace in America, the Hudson's Bay outfit became supreme
over a vast domain. During the first twenty years the company
managed to pay 295 per cent on par value of its stock, in
addition to profits divided without formal declaration during the earliest years. It was not only that some of the finest
beaver came from the Hudson's Bay region and brought the
fanciest prices, but the period included a generally prosperous time in Europe, with the Company holding public fur
auctions two, three times a year, after some prodding from
Parliament, apparently. The first auction, including much
fine black beaver from the Bay region, was held in Garraway's coffeehouse in London in 1672. These public auctions
became gala affairs, with entertainment for the buyers,
largely men of some fashion in their handsomely sashed
coats, plumed hats and elegant fall of lace at throat or wrist.
They came from Spain, Italy, the Netherlands, Germany and
elsewhere, and their chief interest was always beaver, 50,000
and more skins a year although some moose hides, and marten, otter, fisher, fox and smaller furs, surely including ermine, were also sold.

After the impressive dividend of 1690 the Hudson's
Bay Company paid none until 1719, the interval practically
solid war and depression years, including the style change
from sweeping hat brims to the neat and narrow. When the
stock fell from the quoted 260 pounds in 1690 to eighty in
1698, the first step in the retrenchment had been to get rid
of Radisson, back from the French. Discharged by the company he helped organize, he brought suit, was awarded back
pay and restoration of his salary until 1710, deep in Queen
Anne's War, the second great intercolonial struggle in America.

With the decline and closing of Michilimackinac, La

Mothe-Cadillac started a troop-protected post between Lake Huron and Erie, later called Fort Detroit, to cut off the main route of northern furs to the Iroquois traders, and to tap the area to the south and west. This invasion of the Iroquois-English trade region was certain to bring trouble. In 1706 Etienne Veniard de Bourgmont, coureur de bois, replaced Tonty as commander at Detroit. During the war the post was besieged by the Foxes and their allies, in the pay, it was said, of England. A new complaint rose against the bush lopers, the charge that wherever they helped in the war they went loaded with goods. Some managed to carry as many as forty casks of brandy and wherever the French and the Indians came together was a hell. Some even sneaked away to trade with the enemy Foxes. Those who protested this combination of trade and war were told that it was cheaper to let the coureurs de bois carry goods on their way to battle than to transport fighters at government expense. In 1712 a substantial force of Indians, not only Illinois but many from beyond the Mississippi, including Osages and a large party of painted Missouri warriors, came to help break the siege of Detroit. Bourgmont was pleased with these bold and daring western Indians. He deserted his post, went home to live with the Missouris and married an Indian woman. According to Le Page du Pratz, a long-time acquaintance, Bourgmont pushed 800 leagues up the Missouri. He established a fort on the lower river and wrote about the new western regions himself, including a diary of his activities during 1714. Perhaps because his western move proved to be so useful against the Spaniards as well as profitable commercially, his desertion at Detroit was overlooked.

By 1716, before the death of Louis XIV was known in America, there was a clamor for a move against the Spaniards. It was said they had already tried to settle on the Missouri, a very important river now, not only in the fur trade but because the headwaters were surely very near a stream leading to the Pacific. There should be soldiers at Bourgmont's trading post, and Jesuit missions started all up the stream, wherever the Spaniards might penetrate.

Within the next few years Paris of the regent for Louis XV anticipated that fabulous mines like those of New Spain could probably be discovered along the Missouri which, it was assumed, rose in the mountains where the Spanish mines were found. There was urgent need of a fort with an officer, thirty soldiers, twelve Canadian (not Louisiana) traders, such pirogues as might be required, with twelve rowers to each, well selected, in addition to workmen, miners, an engineer, two surgeons and a chaplain. This should be on the upper Missouri, where, the Council of Paris was assured, the Spaniards crossed the river on the way to their mines (another piece of confused geography that any bush loper trading with the Sioux of the plains could have corrected, not to speak of those who had already crossed the Rocky Mountains).

It was thought that the Indians, many of whom raided Spanish horses, could be induced, with enough presents, to help the French get much silver in exchange for their choice merchandise. The Spaniards, it was argued, had no special title to the region, which was as far from New Mexico as it was from Natchitoches, just established up the Red River by St. Denis, where furs proved to be scanty but where Spanish silver and gold were the attraction. Apparently no one thought that Spain should have a title-right to mines she had been working for generations, or questioned the estimation of distances.

Although the discoveries were hearsay and the hopeful suggestions perhaps only shimmering mirages on the far horizon, the Council of Paris decided that a post on the upper Missouri would in fact lead to the long-sought western sea and the silk and spice trade of China. But sending seventy men properly equipped 900 leagues up a swift river with at least twelve pirogues would cost money. Just the pay of the troops would be 20,000 francs a year, which would, however, be spent in France for French goods.

By mid-1716 Gallut, once treasurer to the viceroy of Mexico, wrote that the French had already passed the mountains beyond the Missouri and the further ones too, the last, they hoped, to the South Sea. They had even passed the mountains containing the mines of St. Barbe. Gallut seemed to consider all this Missouri territory neither French nor Spanish and wanted it delimited.

In 1718 Bienville was asking the king to bestow the Cross of St. Louis on Bourgmont for his western service. Because it was decreed that all the beaver trade of France in America must remain with the Canadians, the chief product of Louisiana was to be corn and beans to sell to the Spanish islands, but deerskin, small furs and Indian slaves became more profitable. The Otos and the Kansas, at war with the Padoucas, meaning, in this instance, the Comanches, had just carried off 250 slaves and incidentally reported finding Spaniards with the tribe.

The Indian alignment on the plains was as complicated as in the early St. Lawrence country, and apparently as vagrant as the little dry-land whirlwinds that zigzagged over the prairie, picking up dust here, there ruffling the white rumps of a herd of antelope, or moving sedately among grazing buffaloes darkening the vast plain to the horizon. By making peace with the Comanches the French would be turning their Indian allies into enemies. If, however, they allowed their friends to go on capturing horses and prisoners for slavery from the Comanches the chances of reaching New Mexico through their country would be lost. Any slaves were an embarrassment. If the French didn't buy them, they would be sold to the enemy Foxes, strengthening the ties there. Finally it was suggested that slaves be purchased from the Missouris and that Bourgmont, friend of the tribe, but in France, be sent out to build a post and bring peace among the Indians, and with Spain too, although that was an unlikely prospect so long as French thrusts to the southwest continued. Slaves were rapidly taking the place, commercially, of the beaver. The Osages and Missouris raided the neighboring Panis so often that the very tribal name came to mean slave.

The Spaniards were alarmed by the probes from Louisiana, particularly by Du Tisne making the rounds of Indians considered Spanish tribes in 1719. Finally the viceroy of Mexico heard that France as well as England had declared war on his country, with French troops actually in Spain. He feared English attacks on Chile and Peru and intensification of the threat against Mexican domain started thirty years ago when La Salle planted his post on Garcitas Creek. The Navajos, who made long journeys to Quivira, had been encountering Frenchmen among the Pawnees for some time and brought back trade spoils. In 1697 a Navajo party was completely destroyed by the French and their allies, the rumored dead placed at an exaggerated 4000. Next year an avenging attack annihilated three Pawnee villages and a fortified place. In 1699 the Navajos went out again, and stopped off at a Spanish fair on their way home, loaded with slaves, jewels, carbines, cannons, powder flasks, gamellas, swords, waistcoats, shoes and small pots of brass. They spoke glowingly of French valor and the assistance those white men were to their Indian allies.

Some pueblo captives taken north brought back stories of populous cities and great rivers and lakes hidden in those far mountains. There were even rumors of a northern king who wore a crown, rumors probably started from some pictures, coins or ornaments. Apparently a Spanish expedition in the later 17th century only whetted the avidity of Santa Fe for booty, and by the 18th century it seemed imperative to solve this northern mystery, conquer the interlopers, pillage their holdings.

Much of the time such stories seemed little more than dust stirred by wilderness moccasins, white or Indian, crossing the plaza at Santa Fe. But now, with the war news, the penetration of St. Denis into Mexico some years ago, followed by the journeys of Du Tisne and others, became disturbing. In addition eight Frenchmen made a little attack on a mission outpost in east Texas, apparently setting the chicken yard into a cackling and other settlements into a sort of panic. The viceroy sent Governor Valverde of New Mexico out the summer of 1719 to discover the French fortifications apparently within Spanish territory. Valverde marched toward the Rio Jesus Maria, the South Platte, moving in the usual manner of Spanish expeditions, in two parts. The first consisted of the presidials, the blue-robed priest, white helpers and settlers, led by a small soldier vanguard, the governor, in shining breastplate and on a handsome horse, among them. The second section was the Indian allies. The pack animals and their handlers moved between the two parts, the entire rear guarded by a small group of soldiers, with scouts out all around to avoid ambush. At night there were two camps and two horse herds.

On the way Valverde kept hearing rumors of French guns and ammunition and other trade goods brought to the South Platte but he found little that was tangible. By the end of October he was at the Arkansas River, where some Carlana Apaches told him they had fought a day's battle with the Kansas, who were aided by white men on foot wearing red hunting caps and shooting long muskets. It was said these whites had built several villages on the South Platte and made alliances with the Pawnees and the Jumano.

Perhaps because the snows were near, or uneasiness about the French and their allies grew upon him, Valverde hurried over the mountains back to Santa Fe and sent a courier off to the viceroy. He needed munitions of war, gun carriages for his stone mortars and men to handle them and to train the soldiers of New Mexico in European methods.

The courier stopped on the long route to Mexico City for fresh horses, food, sleep and listeners to his stories, which grew and spread like smoke on the wind. They seemed so alarming to the governor of Parral that he sent a courier to the viceroy too, with dispatches from various points reporting that 6000 Frenchmen were within seventy leagues of Santa Fe and were driving the Apache nation before them. Because his force was entirely too weak to withstand such onslaught he asked for 1000 muskets, 1000 bayonets, 1000 pistols, much ammunition and permission to raise a strong force of volunteers.

The two couriers reached Mexico City almost the same time and although the Parral report was plainly exag-

gerated, for once the colonial government moved with
swiftness. A Spanish settlement should be established at El
Quartelejo, about 350 miles northeast of Santa Fe, with a
presidio of twenty or twenty-five soldiers and several military experts and two or three priests to make friends of
the Apache nation as a barrier against the enemy. There
should also be a military post as near as practicable to the
reported French settlements on the Platte to place a limit
on their advance.

Governor Valverde objected to a settlement so far out
and so did Jose Naranjo, with experience in four expeditions
into the northeast. The country was too remote, too barren
and surrounded by hostile tribes. To hold it would require a
very large force.

Valverde had promised the viceroy he would lead an
expedition out against the French or find a man as capable.
In June or July of 1720—accounts differ—Capt. Pedro de
Villasur marched out with forty-two seasoned soldiers, including Valverde's of last year, some settlers, Father Juan
Minguez, Juan Archeveque as interpreter, Naranjo as chief
of scouts and about sixty Indians. The force was well provided with corn, short swords, knives, sombreros and half a
mule load of tobacco as gifts for the Indians. Villasur's servants had packed the essential utensils for his proper dining
and the feasting of important guests. These included several
silver platters for meats and other viands; silver cups, spoons
and a salt cellar and candlestick. For messages, agreements or
warnings there was a writing case with inkhorn, paper, quills
and perhaps wax for the signet ring on his carefully gaunt-
leted hand. Archeveque, who had been with La Salle when
the explorer was killed, was the interpreter but, always the
trader, he had ten horses and six pack mules well loaded.

The expedition crossed the Arkansas on rafts and
reached the South Platte above the fork August 6, 1720.
They found no sign of the French or their settlements and
Villasur, unfamiliar with the Plains, called a council of war
to decide what should be done. Perhaps if they could find
the Pawnees they might discover something of their French

allies. August 7th they crossed the river and Naranjo's scouts located a band of Pawnees holding a war dance some eight leagues down the river. Villasur sent a Pawnee captive, the personal servant of Captain Serna, out to win the confidence of his kinsmen, but it seemed the large village at the river ford greeted him with tomahawks so he fled back to Villasur. On the tenth the expedition camped opposite the village, on the banks of the flooded stream not far from an island with a large Pawnee band. Twenty-five or thirty of the Indians came to the edge of the water to talk, speaking for peace and asking that the interpreter be returned. Villasur sent the Pawnee back with presents. He was apparently received with kindness and finally came to the bank with some others and shouted that the Indians were friendly but they would not let him go. Of the "Spaniards" (French) among them he had discovered nothing.

The next day some Pawnees came to visit Villasur's camp, and spoke vaguely about a white man. To Archeveque's note written in French the Indians returned a soiled and faded old linen flag and a paper apparently as old, with illegible writing. Villasur was irritated. He sent over good paper, inks and quills for a legible reply to a second letter, this one in Spanish, under the assumption that perhaps Archeveque's written French was weak by now, after more than thirty-five years away from the language of his boyhood. It seems that Villasur waited two days for a reply; then, furious, he urged a crossing to the island to get the information himself. His officers, some with considerable knowledge of the Plains and its Indians advised caution, particularly now that some Spanish Indians bathing in the river had been seized.

The expedition was moved back and camped apparently on the south side of the North Platte, near the fork. Early that night, August 13th, the Indian sentinels reported stalkings, a dog barking and sounds in the river. Villasur sent out a party of Indians along the stream and was told that all was well.

From this point there are many discrepancies in the

stories told by two Spaniards, Tamariz and Aguilar, and those of the Pawnees and the French. One version states that at daybreak next morning the Spaniards were roping horses for the packs when they were attacked by a band of Pawnees, with or without Frenchmen, but at least with French arms. The horse guard, surprised, lost valuable time trying to recover the herd. When the stock was finally rounded up and they could charge the enemy it was too late. The Pawnees were riding around the camp, pouring murderous fire into the disorganized force. Some say the attack was by Indians afoot, sneaking through the tall grass.

However it was done, Villasur and his body servant, caught unarmed, went down, killed at the commander's tent. Archeveque died in the first volley; his servant remained for seven wounds and fled. Twelve or thirteen Spaniards got away in the wake of their escaping Indian allies. Dead and dying in the tall grass were Villasur; the chaplain, Minguez; five corporals and nineteen soldiers; Archeveque and Captain Serna; four servants; the hardy frontiersman Naranjo, too; and eleven Indians.

It was said that the Pawnees suffered such casualties that they were unable to pursue the fleeing. More probably, the powerful attackers were busy gathering the spoils of the battle, chopping the bodies out of the coats of mail, grabbing the silver platters and cups and the candlestick, the signet ring from Villasur's finger, the robe from the priest, and dividing the goods from the pack train of Archeveque. It was an ironic end for Juan, particularly if it was a French ball that found him. When La Salle left his post on Gracitas Creek, driven out by hostile Indians and sickness and pestilence, among those who conspired against him, left him shot through the head, was the sixteen-year-old youth called L'Archeveque, said by some to have fired the telling ball. He and two companions fled to the Indians and surrendered to León's expedition to Texas in 1690, and were sent to Mexico City as French prisoners on Spanish territory. In 1693 Archeveque was sent to Santa Fe. He married, became an Indian trader and was with Ulibarri in his 1706 expedition. Now he lay in the trampled grass far from Texas, but for the wolves here too, and the circling buzzards.

The remnant of Villasur's expedition was tenderly received by the Apaches of the El Quartelejo, their wounds nursed, the men given such poor supplies as the Indians could muster for the defeated return to Santa Fe, with stories to make their rout seem a brave one. Valverde was on an inspection tour when the news arrived but the panic was still high when he returned. The thirty-two widows and many orphans emphasized the danger in the small settlement. Experienced soldiers had been destroyed by the 200 disciplined French riflemen that rumor put into the attack on the Platte. There was even wild talk of abandoning the whole province. October 8, Governor Valverde sent a courier to the viceroy with the news, adding, "I am persuaded that the aggressors must have been the heretical Huguenots, as their insolent daring did not spare even the innocence of the priest who went as chaplain."

Despite this outburst there was no real evidence that any Frenchmen took an active part in the massacre, but this did not change the stories. The white man can accept defeat only from other pale skins. The attack seems to have been the usual Indian ambush of the foolish, although there were certainly traders in the village.

Long before Villasur reached the Platte the war with France was over, but the cry against Valverde forced him to resign in 1722 and in 1726 face charges preferred against him. These were apparently based on the diary of the journey that Tamariz said he lost in the battle but rewrote at Santa Fe later, and the story of Aguilar, another survivor. The verdict was that the governor should have led the expedition himself, not selected a lieutenant inexperienced in military affairs. Villasur was proved incompetent in handling his force, in his awkward attempts to get information about the French and in the protection of his camp, guarded by improper sentinels. Valverde was fined fifty pesos for charity

masses for the souls of the dead soldiers and 150 pesos to aid
in the purchase of mission chalices and ornaments, to appease the relatives demanding his punishment.

In the Pawnee villages there were the fine things
taken in the attack, the shining platters and the candlestick,
the handsomely chased and inlaid guns, the iron shirts, the
silver-mounted saddles, bridles and spurs, the blooded horses
that were to make their herds, already good in 1720, the
finest of the Plains for almost a hundred fifty years.

Falls and springs came and passed and the beavers
grew fat near the place where some of the Pawnee warriors
had died, and where horse bones and those of Spaniards
bleached white as any dropped by the buffalo.

But the search for the "Vermillion Sea" went on.

CHAPTER II

THE ROMANTIC
EXPLORATIONS

DURING the peace that Queen Anne's war brought to the western wilderness animals, the fur bearers started to increase once more. When the Treaty of Utrecht was signed in 1713 it was hoped that the old songs of the voyageurs would once more echo along the western lakes and streams, and that the lopers of bush and prairie would work hard. The merchants intended to get the Indians back into their debt, even though the drunken orgies started all over. Here and there sober and sharp-eared beavers would lift their heads from their work as the trappers returned to the ponds, often to those beside the Indian camps and villages, even the village where two bearded men had appeared out of the dusk almost a hundred years before. They were both gone now, one killed by lightning on the coteau, it was said, the other of age in the buffalo robes. Even the bearding that they brought was lost in the smooth-faced blood of the women's people.

But the eleven years of war silence had not been enough where the trapping was very close, where too much of the seed stock lay in bleaching bones, even out in the Wisconsin region, around the headwaters of the Mississippi and along the Red River of the North. The western posts, abandoned by the French during the war, were reoccupied now, but with diminished returns, and so the traders tried to woo the Crees and Assiniboins back from Hudson's Bay men. The company traders had been pushing westward since 1690, when it became clear that the far Indians could not be expected to make the long journey by moccasin, paddle and portage to the Bay posts, losing a whole year. By now even the Hurons gone west had turned from the French, but beaver was so scarce that the Indians had to go 200 leagues from the lake country, while a good hunter usually took no more than fifty or sixty beaver in a season—October to the end of April. Goods brought 300 leagues from Montreal were divided at old Michilimackinac and then carried another 200-300, a round trip of 1000 leagues to paddle and portage for one trade.

In 1716, after some urging, another amnesty, the third, had been granted to the bush lopers but not many could be coaxed back from life among the Indians or from Louisiana, and certainly not from the English trade. Yet the only hope of reviving the French empire in America lay in the peltries beyond the Mississippi and in the discovery of a route to the western sea and China. But the hardy men from Hudson's Bay were pushing out too, far beyond Lake Winnipeg, west and south, for furs and that same pathway to the Pacific while farther up, their ships tried to fight a northwest passage through the Arctic ice.

The steady expansion of the English and the attempts by Spain to regain the Missouri country stirred France to grasp at her lost trade and endangered areas. The prize coveted by these three international, intercontinental ambitions and appetites was the fresh territory, and the hide, of the plump, soft-bellied creature named castor. His friends and neighbors, the Indians, also had their appetites to feed, appetites grown far beyond the old ones of an occasional feast and the need for winter robes.

A further complication was the lack of definite borders between the French colonies of Canada and Louisiana. All legal traders of the Missouri country and down the Mississippi practically to the gulf were to carry licenses from

Quebec, although the governors of Louisiana claimed their territory extended up the river and north from there to Hudson's Bay, westward too, indefinitely westward, while Canada insisted on her prior jurisdiction straight through to the Pacific and down.

Ignoring any French claims in her way, the Hudson's Bay Company was moving out of the northeast with the inevitability of an ice cap. The royal charter left little room for any national doubt or questioning about either boundaries or management, not even from London. Only once in all the 18th century was the company queried on its management and that was in Parliament, on the charge that the promise of exploration and search for the western sea in return for the many extra-governmental privileges had not been fulfilled. When it seemed that envious and powerful enemies might endanger the renewal of the charter, the company produced a diary of a journey by Henry Kelsey in 1690-92, to prove that the youth had made a long search for the elusive sea. The diary was challenged as a fraudulent account of a fictitious journey, written expressly for relief from the embarrassing investigation. This charge of fraud was a common challenge, one raised against practically every travel diary and journal of the 17th century, including that of Jolliet down the Mississippi with Father Marquette. The Kelsey journal was to come up again, much later, but with enough force to modify the policy of the Company of Gentleman Adventurers.

The Sioux, Assiniboins and Crees, who could furnish vast quantities of buffalo robes from their great surrounds, and many furs, had an alternate market now and looked with suspicion and even hostility upon French trading methods. They came wooden-faced, holding back the beaver until their robes were accepted, huge bales of them, heavy and bulky for the far leagues and portages to the St. Lawrence, at very little profit. Sometimes all the trader's goods went for robes, with nothing left to buy the furs, the valuable and profitable furs. Usually these ended up with the well-supplied men of the Hudson's Bay Company, particularly after their force was increased, the traders as well as the voyageurs often French or mixed-blood, with families in the tribes. It was said that the great-grandson of one of the two bush lopers for whom the Village of the Bearded Men was named worked for the company during these years, trained by his father to go among the Indians, talk for the Bay traders.

Governor Vaudreuil of Canada and the intendant were champions of a passage to the sea through the northern tribes, within their territory, and with furs much more valuable than from a southern route. In 1716 they had sent the regent for young Louis XV a lengthy memorial setting forth a simple route out of Lake Winnipeg from which, they were told, a river flowed to the western ocean. The Indians of the region had Chinese money and could only have obtained it by commerce with the Orient. Plainly such a passage would profit France greatly, and leave the Hudson's Bay Company perched on the bleak shores of the north, but in preparation for this great coup the region as far as Lake Winnipeg should be protected by military posts.

Perhaps because revenue from the fur trade was to finance these establishments, the regent consented to three new western posts and sent La Novë (or Nouë) to build them and prepare for the proposed march to the sea. He found what every trader knew—that the fur riches went to the Hudson's Bay posts, many days off, perhaps because the Frenchmen lacked goods, their suppliers too remote. Only one fort, on Rainy Lake, came of this but the effort stirred up other appeals to the government. After studying several accounts, and apparently accepting Lahontan's literally, Father Bobé prepared a memorial urging exploration of a route to the sea, which was probably only a short distance beyond the continental divide, with rivers leading to it, and to the bearded men who picked up gold dust on the shining shore. The grand vicar to the bishop at Quebec wrote an enthusiastic account of the Missouri country, and of the western sea with huge merchant vessels and men who shaved.

To reach whatever truth lay behind these stories, the regent sent the learned Father Charlevoix to America. Out at the lakes in 1721 he was assured that the climate in the Winnipeg region was milder than the St. Lawrence and from this he decided that the ocean must be near. Further study brought more acumen and finally Charlevoix suggested two possible routes to the Vermillion Sea: up the Missouri to the source and on, which could not be far, or overland west from Lake Superior through Sioux country. For the latter a mission must be established among the tribe, to win their friendship. The good father probably never understood that the Sioux nation had about as many divisions as the French.

Father Charlevoix favored the route up the Missouri but to the authorities the other seemed cheaper and avoided Louisiana, as though that were enemy terrain. They sent two Jesuits and some traders to the eastern Sioux, who had traders and still remained hostile through this and varying additional schemes. It seems surprisingly misinformed, this serious effort to win the eastern division when there were Frenchmen well established with those out on the Plains and along the Missouri and its larger tributaries long before this.

In Louisiana there were other worries, but the English advance down the Ohio involved a powerful nation and arrogant Indians, while the obstacles to the west were lost in the bright prospect that stood out there on the horizon like a morning rainbow, with the hope of precious metals and the shining sea. The scattering of Spaniards who had sought the old Indian mines of the Missouri drainage and followed any color up the streams for 200 years, still furnished elusive rumors of white men killed in twos and threes in one place or another. Gradually these small parties began to carry trade goods, particularly guns and powder and extra horses to appease the Indians, and to bring back furs and handsomely worked robes in lieu of the unlikely gold. John Sen-

ex's map of Louisiana of around 1720 carried a notation on
the upper course of the river labeled Missouri but more
probably the Platte:

> "The Indians say that near this place the Spaniards ford
> the River on Horseback going to treat with some Na-
> tions lying to the northwest whence they bring Yellow
> Iron as they call it."

Even the futile expeditions of Valverde and Villasur
did not convince the Company of the Indies that French
traders in the Missouri valley were enough. There must be
troops if the Spanish monopoly in the region up between the
Rocky Mountains and the Black Hills was to be broken, the
threat of further penetration dispelled.

Bourgmont had returned from France to carry out
his orders to build a military establishment on the Missouri,
make an alliance with the Comanches and bring Indian
chiefs to France. He started Fort Orleans as a headquarters
to re-establish his trade up the Missouri, but was forbidden
to go far beyond the Arikaras, the Rees. September 1725 he
arrived in Paris with all the Indians he was permitted to
bring, apparently one man each of the Otos, Osages, Illinois,
Chicagou, a chief and a young girl from the Missouris and
the ambassador of the Metchegamias (Michigameas). In their
varying headdresses, their beads and paint and robes and with
their fine physiques, scarred and tattooed, they caused a romantic stir in the city and the nation already festive for the
marriage of young Louis XV.

By now the power of Spain in Europe seemed sufficiently reduced so that Louis could marry the daughter of the
deposed king of Poland instead of the Infanta Maria of
Spain, long planned as the means to an expedient alliance.
With Mexico also weakened now, Bourgmont was recalled in
1726; his post was abandoned two years later when the Company of the Indies, discouraged, sold the monopoly of trade
in the region to two Canadians who agreed to buy all their
supplies from the company warehouses in New Orleans and
deliver the pelts there—20,000 livres of castor each year, all

prime and winter-killed, at contract price, and all the deer-skins they could gather. The monopoly was revoked in 1736 and the trade of the so-called upper Louisiana opened to everyone, every Frenchman, in addition to the Spaniards there illegally, according to the French.

The number of traders, bush lopers and voyageurs in the region multiplied and while there was less alcohol in the Missouri trade than in the debauched early years of the St. Lawrence, trouble rose with or without it, helped along by both the Spaniards and the French agitating among the tribes. There was a report of eleven Frenchmen killed on the Missouri by the Osages, perhaps because the traders were short of goods, as happened, particularly if they had bought furs on owing sticks and then were unable to redeem them. Two months later nine of the men reported killed arrived in Illinois. They had become alarmed when a slave and a tramp engagé were murdered and hid out. Then in 1734 the mine rumors were started again, this time by a Frenchman some years with the Pawnees. He had gone up the Missouri to an earthen village of the Rees and on his return told of finding silver mines.

Before this the authorities of Canada, seeing more and more of their castor drained away northward to Hudson's Bay and south to New Orleans, had decided to send out an explorer for new fur regions and that everlasting phantom, a passage to the western sea, one following the northern waterways from Montreal. Fairly accurate dimensions of the world were known by now, had been for 150-200 years, ever since Magellan and Drake, with astrolabe findings certainly giving the approximate position of the northwest coast that Drake saw, and the leagues west of Lake Superior to the sea roughly calculable. But somehow explorers refuse to hamper themselves with actuality. Each one seeking the Pacific and the route to the Orient hoped to glimpse the sea over every rise.

Perhaps the most serious of these explorers was Pierre Gaultier de Varennes, sieur de La Verendrye. He was the eighth of ten children, the son of the governor of Three Rivers, and grandson of a former governor. Pierre's father was not wealthy but had to maintain a menage befitting his position and when he died in 1689, his widow was probably not in affluent circumstances. Young Pierre entered the army at twelve and went against New England under Hertel de Rouville and was probably at the capture of Deerfield in 1705. In France he was a lieutenant in the Regiment of Bretagne in three campaigns, received four saber wounds and a bullet through the body at Malpalquet and was apparently left for dead. It was impossible for an officer with no private fortune to maintain himself in the army in France so Verendrye returned to Canada. With four sons born between 1713 and 1718, he needed a substantial income and was given command of the trading posts out at Lake Nipigon, north of Superior.

As a boy at Three Rivers, Verendrye had heard great stories of the western country from the builders of forts on the border and from the coureurs de bois back from the Indians. Some of these bush lopers were young men of good family, perhaps neighbors of young Pierre. Both groups spoke of the *Mer de l'Ouest,* with adventurous tales of the lakes and streams that led to that sea. While Verendrye was out at Nipigon he met Father Gonner, another enthusiast for reaching the Pacific, one who had enough experience with the Sioux at Fort Beauharnois to recommend a route past them.

Back at his posts, Verendrye asked his Cree friend, Chief Tacchigis, who said that he had traveled as far as the lake of that great river of the west. Others said this was true, and repeated reports of men who had followed the stream. A slave among the Crees said that those western lands were full of game and fruit, with many tribes who raised quantities of grain but who did not know what a canoe was, and had no wood to burn, using buffalo dung instead. The slave had seen a mountain of stone that glistened night and day, and from which one could notice a rise and fall in the waters below. An Indian called Ochagach claimed he had paddled down the river flowing west from a great lake to where the water ebbed and flowed. Men of terrifying mien lived there, in the fortified towns. They wore armor, rode horses and had great ships. He made a rough map of this stream on birchbark.

With this and all the stories of lands full of animals, so rich in beaver that the Indians threw their winter robes away every spring, of cities and fortresses and white-skinned people in metal clothing, Verendrye was prepared to appeal to the government for permission to go exploring. As a final thrust he reminded the authorities that England had every interest in reaching the sea first.

Once more there was much talk in Paris of an American passage to the Grand Ocean and China, whose exploration had been proposed under Henry IV, under Louis XIII and XIV and taken up with renewed enthusiasm in 1717 by the regency, with 50,000 livres appropriated for Novë. Yet for all the revival of enthusiasm Maurepas, minister of France, stated firmly that the officials were not looking for a sea of the west but a sea of beaver. It seemed that Louis XV had other places for his money.

Verendrye understood the Indian's fondness for the attention and presents that tall tales brought from the white man and certainly realized the misunderstandings that can rise from inadequate and faulty interpretation. He must have known that a little calculation with the world's dimensions might have revealed a discouraging distance to be covered to the Pacific, but apparently he also suffered from the curious romanticism of many explorers: a preference for any fable, folklore or plain lie to dull fact. Perhaps this was deliberate. At the upper lake posts Verendrye could have seen and talked to coureurs de bois who had been to the Missouri country, men who knew that the earlier, wilder breed of bush lopers had been there long ago. Of course the coureur de bois did not have to convince a governor general, a minister of the colonies or a pampered monarch to get permission to go, nor needed to glorify the findings on his return.

Still, many an ambitious merchant covered his purpose with the flowing mantle of the explorer.

The core of the Indian stories seemed so probable to

Verendrye, at least in his presentation to the authorities, that he apparently convinced himself. He gave up his posts, got the permission and support of Beauharnois, whose request for a hundred men and supplies for the expedition was denied by young Louis XV, but the king did grant the hopeful explorer a monopoly of the western fur trade so he could build the necessary posts himself and certainly make a profit. Verendrye was not happy; perhaps he had to admit how much of the fur harvest was already being carried south, down the river, or north on the ancient trails to the Hudson's Bay men. He did want the honor of a route to the western sea for his country and the territorial claims of it, but he had no fortune either for his family or to finance his explorations. Most of the profits from his posts, at Nipigon and any built in the future, would have to go to the men who managed them while he was seeking the salt sea. Still he agreed, and the spring of 1731 he talked fat fur harvests to the Montreal merchants and obtained the most essential goods and supplies, but, as he had feared, for a large share of the possible profits.

The Verendrye expedition included the leader's nephew, Jemeraye, second in command, some blacksmiths and carpenters for the posts to be built and fifty voyageurs young in years but already grizzled in experience. He took the three eldest of his four sons along, none over eighteen. On a summer day in 1731 the wide gates of Montreal swung open and the merchants, with the townspeople scattered along the slope, watched the expedition march out: Verendrye and his relatives handsomely attired for the proper departure, the artisans and voyageurs behind them, first those with the great canoes on their shoulders, followed by the long string of men bent under the packs. Slowly they headed out on the road to the Ottawa River, past the roaring rapids still called Lachine from La Salle's seigneury.

At the Ottawa the canoes were loaded until they sat deep in the welcoming water and were pushed out in single file on the long journey westward. Surely the voyageurs sang to ease the thought of the months ahead, perhaps one of the oldest of the Canadian chansons, the sad tale of Cadieux, the white hunter who, in the early Iroquois wars, was put ashore to divert the enemy while his companions escaped. Instead of Indians he meets the *folie des bois,* the folly of the woods, which sets men traveling in circles until solitude, weariness and hunger bring the end planned by folly—death. Another less popular version, it seems, ends more happily, with the Great Beaver singing to the lost one: "Follow the waters, run with the stream."

But troubles closer than those of any luckless Cadieux, without beaver advice, cropped up for Verendrye. After seventy-eight days of steady paddle and portage, with only a short stop at Michilimackinac to pick up the guide, Ochagach, and a Jesuit blackrobe, the rising sullenness among the voyageurs broke into revolt at Pigeon River, with miles of portage around the wild rapids before them. Verendrye thought that two or three of his boatmen had been bribed by enemies at Montreal to relate tales of horror and dire dangers along the shores ahead, with demons in the waters, the windigos along the banks. Probably it was the lateness of autumn, morning ice already fringing the lakes, the little snows promising great storms to come, and so much arduous winter work still before them that scared the eastern voyageurs. Some of the men who had been with Jemeraye on the Mississippi scoffed at the idea of demons but they couldn't deny the coming hardships.

Unable to reach his destination before the freeze-up, Verndrye sent Jean, the eldest son, on with the energetic Jemeraye and twenty-eight men in four heavily loaded canoes to race the winter over the forty portages to Rainy Lake, where Novë had once started a post. They got through and built the first of the planned forts, St. Pierre.

Verendrye was compelled to return to Fort Kaministiquia on Superior for shelter for his men and goods. Fortunately food was plentiful there, particularly fish—muskellunge, bass, lake trout, wall-eyed pike and pickerel. The Indians caught these big ones in the transparent depths of Superior by building huts or shelters over holes in the ice. In such shadowing they could see deep into the water, the poised spears, sometimes as much as forty feet long, tipped with the white man's iron or even with the old bone or stone barbs.

But the desperate struggle was just begun. Jemeraye and young Jean did return in the spring loaded with good winter-prime beaver and then had to go on clear to Montreal to impress the merchants with the quality of the fur, hoping to obtain more credit. Beauharnois tried to help. His report to Paris in 1733 and another, undated, gave Jemeraye's plans to go to the country of the Ouachipouennes called "the Sioux who go underground." These people, the Crees and the Assiniboins said, lived in eight fortified villages on the River of the West, about 300 leagues from Lake of the Woods. They had "fields of Indian corn, melons, pumpkins, beans," also horses, cats, goats and poultry,* and lived in dwellings of wood and earth built like French houses. Some of the tribe had light hair, some red, some black. "They have beards which they either cut or pull out, although a few allow it to grow." Their language bore some resemblance to French but was quite unlike the English. They dressed in ox hide, never went to war but did defend themselves. Jemeraye had brought three children of these underground Sioux to Montreal, children he bought from their enemy captors. They neighed like horses in their play and when they saw cats and horses said they had these at home.

The French officials and the Montreal merchants demanded more concrete results. Out west St. Charles was built on Lake of the Woods and Jean Verendrye and his younger brother Pierre went on farther to locate the site for the third fort, Maurepas, on Winnipeg. These later posts suffered real threats of winter starvation and young Jean made

* The "goats and poultry" could have been misinterpretation, although the French called the prong horn *cabrie* goat, and most tribes had young antelope around the villages at various times. Verendrye's journal to Beauharnois in 1734 reports that the Assiniboins spoke of the Ouachipouennes as raisers of goats and horses. The cats could have been wild cats captured as kittens. Most tribes, particularly the sedentary ones, had many wild creatures as pets.

fantastic journeys of hundreds of miles on snowshoes to get supplies to his men.

All these difficulties delayed the exploration, with the men unpaid, although Verendrye had sunk between forty and fifty thousand livres of his own in the expedition. He made the 2000-mile journey back to Montreal, prepared to beg, and was faced with condemnation for stooping to trade, when, by agreement, he was to finance himself through commerce in furs. To the merchants he said that the Crees and Assiniboins had welcomed him and promised to bring many furs to his new posts, although these Indians had had to be weaned from the Hudson's Bay men penetrating everywhere, with posts growing up at such places as the Red River. To hold these Indians he must have goods.

The merchants, with only two smallish yields of beaver in four years, were sour but they doled out some supplies, late enough to be caught in the swift ice of the west.

The winter at Maurepas was a desperate one. The fishing failed and the game departed before the snows. The men were reduced to eating roots and rawhide and finally the hunting dogs. In the spring, 1736, Jemeraye took the furs and such provisions as he could gather up and started to rescue St. Charles, also starving. He was ill when he set out and died on the way, to be buried in the north country in his hunting robe, at twenty-seven already with a lifetime dedicated to the wilderness and to the dream of his uncle—to all dreamers.

At St. Charles Verendrye checked his shrunken provisions and powder. The Crees were due in to trade their winter furs and if they discovered the weakness of the post they might seize everything for their war against the Sioux. Jean, twenty-three now, was sent with three loaded but swift canoes and twenty men to Michilimackinac to trade beaver for food and powder. It was not a good time to go. Some Crees, trying their new guns, had shot at a party of Sioux and then blamed it on the French. The implacable Sioux of the Prairies considered the Canadians allies of their enemies, the

Chippewas and Crees, and were doubly angered. When a party traveling the regular Sioux war road against the Chippewas discovered Jean Verendrye's party, they killed them all, the leader and a Jesuit missionary and the voyageurs, the bodies left in a circle, apparently overcome by a charge while resting. The heads, cut off in the Sioux manner of those days, and left, were wrapped in beaver skin, perhaps as a jibe at the white man's eagerness for fur, as in later fights they crammed the mouths of dead white men with earth to satiate their hunger for land.

The Crees were certain that the French would fall upon the Sioux now, destroy them, as the Hurons had hoped that the Iroquois would be exterminated after the horror tales of the torture and death of the Jesuit fathers in 1649. But the grief-stricken Verendrye spoke for peace. War would set the whole region aflame and prevent any search for the western sea, as well as destroy the beaver trade until it was over. Under his double sorrow and his load of debts he still tried to put together the most recent accounts of strange men in the western regions. He realized that they might be Spaniards but he decided he must still go. His Indian maps had proved true so far, and should be reliable the rest of the distance, perhaps even to the sea.

Through the Assiniboin friendship with the underground Sioux, called Mantannes, it seems, as well as Ouachipouennes, their chief had sent Verendrye an invitation to visit their village. The explorer had hoped to go, perhaps in 1736. In preparation he sent two men to make friends with the Indians in that direction and one of his sons to reach the Missouri, but there were no canoes available for the river part of the journey. And now his best support had died.

Once more Verendrye had to make the long, long trip to the St. Lawrence in search of support. He took fourteen heavily loaded canoes. At Quebec he hinted that, in his early fifties now, he would like a captaincy, and the Cross of the Order of St. Louis for his nine battle wounds. Instead, bewigged, perfumed and lace-jaboted Versailles concerned itself with surprise that he had made so little progress toward the western sea. Maurepas, minister of colonies, described the beheading of twenty-one men by the Sioux as most annoying—annoying, when the eldest son of the pleading explorer was among the dead.

Beauharnois, governor general, defended Verendrye by letter to France. He had heard much of the difficulties of wilderness winters and the hardships of the trade. Privately he blamed Verendrye for leaving his post and warned him that the next time he would not be permitted to return to his wilderness.

In desperation the explorer promised to go to the Mantannes that winter. With such supplies as he could coax and threaten out of the merchants, and with La Marque, their representative, watchdog and investor, along, he reached the western country in September 1738. It was very late for a venture out upon the vast open prairie, soon to be bleak, iron-hard and blizzard-swept, but with the nagging of Quebec and Versailles at his heels he hurried the preparations.

The Crees were dark-faced at the prospect. Water in the river was low and would ruin his canoes. Besides, the Assiniboins out there were an unpredictable lot at the best, without proper knowledge of beaver killing, a people dressed in rough buffalo skins, without intelligence, who could not get along with the French. Verendrye must have realized that although the Crees were trying to keep the trade in their own hands there was danger in this winter travel. He left his son Pierre in charge at St. Charles and with the two youngest, both under twenty, he pushed up the muddy Red River to the mouth of the Assiniboine, as far as he dared take the canoes. There had been no rain all summer and instead of watching for beaver he sought conifers among the trees of the banks and found none to provide gum or resin if the bark canoes needed repair or replacements had to be calked. Beyond the river the plains stretched away into the haze, with multitudes of buffaloes and deer to the rolling

hills of the horizon. At Portage of the Prairie he built La
Reine, named for the queen, and leaving his men to bring
the necessary cargo from the canoes, Verendrye struck out
overland the middle of October with a party of about fifty,
his two sons, the watchdog La Marque and his brother,
fifteen, sixteen workmen, the rest Crees and Assiniboins.
They walked the ancient trail used by the agricultural Indians of the upper Missouri to trade their surplus corn and
beans as far as the Bay country in exchange for white fox and
bear long before a fur man set a foot on its packed earth.

There were many delays. The leisurely Indian guide
traveled when he felt right, and the hospitable Assiniboin
camps along the route, or even at some distance, insisted on
visits. At one village each warrior put his hand on Verendrye's head, acknowledging him as his father, and then on
the heads of the other Frenchmen, taking them for brothers,
tears running down their rugged faces, a habit that gave
them the nickname, the Weepers. When Verendrye got the
guide to move again the whole Assiniboin village came along,
to visit with the Mantannes, white men too, they said, white
as the French here, their new-found friends.

The first rest stop was at Star Mound, on an old
Plains Indian trail to Hudson's Bay. The mound was the site
of an ancient earth-lodge village, where a long time ago the
Assiniboins had traded furs to white men from the far north.
But the Sioux were troublesome and then for a while they
had to take their beaver clear to the Bay or to the French of
the lakes until traders began to move out and new posts were
set up. The old hut rings and the village ruins were still very
plain, and the ancient trail.

Verendrye's next stop seems to have been at the north
edge of Turtle Mountain, near more earth-house ruins, left,
it was said, by the last Hidatsas, underground Sioux, of the
region, before the Chippewas were pushed west and drove
the small tribe out. Part of those people were still in the
Devils Lake region and south and west of the Souris River,
but most of them had moved to fortified villages on the Missouri. There was another old Hidatsa site near the mouth of

North Antler Creek, still a good camping spot, with a large Assiniboin village of skin lodges, also eager to join the white man's expedition.

The old soldier in Verendrye admired the disciplined march of the accumulated Indians. Scouts were out ahead and detachments of warriors moved on each flank, with a strong rear guard, the women, children and dogs, the aged and infirm, all in the middle, the stronger women bent under babies or packs, with big dogs loaded too, on leashes at their sides. When the frequent signals of buffaloes came, most of the active men ran out to the hunt, with bow and spear and their few guns; the surrounds too, if managed at all, well-disciplined. It was dangerous, on foot,* but soon they had plenty of fresh meat.

Messengers went ahead and near the end of November the chief of the Mantannes came with thirty of his people carrying Indian corn and a roll of tobacco—small gifts, but speaking of Indian friendship. Verendrye was bitterly disappointed in the men, much like the Assiniboins, with the same clothing: moccasins, breechclouts and buffalo robes. The long hair was black or with faded reddish streaks in the sun, falling loose below the waist except that a few wore it rolled into a big knot above the forehead. The chief made a speech. His village was the nearest of their six, but smaller. He welcomed his white friends and the Assiniboins too. Then because he was not anxious to draw this large delegation to his village, to be feasted as guests none could tell for how many moons, he said that the Sioux were on the warpath

---

* The Verendrye reports and journals suffer from the tendency to exaggerate the difficulties, a common flaw in such accounts. It seems incredible that there were no horses in the expedition. The Assiniboins had horses long before this. Sioux wintercounts mention several raids on them: 1709-10 and 1717-18 are called Brought-Home-Assiniboin-Horses winter(s), and 1728-29 is Brought-Home-Gros-Ventres-Horses winter. These were the Hidatsas, an underground Sioux people. The Arikaras probably brought the first horses to the upper Missouri, from their relatives, the Pawnees, who obtained Spanish horses in the southwest early in the 17th century, some before that. The Mantannes and their neighbors would surely hide their stock before the overwhelming number of Assiniboin warriors, expert horse thieves, but horse sign could not be hidden.

and his heart was warmed to see so many brave warriors to help stand off the attack on his people.

The Assiniboins, wary of the Sioux at the best, were far from their fellow tribesmen and with many women and children along. They prepared to retreat, but a heroic old warrior sprang to his feet and shamed them for abandoning their father, Verendrye, to the enemy. So most of the men went on, leaving the women and children behind in a well-protected spot at the Souris.

Once more they started southwest, over the browned fall prairie toward the Missouri, the several hundred warriors gallantly, and hungrily, moving in their formal march on the trail that was more worn as they advanced. When they neared the village the Mantannes brought the buffalo robe of welcome for important personages and, placing Verendrye on it, carried him behind one of his sons bearing the banner of France whipping its fleur-de-lis in the wind. The Frenchmen came next, the Indians strung out over the prairie. They were met by the four old councillors bringing the pipe, the calumet, escorted by many young warriors. The Assiniboins who had guns joined in the three-volley salute to the village, with people running out along the bluffs to see.

All the disappointment at discovering that these Mantannes were not white men or of some new race did not dull Verendrye's interest in their village, different from any he had ever seen, more familiar. Located on a rise back from the broad river valley and the fields, it was surrounded by a stout palisade with bastions jutting out to give the defenders a flanking fire along the walls, which were surrounded by a ditch fifteen to eighteen feet wide and about as deep, the only entrance by wooden steps that could be withdrawn. Out from the palisades, on a high windy spot, stood the death scaffolds, and farther away was a scattering of smaller forts. Each enclosed a small community of earthen lodges, evidently for use in the summer when the women were in the fields or on the prairie, or perhaps to flank an attacking enemy.

The main village, called Fort Butte by the Frenchmen, was laid out in streets and squares, clean and orderly. The 130 domed earth lodges, some trailing a little smoke from the central hole into the chilly wind, were large, the supporting poles inside eighteen to twenty feet tall. The chief's council house, wide enough to accommodate 200, could not hold the Assiniboins. In the confusion someone stole Verendrye's bulging skin sack of merchandise, his presents for the hosts. The chief said he was sorry but there were many rascals here among them.

After the feasting and a little dance to entertain the visitors, the village let the weary travelers sleep. The next day Verendrye made a few gifts of powder and ball, apologizing for their smallness. The Assiniboins had traded the few northern goods they brought for handsomely colored buffalo robes and finely worked skins of deer, and for corn and beans and dried pumpkin rings. Still they did not leave and the chief, seeing the winter supplies melting before all these guests, announced that the scouts had discovered a great Sioux war party very near, ready to attack. The Assiniboins expressed great anxiety about their families on the Souris and left, but unfortunately Verendrye's Cree interpreter went with them, following a young woman who had taken his fancy.

Now the Frenchmen couldn't make themselves understood, and so there was more drumming, more feasting on squash, pumpkins, nuts, fruit, corn, and meat—buffalo, deer and small game. Certainly there was roast beaver for the guest feast, as had been offered the first white men here, although perhaps no longer roasted in the skin. The Bearded Ones of a hundred years ago had shown the magical goods the plews could bring.

The white visitors examined the dwellings, the usual lodge with easy living space for ten to twenty, or forty to fifty in a crowding time of need. The walls were several feet thick, cool in summer, and comfortable, with the central nest of coals, even in the biting cold of the Plains winters. The sides were divided into small alcoves hung from wall and roof with personal belongings, the beds raised two feet from the ground on stakes, the buffalo sleeping robes laid over the tightly drawn rawhide.

Verendrye explored a little. He found the river broad enough for a pathway to the sea, and certainly very deep in the spring as the flood plain indicated, although the water was brackish now, which reminded him of the salt and sulphur marshes and pools they passed on the last stretch of the journey here. That accounted for the village water path leading from the small spring-fed creek instead of the river. The Missouri, which Verendrye called the River of the Mantannes, was full of sand and mud bars, and piled with snags and tangled stumps and trees whitening in bleach and alkali. Yet the muddy current was swift and led, it was hoped, to the western sea, but to the questions of the white men all the Indians talked at once, perhaps hoping, if they understood the questions at all, to convey their meaning by volume if not by words.

The bales of dressed trade robes from the season's hunt would bring guns and ammunition, the Indians indicated by signs. They had many trade products and knew about the white men who lived down the river and the Spaniards too, as well as whites among some of the tribes. Beavers were plentiful everywhere, but it seemed no plews remained from the winter.

La Marque and one of the young Verendryes went down the river to another village of the tribe and couldn't make themselves understood much better there. When they returned the son, who had studied mathematics and shooting the heavens with the astrolabe for the explorations, recorded the village at 48° 12′ north latitude, which put it above Old Crossing of the Missouri, where the trails from the Souris and the Devils Lake region converged, perhaps the same village or near the same site as the one to which the two bearded men had come long ago.

Without the interpreter and with little powder left for hunting, it was plainly not profitable for Verendrye to stay among the Mantannes all winter as he had planned. It was true that those who went to the village down stream had found a promising southwestward turn of the river but, unfamiliar with Siouan languages or sign talk, they could discover nothing further. Besides, if they were to get back over the winter prairies in time to maneuver the canoes down the Assiniboine between ice break-up and the big spring floods as the snow thawed off, they should start. Verendrye requested that his personal servant and one of La Marque's men be permitted to stay with the tribe to learn the language and scout the region for the route to the sea.

In farewell Verendrye gave his host a flag, and a lead tablet with the four corners adorned in ribbon and fitted into a box, to be held in perpetuity by the tribe as a remembrance of the day he took possession of the region in the name of the king of France. The plate was to be carefully preserved within the family as a sign of this honoring above all others, and handed down from father to son. He said these things with gestures, hoping to be understood.

The night before his departure the Frenchman became ill and was too sick and weak to move for three days, with all his medicines, his tinctures and physics, in a box of personal effects carried away by an Assiniboin. It is not recorded whether any of the fabulous medicinal qualities of the beaver, lauded and prescribed by white doctors and Indian medicine men, were tried on Verendrye. By the 13th he was sufficiently improved to start across the winter plains to the Assiniboin village at the Souris. He reached there the evening of December 24, very ill, very cold and worn. Fortunately his personal box was returned to him with nothing disturbed. Treated with the remedies he carried, rested and fed, and with the interpreter once more available, he reproached the Indians for lying to him about the Mantannes, who were neither white nor living like white men.

In reply to this charge, which the interpreter must have hesitated to convey to the Indians, one of the headmen rose, saying that they had meant a nation much farther down the river, a people who worked in iron.

This reply seemed too tame to another Indian. Springing up, he shouted, "I am the man best able to talk to you about this! You did not rightfully understand what was said to you. I don't tell lies. Last summer I killed one (of that nation) who was covered with iron as I have already said several times. If I had not killed his horse first I should not have got the man."

"What did you take from the body to let us see that you are speaking the truth?" Verendrye demanded.

"As I was about to cut off his head I saw some men on horseback who were intercepting my retreat, and I had much difficulty escaping. I couldn't bring anything with me. I threw away everything I had, even my blanket, and I ran away naked—"

After three days of rest Verendrye continued his journey and by January 9 reached the first mountain. Here the party dug in out of the storms, with water and wood. La Marque decided to go on ahead and send help back for the sick man. The winter trip to La Reine was hardship for even the able-bodied Indians. Most of the way was over open prairie, the only shelter great drifts of frozen snow, with no firewood, the moose and deer and buffalo so plentiful in the fall all gone. Finally Verendrye arrived at his post, sick and worn, his heart heavy as the wet and frozen pacs of his feet over the long route. Perhaps he sensed that he would never see his River of the Mantannes again, or any stream running toward the Pacific. As a sort of reward for his desperate winter journey he was served with papers for the seizure of his possessions and had to set off for the St. Lawrence to contest the suit.

But the Verendrye vision was not to be lost. One of the sons went up the Saskatchewan, flowing in from the west. He met Indians who told him of the great mountains, far away, but standing between the river and the sea. He returned, helped establish more trading posts in good beaver country, but the mind of his father still turned toward exploration.

The two men left with the Mantannes returned, saying that early in June 1739 several tribes of mounted Indians came to trade for the beans and grains of the villages—200 lodges, of different horse tribes. The men talked with some Indians who had come overland from Spanish territory, and heard descriptions of white men who lived in forts of brick and stone, with women very white and handsome, playing music. It seems that Verendrye sent one of his sons back to the Mantannes on a fast trip for further information. He returned with two horses and some cotton cloth and porcelain beads of Spanish manufacture but could find no guide to go beyond the village.

Once more Verendrye tried to get further financing and obtained little except a small lead plate not quite nine by seven inches, an eighth of an inch thick, to be left, perhaps, where the westward river joined the sea. The inscription of this plate made no claims to the region for the king of France; the wording, translated from the Latin, is plainly inconclusive, left open, perhaps, for additions:

> "In the 26th year of the reign of Louis XV the most illustrious Lord, the Lord Marquis of Beauharnois being viceroy, 1741, Peter de La Verendrye placed this."

Because the cost of a real expedition was beyond Verendrye now and he had trouble enough maintaining peace between the local tribes and the Sioux, he sent Francois and Louis-Joseph out. The sons would require no wages and took along only two men, probably those who had wintered with the Mantannes, although it is difficult to be certain of this or much else of the journey from the very vague account.

April 1742, the Verendryes started on the familiar trail of the Souris and over the Missouri coteau to the Mantannes and waited three weeks for a tribe of horse Indians due in, to provide mounts and guides. According to that hazy account they finally gave up, and July 23, with two Mantanne guides, struck out afoot loaded with provisions, heading southwest across the prairie, apparently between the Yellowstone and the Little Missouri. After a twenty-day

search for the Horse Indians, the guides slipped away and
the Indians discovered the Verendryes. Well supplied, even
with mules and jackasses, they furnished mounts for the explorers, who traveled rapidly now. They met several tribes
but the names they reported from memory proved unrecog-
nizable, and not surprising, with the language difficulties in
that region of Algonquin, Siouan, Uto-Aztecan, Caddoan and
probably Athapascan dialects.

It seems that the Verendryes finally joined a band of
Bow Indians going against the Serpents (who may have been
the Snakes or some division of Sioux) and plodded for days
toward the rising line of mountains, surely snow-covered on
New Year's Day, to discover that the Serpents had moved.
The Bows, expressing fear that the enemy had slipped
around to attack the camp of their women and children,
started back. More probably it was the usual Plains Indian
dislike for winter fighting that sent them home. The white
men made the grim retreat with the Bows through bitter
cold and deep snow. From there they struck out alone, apparently with the northwest wind blowing the horses' tails
between their legs, the men hunching their backs against the
force of it. By March they had reached the tribe they called
Little Cherry and found one of the rumored Spanish-
speaking Indians among them, but never located "the Frenchman" apparently with a village not far away.

Finally the Verendryes buried their lead plate under
a pile of stones on a rise overlooking a stream they called the
river of the Missouris, a name often applied to the Platte.
They had scratched on the back of the small plate, in French,
the information that it was "placed" by the Verendryes
March 30, 1743, without any indication or guess at the site.
Then they went north-northeast and sometimes north-
northwest, back to the Mantannes, and were home at La
Reine by July 2, where the only account of the journey was
written.

Not only are most of the Indian tribes unidentifiable
in the account but, with no place names and no recognizable
descriptions except the one of the colorful badlands of the

Little Missouri, it is impossible for one familiar with the region to follow the wanderings of the Verendryes. The mountains mentioned stand against the west along the whole American continent. Although Louis-Joseph had learned to take observations with his astrolabe—"Shooting the sun," the Indians called it—apparently he did no more than glance at a compass now and then on this trip. It seems improbable that the four men actually walked from the Mantanne village to the Horse Indians when the whole Missouri country was full of Spanish horses, some with herds for generations. Besides, what became of those brought back from the Mantannes earlier?

Perhaps Verendrye hoped that walking the wilderness would sound more impressive in Beauharnois' reports to Maurepas, who could have no conception of the vastness of the American west, and would measure distances by his provincial yardstick.

The initiative, the toil and hardship of the journeys brought no great honor to the Verendryes. In 1744 the father, with the nine battle wounds and most of a lifetime spent trying to expand France in America, was relieved of his grants and command of the Post to the Western Sea whose forts the family had built. It seems he was not only supplanted but was obliged to pay his successor 3000 livres a year out of profits that existed only in the mind of Maurepas. With typical governmental ingratitude the sons were forbidden to carry on the father's work. Finally old Pierre was granted permission to go west once more, in May 1750, but he died the December before.

When France was finally defeated and driven out of North America in 1763, many Canadians followed the fleur-de-lis. Louis-Joseph was on the *Auguste* that was wrecked with a loss of over 300, young Verendrye among them. Francois had helped Langlade gather up 1200 Indians, including some of the tribes they had known on the Plains, and went with the expedition down the Ottawa against the British. He

fought with the gallantry of his father through the war, and
when Canada fell he remained in the land that had taken
two brothers and his father. He lived thirty-four years under
British rule, a bachelor to his death. Before he died the
dream of the father, and of all the sons, was realized, but by
an Englishman, and far north of the River to the Western
Sea. Alexander Mackenzie was no romantic. He worked with
all the maps and knowledge he could gather anywhere, including the Spanish, and certainly the British from Drake
and Cavendish on through the rest. When he followed a
river that led him to the Arctic, he tried again, and reached
that Western Sea.

CHAPTER III

THE GENTLEMEN
ADVENTURERS

"The beaver does everything well, it makes kettles, hatchets, swords, knives, bread; and, in short, it makes everything." Indian remark to Father Le Jeune, *Jesuit Relations.*

FOR more than two hundred years the beaver had been the most important export from America, commercially the most important fur bearer that the world had seen, and the subject of imperial competition and warring by the great powers of Europe. Now at last the beaver received a little attention for himself, not merely the hide he wore. To be sure, the attention was not scientific; that would not come for almost another hundred years, not until 1820, when Kuhl published a description of the Canadian beaver in the British museum and named him at that late day, *castor canadensis.*

Although still scientifically ignored back in 1738, that year Le Beau's account pictured this castor as a fabulous creature, with fabulous ways fit to stir the councils of Europe and even the most self-centered and foppish courts ever since Cartier first saw the beaver skins and robes of the American Indian. While the romantic stories of Le Beau and his kind could be told and retold elsewhere, the fur men of the wilderness knew the beaver in close detail, knew him better than they knew themselves, because they had studied the castor.

Man was the beaver's only real enemy. Cougars, bobcats, lynxes, wolves, coyotes, bears, wolverines and otters sometimes killed beavers, and even a fox, an eagle or a hawk might take an occasional young kitten. All but the otter had to surprise the beaver on land, while at work or traveling and at his most awkward and helpless. A bear might rip up a house, slavering in his eagerness for the sweet meat, but the smell was usually all he got, the beaver gone. Apparently otters sometimes drained ponds in winter to hunt under the ice, or pursued the beaver in the water, perhaps to be wounded in the attack by the sharp teeth or the powerful slash of the hind claws.

The beaver's eyes are small and probably limited in range but he is very quick to detect movement and his nose is sharp. The short ears, fur-lined, close under water but even there the hearing is keen. The forepaws, small, with fairly long claws, are used like hands for digging and to grasp and hold. The hind paws are very large, sometimes seven inches long, with a spread of five inches, and webbed like the foot of a goose for speed in the water, the toes strong and sharp-clawed. The two inner ones, called combing claws, are drawn through the hair to clean it, and to spread the waterproofing oil of the sacs near the castoreum outlet. A beaver might spend hours combing and smoothing his fur, a pleasant occupation on a lazy afternoon spent on the top of the house in the sun.

The paddle-shaped tail is perhaps the most romanticized portion of the beaver. Contrary to some accounts, it is not used to sled mud to the dam, or as a trowel to apply and spread it. Or to drive stakes. The beaver does not sleep with the tail in the water to feel a drop in the pond level. He detects any breaks in the dam by the noise of rushing water, even while sleeping curled up, snug and dry in his bed of soft grass and fine wood chips.

Romancers liked to picture the beaver sucking air from wood to make it sink, but actually he weights his winter supply down with mud and stones in the bottom of the pond, well below any ice level. He does not fell trees across streams except by accidental leaning. He smells out traps if they are not well concealed but he does not carry a stick to trip them, not even the wiliest whiskered old-timer who has

been caught and escaped, despite the credence John Bradbury, the Scottish naturalist, put in such stories told him by
hunters during his travels up the Missouri. Stringing the tenderfoot along was an old pastime by 1810.

The Indian was a prudent husbander of the beaver
before the white man's tempting goods arrived. The villages
lived beside their neighbors in the ponds much like remote
Texans might with the self-sustaining herds of Longhorns before there was a market for them. When the Indians needed
meat or skins they went out and killed a supply, much as the
beavers cut birch and poplar, cottonwood and aspen. Their
methods of catching the beavers varied with the region and
the season and were intensified as the traders arrived and the
appetites they fostered grew.

Some methods were rather widespread, as the trench-
ing with dogs seen by the two bearded men who came to the
Indian village at the Old Crossing of the upper Missouri in
the 1630's. They might have seen the same kind of hunting
as far east as the Micmacs of Nova Scotia. Perhaps all the
tribes with icing winters speared beaver when the ponds were
covered, either through blow holes or those the hunters cut.
Afterward they chopped into the frozen top of a house to
scare the beavers out into the water and then stealthily approached the holes, "ahead of your shadow," as the Indians
called it, to catch any gentle movement in the water below
from beavers breathing. A swift thrust of the spear might
take an animal, whether the barb was of bone from the small
white whale in the Saguenay River and spread far by trade,
or of elk, deer or moose horn or shaped from the lighter,
keener-edged iron of the white man.

The head snare, the high noose, was seldom used
against animals with thick necks but the beaver was often
netted, largely by the fishing tribes, experts in mesh and
trammel weaving. Netting required care against the beaver's
sharp incisors and his ripping hind claws. Either the animal
had to be so enmeshed by his first struggles that he couldn't

cut his way out before drowning or the hunter had to be ready to drag the net out and club him on the head.

Indians of wooded regions were expert with the dead-fall and sometimes caught beaver that way. These traps were usually set on the dam, the opening facing toward the pond or lake. A frame was made of stakes, often six (three to a side, and tied together with rawhide for firmness), the middle stakes low-forked to hold the crossbar that triggered the heavy, tilted log waiting, with green birch or other favored wood behind the trigger. To reach this bait the beaver stepped on or dragged over the tread bar, sprung the trap and was killed by the falling log.

Because of the weight and the scarcity of properly flexible saplings or trees close enough to beaver workings, there was less use of the spring pole that swung the captured animal off the ground before he could gnaw or more probably twist the foot off. There seems to have been little use of the set arrow, to be released and driven into the prey, against beaver, but the Indians were experts in still-hunting with the bow. Between sundown and darkness on fall evenings beavers come out of their houses and rise to the top of the quiet pond, to leave widening wakes in the sky-bright water toward the shore. Awkwardly they pull themselves out over the chilling bank and feed on the bark of young birch or poplar or willow, aspen or cottonwood. In a large pond or lake the still hunters might move up from the distance but if small they probably launched their canoe earlier on the down-wind side from the houses, to hide in the first shadows of the lowering sun before the beavers began to stir.

Later they came gliding out upon the dusky pond, the paddler making no more noise than the fall of a dead leaf settling upon the water, the hunter, in the prow, ready with an arrow set to the bow and an extra one held in his mouth as he peered into the depths and listened to the movements of the beavers on the shore. With silent hand motions he signaled this way and that, or gave the downward patting that meant drift, stop, and then once more motioned the canoe ahead. Silently they edged through the shadows toward the sound of feeding, the grunts and crunches and soft squashy noises of beavers chewing young twigs on the bank and in the water's edge.

The hunter signaled to let the canoe drift forward. The bowstring twanged and then again. There was a kicking on the shore and a splashing around below it. The hunter leaped out to catch the beaver in the water before he could reach any depths and be lost, dead or alive, while the paddler sent the canoe into the soft bank and sprang out for the one on shore. The plungings and splashings all around the pond were dying, the ripples quieting in the agitated water.

Now the men could talk and laugh in the gathering darkness, for the still hunt was over, as it would have been with spear too, or powder and ball. They had two grown beavers, fat and heavy, the furring dense under the stroking palm. Together they would paddle across the pond, the night already chilling toward the ice of morning.

What the Indian of the beaver regions called his hunting bundle, his medicine bundle used in his ceremonials to bring the game, was sometimes actually carried on the hunt. This often contained a bit of the beaver oil sac—with the thick, cream-colored oil that helps keep the fur glossy and water-shedding. The odor is unpleasant to man but as bait for various traps it draws all other creatures that hunger for the meat of the castor, particularly the lynx but also otters, fishers, martens, mink and that trap robber, the wolverine, the beaver devil, and even the bear, who may chew up a lure stick rubbed with the oil. For the beaver the castoreum of his kind is the best summer or open-water lure. There are even cases of an occasional beaver with a trap on his foot coming to another baited with castoreum.

The sign heaps, near pond or stream and apparently a beaver means of communication, look like foot-wide mud pies about three inches thick with castoreum deposited on the top. There seem to be several theories about these heaps but they are probably territorial warnings, as the dung heaps built up on rises by mustang stallions, and the urine stumps or stone piles of the gray wolves of the prairie, all apparently renewed each time that the animal makes a round of his domain.

Whatever the purpose of the sign heaps, the beaver is drawn to them, and to the castoreum emitted along the banks of ponds or other water. This attraction was apparently not exploited to any extent until the white man came with the urge to kill off whole beaver populations, and infected the Indian. Castoreum was most useful with the steel traps, brought in by the fur men but withheld from the Indians for some time and then generally loaned to them, to keep them tied to the trader-owner. The valuable hide was the one taken from the adult in winter, usually between early November and mid-April, or longer in the northern regions where the ice lasted. In the prime plew the skin underneath is firm and whitish, with all the blue transparency of the summer thinness gone, the fur dense, soft and silky under the long glistening king or guard hairs. There was usually a short time, between the first swift storms of fall and the freeze-over, when traps could be set near the shore where the beavers had been crawling in and out. The trap was placed carefully, in about three inches of water, the chain staked firmly, a space left under the trip or pan for its fall, and then all the iron, including the pan, covered lightly with fine soil sifted from the fingers to settle naturally. The lure was usually a small bit of castoreum left on the bank or in a split-end stick set about ten or twelve inches beyond the trap. In the west and the mountains the castoreum was often pounded with buds of aspen, the top of the lure stick rolled in this as a sort of year-around bait. Every trapper worked out a favorite recipe, usually carried in a bait vial, bait bottle, the Indian's usually modified by suggestions derived from his puberty dreaming or a later fasting time.

Some trappers cut shallow breaks in the top of the beaver dam and set traps in these under about two inches of water, to catch the old ones come out to make repairs. As important, however, as catching the beaver was holding him after he put a foot into the trap. The slender bones of the leg were usually broken by the snap of the iron jaws or in the desperate struggle to get free, and the ligaments and skin twisted off, leaving only the foot behind, and another crippled beaver to live the best he could. Sometimes he fought the trap, perhaps splintering or breaking the sharp yellow incisors, and with his leg twisted off he was free, free but caught in the vaster if slower trap of a tooth that might grow to monstrous length until the beaver died of open-mouthed starvation.

To prevent these losses and the fur damage from long struggles on trap lines that couldn't be run within a few hours after setting, as well as to avoid catching young, under-sized animals, the experienced fur man often set his trap in four to eight inches of water, on a shelf or little bench at the edge of a step-off into a deep place. The trap chain was extended to fifteen or more feet by wire and fastened to a stake, a stone tied close to the trap spring and laid so that the first jerk toppled it into the deep water, to drag the beaver down to drown quickly as well as to hide him from trap robbers—wolverine or man. In regions free of compact, usable rock or stone the trapper might carry deer-skin sacks to be filled with earth or gravel and used as the stones would be.

Another and more difficult device for drowning the trapped beaver was the sliding stick or pole, of dry, dead wood, to keep the beavers from gnawing it away before they were caught. The pole might be a thin sapling or cut from a clump of dead diamond willow, always with a few branches to be lopped off at about a half or quarter of an inch from the trunk, leaving little knuckles, small enough to let the trap chain ring slip down over them but not back up. The trap was set as usual but on a short chain, the ring slid over the butt end of the pole, which was thrust, branched end downward, slant-wise into the bottom of the pond, out in perhaps four, five feet of water. Caught, the beaver struggled and dived, his instinctive way out of trouble. The trap ring slid down the stick but not up, and the animal drowned.

The sliding pole was also useful in deep winter. The hunter cut a hole about three feet wide through the ice near the shore and near a house if possible. Then a green swamp magnolia, birch, alder, aspen or young cottownwood tree, branched, about two inches in diameter at the butt, was pressed together and pushed top first through the hole and off under the ice, in the direction that the beavers would pass, the trunk end staked down securely to keep it from being dragged away. If there was no shallow bench or shelf near the anchored butt, a little platform was made with stakes and the trap set on this, covered, the chain or wire of it fastened to the usual sliding pole. Then the hole was roofed over with snow to freeze. The beaver, finding the little green tree, tried to cut it off at the butt, and stepped into the trap. The first jerk loosened the chain or wire ring to slide down in the struggle and the dive. The icy water kept the fur in good condition even if the hunter was several days late running the trap line.

Beavers are skinned open, as it is called, in contrast to such animals as otter, marten, mink or ermine, whose hides are kept cased, closed, and pulled off over the head like an Indian getting out of his buckskin shirt. The beaver skinner turns a thin, pointed knife around each leg just above the foot and around the base of the tail. Then he runs the blade from the foot up the inside of each hind leg to the anal vent and from there up the belly and the breast to the middle of the lower lip, and from each forepaw up the inside of the leg to the center slit at the chest. The skin is loosened at the edges and the legs and pulled off, to be stretched tightly on a circle of willow withe and left to dry a day or so out of the sun. Then the flesh side is carefully scraped of every particle of tissue or fat, the hide hung up on the stretcher to cure and finally be piled away in a cold, dry place for market. East of the buffalo ranges the Indian women sometimes tanned beaver for sale, tanned the skins soft as velour, and these brought a special price, if the Indians could hold out against the lure of alcohol long enough to get the full value.

Sometimes, in the regions where the Hudson's Bay men were in competition with the French and an occasional trader from the British colonies, the Indians got fabulous prices for their furs, prices that were really attempts to drive out the competition, really bribes, as the wily redskin well understood. In August of 1741, Beauharnois, nephew of the governor general, wrote, "The fair sex, among the Hurons with us, has absolute power over the minds of the men." He had a number of fine collars of 1500 porcelain beads made to give to them, with some bags of flour to win them over. The large collar he had been sent was found too white. He was having 1400 black porcelain beads added to it. Evidently the Huron matrons understood their prime bargaining power, with the English not far away.

Rough standards of values had been set up at various trading points almost from the start, always with the beaver the unit of currency. For instance, one fat winter-prime adult beaver hide usually had the trade value of each of the following:

3 martens	2 ordinary otters
1 fox	(1 if exceptionally fine)
1 moose	2 deerskins
1 weejack (fisher)	1 lb. castoreum
1 bear cub	10 lbs. feathers
2 queequehatches	8 moose hoofs
(wolverines)	4 fathoms of netting

One good black bear hide was worth two beaver skins.

The Hudson's Bay Company established the value of their trade goods at the various forts, particularly the main ones, with more flexibility permitted at the little outposts, as the one on the Red River. In 1733 at Moose River on James Bay, made-beaver, an adult prime hide in good condition, paid for any one of the following: 1/2 lb. beads, *le milk;* 3/4 lb. beads, colored; 1 brass kettle; 1 lb. lead, black; 1 1/2 lb. gunpowder or 2 lbs. sugar. Near Fort York and up at Churchill, both farther up Hudson's Bay, the price of trade goods was increased because the French were remote, although these posts were much farther, by pack and paddle, for all but the tribes west of the Red River.

The Indians arrived at these posts with their long strings of loaded summer canoes and were taken into the trading room one at a time, where a clerk or trader separated the bundles of furs into piles by variety and condition, estimated in made-beaver. For these the Indian received little pieces of wood. Later these were grooved to represent numbers of beaver, say one to ten, to simplify the process.

With his pouch full of these tally sticks the Indian was taken to the store room to wander along the aisles of bales and bundles, boxes and barrels of goods: blankets and slop coats; guns, lead, powder and flints; knives and axes; tea and sugar; paint, beads and so on, at fixed prices. A slop coat might be twelve made-beaver, a gun twenty or more, a knife two. Usually the Indian had requests from the women of his family at home or some maiden of his fancy, perhaps a deerskin list, the items in picture writing. These might be long meat knives, kettles, vermilion, finery. Often there was the rum of the company to be considered first, particularly at the competitive posts, although there was apparently no repetition of the appalling drunkenness common at the Montreal fur fairs or at the later trapper rendezvous of the far west.

Not that the Hudson's Bay outfit was without blame. Complaints and petitions were general around London and Parliament, growing in insistence during the 1730's and 1740's. When the company applied for reconfirmation of the charter, back shortly after the accession of William III, in 1688, during the period of fantastic profits, there was opposition by Feltmakers Company and again seven years later, also unsuccessfully. The glutted market around 1700 and the colonial wars quieted the opposition but in 1737 there was a more determined attack on the charter, led by Arthur Dobbs, who gave a glowing picture of the interior of North America and the lucrative trade that could be opened by London merchants. He called the Hudson's Bay Company unenterprising and repeated the charge that no attempt was made to discover the passage to the south sea. His Irish eloquence, describing the advantage of a northwest passage, got orders from the Lords of the Admiralty to Captain Middleton, formerly of the company, to search for the passage. When he failed, Dobbs attacked him, and Parliament voted a £20,000 reward for the discovery of such a route. Dobbs led a campaign for public subscription of £10,000 to finance the new voyage, but the attempt failed.

Now Arthur Dobbs extended his charges against the Bay Company to include neglect in fostering the settlements required by the charter, abuse of the Indians, neglect of the forts, ill-treatment of company servants and encouragement of the French. The company submitted a detailed list of vessels sent out along the northern coast—to draw attention from their unaccountable neglect for eighty years, some accused, of their fabulous domain in the interior. About this they had done practically nothing while the French pushed clear out to the Missouri and beyond, Frenchmen who wrote of their journeys, no matter how dubious the accounts. It was apparently true that the company had tried to get men out to explore but no one wanted to stir from the Bay posts, no one except the traders eager for hides.

In 1748 Dobbs, spokesman for a commercial combine, presented a petition to the Parliamentary Committee for privileges in America similar to those of Hudson's Bay, offering to undertake extensive colonization and the explorations never made by the company. In rebuttal to this the directors had offered *A Journal of a Voyage and Journey* by Henry Kellsey,* to discover and endeavor to bring "to a commerce the Naywatanee Poets," dated 1691, which was attacked by Joseph Robson. He was a stone mason who had built Fort Prince of Wales at Churchill, and wrote under the title "Late Surveyor and Supervisor of the Buildings to the Hudson's-Bay Company." He had been induced to return to the bay from England in 1744-47 and believed that this was done to keep him from getting to Dobbs. Others added color to the

---

* See *The Kelsey Papers*, listed in the Bibliography.

charges by saying that Kelsey had lived several seasons among the Indians of the interior, but as a refugee from the Hudson's Bay Company.

With Kelsey safely dead since 1730, Robson's account of his six years' residence at Hudson's Bay and his comment in 1752, "I no more believe that it is Kelsey's than it is mine," brought more doubt upon the journal. In the handsome 250th-anniversary volume of the Hudson's Bay Company, their spokesman says that they made a "fairly effective reply" to the charges about the Northwest Passage but were less convincing on the development of their territory. That their defense was a little shaky was admitted in 1820, when, during the struggle with the North West Company, they feared revival of the charges made in 1737-49. It seems plain that during the eighty years of their fur monopoly the company had been content with the profits and did little to develop the region or to push trade, and yet refused to let others in. The company won, but rumors of cheated Indians and flogged servants persisted. True, everybody cheated Indians and flogging was common in Europe and America; even an occasional woman still felt the sting of the cat at Montreal and elsewhere.

After the inquiry of 1749 and the end of another war between France and England, the Hudson's Bay Company spurred itself to a policy of imperialism; not subject to the same government control as the British colonies, the company moved against the French traders in both the east and the west and southward. Not that this was all new. The impression given during the investigations was not completely just. Since late in the 17th century men went out from the main posts to channel furs toward the Bay, men as far as Turtle Mountain and west, out toward the headwaters of the Saskatchewan and down along the Rockies. The lauded westward thrust of the French was less initiative than pure necessity. As they destroyed the beaver they had to move on to remain in business at all.

After the Verendrye expeditions, the trade of their region declined. The Sioux returned to the warpath and, partly to avoid them, the Crees once more took the furs of their catch and trade over the long water haul to Hudson's Bay. Hostile Indians destroyed the Verendrye posts of La Reine and Maurepas and in 1750 what remained to the family was rapidly being expropriated. A so-called expert in Indians and the fur trade undertook to stop the Sioux war, placate the Crees and get the hunting started once more. He failed in everything but did send a man to build a post on some far tributary of the Southern Saskatchewan, to compete with the Bay Company in their trade among the Blackfeet. More disasters fell upon the French, from the Sioux, from the Crees who destroyed posts and from the competition and the government, to whom the small trader was still often a sort of bush loper, although out in new regions he had his usual success with the natives. Another little post was started for the Blackfeet and the Assiniboins, with men pushing down toward the headwaters of the Missouri and sifting through the passes to the ancient Indian trade fairs in the summer mountain valleys draining westward.

Then suddenly the trade goods no longer reached the outposts in the spring and some of the newer bush lopers didn't discover for years that in 1754 another French and Indian war against the English had started, drawing men and resources from the posts of the west, and with them all French control forever. During these years some of the bush lopers, particularly the mixed-bloods, not only became more solidly members of the tribes of their wives but had gone over to the G-string completely.

In the meantime Graham, factor of the Bay's York fort, had started Anthony Hendry (or Henday) to the western Indians. Hendry was young and new to the country but he went a thousand miles inland without a white companion, to the upper South Saskatchewan country, where the company still claimed Kelsey had been. Apparently the directors did not know that Hendry was outlawed for smuggling in England. They gave him a valuable supply of trade goods. He was to be free-handed with presents and to undersell the French. His journal, graphic, easily followed, a unique quality in such writings, shows him pleased with what he saw: a wide, promising country, with great buffalo herds and the Blackfeet tribe, who far excelled other Indians. They were well-mounted, with pack horses, were good firemakers, carrying a black stone that they used as flint and a kind of ore for the steel, a well-fed, orderly, hospitable people. They made slaves of captives, the young ones adopted into families who had lost children, but it seemed to him that they tortured the aged of both sexes.

Unfortunately these Blackfeet killed game mostly for their own needs, taking only ten beavers when they might have killed 200. Hendry bought beaver, wolf and fox hides from them, wintered in their villages and made friends but he had to hear their complaints about the long killing journey to the Bay. They were not canoe men, they said, with perhaps a little of that general contempt of the Plains people for the water-bound.

South and east of the Blackfeet the Indians remained more or less loyal to the Frenchmen. Each summer from 1754 to the surrender of Canada war parties from as far west as the Missouri and the Plains beyond went to join Charles Langlade, the mixed-blood trader of Green Bay, leading a breed and Indian force against the British. He was credited with planning the ambush of Braddock's troops, where over 900 were reported dead and wounded, including sixty-three of the eighty-nine officers, killed trying to rally the soldiers who were running away. Many more would have died if Langlade's Indians had not stopped to do a little scalping and jerking red coats off. Two years later they defeated a raiding party of Rogers Rangers, and many served in the Quebec campaign under Montcalm in 1759. Each year other young Indian warriors had gone east, to replace those who came home with stories that would grow into vague, cloudy legends, with coats of red cloth that would fade too, and yield their wool to hungry crickets.

With the surrender of Canada in 1760, the Hudson's

Bay Company moved to consolidate what had been taken over from the retreating French traders. In 1761 the company once more petitioned the Crown to have their southern boundary moved down to the 49th parallel, and plainly with no intention of stopping there, although French cession of Louisiana to Spain to keep it out of English hands might be a temporary barrier. The treaty of 1763 put most of the beaver regions of the world if not under actual British control at least by infiltration and design under British influence. The vast territory west of the Mississippi, very rich in robes and fur, was technically Spanish but with little show of interest or power. The hope of an absolute charter to the 49th parallel and eventually over the Spanish fur territories—a monopoly of the earth's supply of beaver—was "aiming high and taking a good lead," as the old hunters used to say, but the quarry was worth the powder.

Because the French traders and trappers had a long and intricate family relationship with the Indians (one man often with wives in serveral tribes) those who wanted to work during the war had been given a friendly hearing by the Hudson's Bay officials. But some remained out even after 1763, the Bay men reporting that a few old "Pedlars from Quebec" as they called them, were still living in the French houses of the Saskatchewan region. In 1765 Louis Primo (probably Primeau) found his way to York Factory, complaining of his hardship with the Indians the last five, six years, perhaps because he had no trade goods and could not explain the reason. The post journal described Primo as a native of Quebec, talkative, illiterate, "compleat master of the Indian language," although one might have asked: which one—Cree, Sioux, Blackfeet or Assiniboin?

Primo was hired and was probably useful in the company's system of watching any opposition, now largely those Pedlars from Quebec, including an increasing number of Scotsmen from Montreal. Everything seen and heard of the competition was entered in the required journals and diaries. The master at Moose River reported that the Indians had found the English "thick as Muskettos" on the Nottaway

River, also flowing into James Bay—but not company English. Pontiac's uprising stopped the lake traffic for a while, with probably many killed trying to get through, but as soon as the Indians were defeated the St. Lawrence traders once more followed the sweet smell of the castor westward, seeking unspoiled fields.

The post journals of the Hudson's Bay Company during the 1760's contain the Indian names, in a sort of phonetic spelling, of an assortment of old-time French traders and trappers still found in the west, some traceable by their licenses but more without paper. The man called Saswaw was recorded as Francis Sirdaw, probably the Franceway of the fur business, for thirty years in the upper country and known to the Indians as Saswee. It seemed that in 1768 he occupied a trader place one day's paddle below the later Finlay House on the Saskatchewan, and before that was at Old French House, another day's work down the river. Evidently he was a real irritation to the Bay force in the Saskatchewan region to 1776, perhaps because he joined the new men coming out of Montreal, finally serving as guide and trader for Todd and McGill.

But Franceway was only one of the many Canadians scattered over the wilderness gathering furs for market as the routes reopened. Most of them restored their connection with Montreal through the new merchants but some turned their faces, at least their bullboats of furs from the Blackfeet and neighboring tribes, southward on the spring floods, perhaps from near the headwaters of the Missouri or through the passes from beyond, all knowing that there must still be French merchants somewhere down the river, even if it was the far New Orleans, and in Spanish hands.

The political peace of 1763 brought no commercial peace to the Hudson's Bay Company. To be sure the rival traders were all small, their take seldom more than a few loaded canoes, but the combined result could be significant. There were stirrings toward a formal organization down on the St. Lawrence in 1776 but the rebellion of the American colonies brought arms to the lake routes, closed them. In

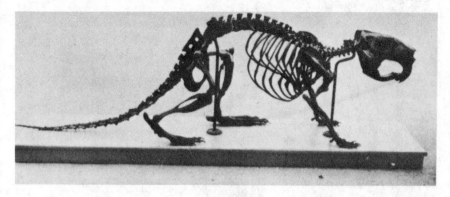

Giant prehistoric beaver, *Castoroides Ohioensis,* found in Randolph County, Indiana. Length, 6 ft., 2½ in. — with fleshy tail, would have measured full seven feet. *Joseph Moore Museum, Earlham College, Richmond, Ind. Photo by Susan Castator.*

Beaver making a stand. *Nebraska Game Commission.*

The Cataract of NIAGARA some make this Water-Fall to be half a League while others reckon it no more than a hundred Fathom

A View of ye Industry of ye Beavers of Canada in making Dams to stop ye Course of ye Rivulet in order to form a great Lake, about wch they build their Habitations. To Effect this; they fell large Trees with their Teeth in such a manner as to make them come Cross ye Rivulet, to lay ye foundation of ye Dam; they make Mortar, work up, and finish ye whole with great order and wonderfull Dexterity. The Beavers have two Doors to their Lodges, one to the water and the other to the Land side. According to ye French Accounts.

Inset from Herman Moll's "Map of the Dominions of the King of Great Britain," 1709-1720. *The World Described.*

THE HUDSON'S BAY COMPANY'S BEAVER TOKEN.

The *N.B.* was engraved by error — should have been *M.B.* for "made-beaver," value one large adult, winter-prime hide, or the equivalent.

Pierre La Verendrye's expedition to search for the Western Sea, and furs, leaving Montreal, 1731. *N. Y. Public Library Picture Collection.*

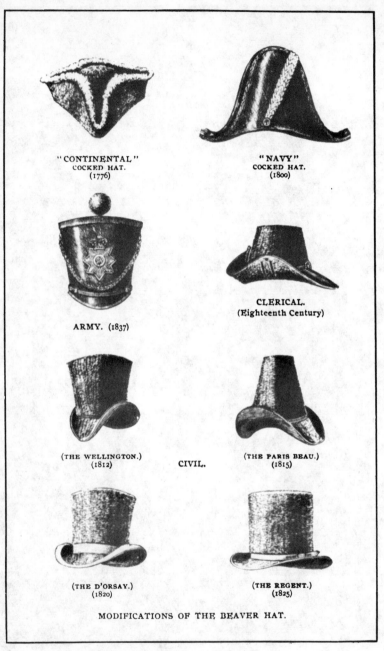

"CONTINENTAL"
COCKED HAT.
(1776)

"NAVY"
COCKED HAT.
(1800)

ARMY. (1837)

CLERICAL.
(Eighteenth Century)

(THE WELLINGTON.)
(1812)

CIVIL.

(THE PARIS BEAU.)
(1815)

(THE D'ORSAY.)
(1820)

(THE REGENT.)
(1825)

MODIFICATIONS OF THE BEAVER HAT.

From *Castorologia,* by Horace T. Martin.

Ball play of the Dahcota (Sioux) Indians. *N. Y. Public Library
Picture Collection.*

→

TRAPPER AND
TRADER OF THE
OLD REGIME.

From *Castorologia,* by Horace T. Martin.

Hidatsa (called Minnetaree on picture) village of Upper Missouri, painted by George Catlin. *Smithsonian Institution.*

Trapping for Beaver. Note simplified sketch of steel trap, later perfected by Newhouse. *N. Y. Public Library Picture Collection.*

Beaver, ceramic plaque in subway station, Astor Place, New York City, named for John Jacob Astor.

Pawnee council at Major Long's Expedition encampment, overlooking Missouri River, 1819-1820; drawn by Samuel Seymour.

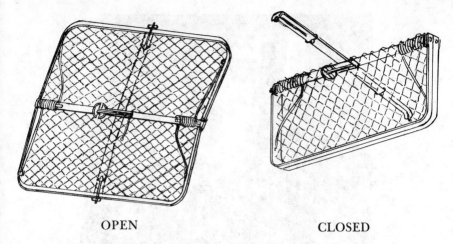

OPEN   CLOSED

Sketch of modern trap for catching beaver uninjured, to be transported to regions where dams will hold back run-off water, prevent soil erosion and stabilize streams. Planes parachute-drop beavers, in pairs, in such regions as the Big Horn Mountains.

Summer work of beavers. *Nebraska Game Commission.*

1784 a group of the most efficient traders of Montreal started the North West Company. This was a remarkable combination of genius, energy and business acumen. In the meantime, at the mouth of the Missouri, in the growing little settlement named St. Louis, a young man was developing into a major figure in the fur trade of the west, while in Scotland a boy yet to be born would some day not only head the Hudson's Bay Company but become its knighted symbol. At times there would be desperate competition between the Scotsman and the son of the young trader from St. Louis, each to become ambitious under the ruthless spur of an illegitimate name.

But in 1784 there were still a few remote regions where the beaver went his quiet, industrious way, undisturbed.

CHAPTER IV

A DARING RACE OF SCOTS

THE war years of 1745-48 had been comparatively quiet around the northwestern beaver regions. In many places no new bones were added to those bleaching and fragile as dry aspen twigs around the powerful-jawed skulls and the long yellow teeth. These were the years when the La Verendryes were dispossessed and the Hudson's Bay Company was still fighting off Arthur Dobbs to protect their monopoly on the vast fur profits.

For the beaver the portentous event was neither of these. During the war between France and England Bonnie Prince Charlie, with his Jacobites, had landed in Scotland with plans to re-establish the line of James* II, who had fled from London to Paris in 1688. They were defeated at Culloden Moor in April 1746. Charlie fled to France, and many of his Scottish Highland followers to the French too, but at Montreal. Some of these became merchants there, and once more Montreal was the gathering place of men in a strange land learning a strange trade, this time Scottish immigrants looking toward the beaver of the western regions vacated by the French government and merchants if not by all the coureurs de bois.

During the warring of the 1740's the Canadians were

* *Jacobus* in Latin.

busy trying to defend Louisbourg and Quebec and neglected their attempt to control the fur trade of all Louisiana, never to be reasserted. In the meantime the French of the Mississippi and Missouri posts obtained trade goods through New Orleans and completed a treaty with the Jumanos and Comanches to permit expeditions led by Spanish deserters, private traders and official agents through to New Mexico. Most of the southwest was poor beaver country, with vast reaches of summer-dried lagunas and buffalo wallows and wide empty stream beds with the sweeping current marks of spring floods and summer cloudbursts upon the shining yellow-white sand. Besides, the pelt of the southern beaver was much lighter, thinner-furred, although just as stinking in the hot moist New Orleans warehouses as the densest northern fur, and as injured by heat.

But the Spanish southwest had other attractions, including old settlements with many trade needs, and many handsome duenna-guarded young women, white or nearly so, those of even the best Spanish families marrying at twelve to fourteen, with dowry and proper wedding ceremony, feast and dancing. The thought could make a tangle-bearded trapper recall his youth in France or even Three Rivers. For others there were the stories of tequila and fandangos and girls with flowers behind their ears. And always there was the silver and gold, and for some even the thought of territory and governorships.

Early in 1748 thirty-three Frenchmen were trading with those prime raiders of the Spanish settlements, the Comanches, who, like the Blackfeet, very often did not get their furs from the animals that grew them. Some French expeditions to New Mexico went up the Missouri and the South Platte. In August 1752 a couple of bolder traders were guided clear to Santa Fe by the Comanches. The men lost their goods, were thrown into prison and apparently sent to Spain, probably for questioning about French penetration and plans.

There was a growing violence in the Missouri and Arkansas River country, caused by the combination of law

less bush lopers drifting toward the wilder regions, the traders driven down by the closed lake routes, and those from
Illinois, all stirring the Indians up against each other almost
as much as the French and Spaniards did. The calamities of
alcohol and disease accentuated the troubles. The Big Osages
were in a continual war with the Panis-Noirs and Panis
Picques, trade allies of the Spanish. When measles and smallpox decimated one of the Pani villages they appealed to the
Laytanes, the nomadic Apaches, for protection. Together
they struck a Big Osage village during a formal buffalo surround. In the swift attack the Osages lost twenty-two of their
chiefs and came crying to the French for help.

But the authorities, with only a handful of soldiers,
and wiser than Champlain and some who followed him,
would not take sides in intertribal conflicts. Besides, fighting
killed trade; nobody hunted. Further, some divisions of the
Osages had been sending furs to the British coming across the
Mississippi and this the French also remembered.

By 1752 Macarty, the new commandant of French
Illinois, complained loudly against the lawless bush lopers
from Canada who traded and doled out brandy on permits
for hunting only. In addition the Spaniards were reaching
up the Platte again, and to the Niobrara and the Arikara villages beyond, their goods going as far as the Assiniboins.
Macarty wrote of the Missouri as a path to the western sea
but he considered the search beyond private means. Still, the
French had climbed every consequential branch of the Missouri to the mountains, and some beyond, to pack their furs
back through the passes, but they spread themselves out.
Down in Texas, when missions and forts were attacked by
large forces of Indians during the late 1750's, the French
were still blamed with the instigation. Finally Captain Par-
rilla was sent to the Red River with troops, Indian allies and
cannon to dislodge a stockaded gathering place for raiding
Comanches, Wichitas and other tribes under the French flag.
He attacked, was repulsed, lost his baggage and cannon.
Plainly the French were not only ubiquitous but very strong.

Four years later France was out of America. Her retreat, even with the transfer to nominal Spanish rule, had little effect on the trade draining through New Orleans. Early in 1763 D'Abbadie, French director general of Louisiana, granted the exclusive trading rights of the entire Missouri valley to Maxent, Laclede and Company. When the established traders complained of favoritism, he forwarded their protests to Paris in June 1764 with his denial of the charges, just as though these were still French concern.

The new trader Laclede had come up from New Orleans in 1763 and early in the next year started St. Louis, named for Louis XVI, on what turned out to be Spanish territory. He had founded not only the settlement that was to grow into the queen of the later beaver trade but also the greatest fur-trade family of that city and the entire Missouri country—unfortunately, not in his name. When he came north he brought the thirteen-year-old Auguste Chouteau along, and the boy's mother, who had left Chouteau and gone through a civil ceremony with Laclede. The marriage had no status in French law and so the four children she bore him carried the Chouteau name, including Pierre, who would, with the help of his father and the half-brother Auguste, become the power that could even withstand Astor and his American Fur Company for years.

Many Frenchmen, particularly from Illinois, followed Laclede to the St. Louis region, which was left free from Spanish interference for six years. Many heavily loaded batteaux and pirogues came up from New Orleans and went back piled high with furs and robes, often guiding great rafts like high floating islands—more furs. Laclede kept to the lower Missouri trade and let others operate elsewhere, often with his financial help.

While the Spaniards were slow in asserting their supremacy over the burgeoning St. Louis, the Scotsmen of Montreal moved with great speed to take over the trade of their west. Canada had barely surrendered in 1760 when Alexander Henry started from Lachine, still avoiding the rapids as surely now as the earliest explorer. Henry hoped to take over the farther posts vacated by the French before the Hudson's Bay men moved in. He was twenty-three and a greenhorn to the wilderness and its commerce, but he took a stout old French trader and hunter along as guide and adviser. Certainly no newcomer could have anticipated the mood of the Indians, dependent upon white-man goods for a hundred years and then suddenly deprived of them, often with the game scarce and wild, the region beaver-stripped and barren.

Henry planned to trade on the Indian passion for alcohol but practically the first ones he met stole his rum and then explained, as they told the story almost a hundred years later, "You lose all anyhow, farther on; we take now, keep from bad enemies."

They were right about the robbers farther on. Henry lost the last of his goods at Michilimackinac and may have been lucky to get away alive, although there are some who question the complete accuracy of his account.

Five years later Alexander Henry got a license to the exclusive trade of Lake Superior and once more he led his canoes out, with Cadotte along—well known around the lakes, well established among the Indians, with an Indian wife. This time Henry stayed out for years, successfully.

Others besides Henry were robbed because they had to go through the older, fur-impoverished regions, past the debauched and pauperized tribes, to get to the Indians with more independence and furs. Blondishes Fort on the Assiniboine may have kept open all through the warring years in spite of the pressures from the Bay men on him, and from the Indians too, with trade goods so scarce. There may have been some seepage of supplies from the Hudson's Bay trade, some from down the Missouri, perhaps, or even from the far-ranging pack mules of the Spaniards—a little powder, probably, and hoop iron for arrow and spear points. Goods did reach the earthen villages of the upper Missouri with some regularity, probably managed by coureurs de bois living there and the descendants of Long Beard and Little Beard, in addition to those gone north to work for the Bay Company around York or out along the rivers.

There was some disagreement about government disposition of the Indian regions taken from the French, and particularly their tribal allies. After a little fumbling General Gage was given the task of subduing the Indians. His terms of settlement, 1764, required them to surrender all prisoners, deserters and Frenchmen among them, and to drive out the Jesuit missionaries, a sort of retribution for the exclusion of all non-Catholics from settlement in New France, and the encouragement of the missions for continued Indian raids against the "heretic" English settlements. Not that this stricture against the Jesuits was unprecedented. In 1759 they were expelled from Portugal and Portuguese colonies; France suppressed them in 1764, the year Gates ordered them driven out; three years later the Spanish dominions were closed to them and in 1773 Clement XIV, under pressure from the Bourbons and some of his cardinals, dissolved the order, to be restored later, by other hands.

The disagreement about the proper disposal of the Indian country went on. Lord Barrington, British Secretary of War, argued that the country west of the Alleghenies should be left to them, and Croghan wanted the region preserved as a hunting ground for the Indians and for the fur trade. But there was land out there, and most of the people of Europe land-hungry.

In 1765 Maj. Robert Rogers of the Rangers, was recommended as commandant at Michilimackinac, which had been a central point under the French for the trading posts north, west and south, with high payment for monopoly privileges, such as 25,000 livres a year for Green Bay, less for smaller posts. Under the English, payments and monopolies were discontinued, at least in theory. Rogers was bold, energetic and clever and ambitious. He spoke of exploration and expansion and, it was said, exacted presents from the Indians and traders when they entered the post and left it. Not that this was unusual but it made hard feelings, adhering neither to the old French system of paid privileges nor to the austere Hudson's Bay practices, where all posts belonged to the company. Rogers turned trader and was accused of taking his preference of all furs and skins brought there before the marketing, as well as violating the ban against rum in the Indian trade.

Rogers had definite ideas about Indian goods. He recommended that 100 canoes be alloted to his post and its territory. These should carry 6000 pounds of merchandise and 1000 pounds of supplies each, Henry reported, the contents to be: eighteen bales of strouds, blankets, freize, coats, bed gowns, coarse calicoes, linen shirts, leggings, ribbons, beads, vermilion, gartering and so on, and in addition: nine kegs of gunpowder, one of flint steels and gun screws, and ten of British brandy; four cases iron work and cutlery, two of guns, two of looking glasses and combs; two bales of brass kettles, two of manufactured tobacco; twelve bags of shot and ball, and a box of silver and wampum. The value of each canoe would be £450 at Quebec, the total cost of operating the 100 canoes one season estimated at £60,898. This Rogers declared would keep out traders from Spanish Louisiana and win the Sioux, help open new regions, insure the northwest to the British, promote English manufactures and bring prosperity to many subjects of the empire.

When abolition of the most of the small posts around him was suggested, Rogers objected. The traders supported him but wanted the French removed from the west. He sent his requests straight to the Board of Trade, ignoring all intermediaries, and proceeded as though his ideas had been approved. In 1765 he submitted a "Proposal for the Discovery of a Northwest Passage," certain that the achievement would conciliate the Indians, particularly those a thousand leagues away who never came because the journey would cost them a year's hunt.

In 1766 Rogers sent Jonathan Carver west to make the discoveries wanted. At Grand Portage he found many Crees and Assiniboins waiting for the traders due in July for the long-established rendezvous. General Carleton, hoping to prevent French and Spanish trade extensions, recommended that the Canadian French be permitted to roam freely for furs provided that they take some English in every canoe to become familiar with the remote regions and with the languages and customs of the Indians.

Before much was known of Carver's explorations Rogers was arrested for treason: planning to enter the French service, with the lesser charge of winning popularity with the Indians by buying lavish gifts for them on credit, apparently from the 100,000 livres he owed the traders. A Canadian told Captain Spiesmachus (Spiesmacher), the post's second in command, that Rogers said he was working for French interest and would make a fortune, to which Spiesmachus added that Rogers planned to decoy him from the fort and then "bring savages to capture it and not go to the French empty handed." He also intended to capture Detroit and Illinois for them, it seemed, although some thought Rogers hoped to erect the country around Michilimackinac "into a separate Province and make him(self) governor of it." If this failed he would retire to the French down the Mississippi.

The major was taken to Montreal in chains, court-martialed and acquitted for lack of evidence but, the Deputy Judge-Advocate of England wrote, there was great reason to suspect Major Rogers of "entertaining an improper and dangerous correspondence" and so on. The Michilimackinac trade suffered greatly. The debts to the local merchants were not paid and most of them were ruined, leaving the wilderness open to the traders from the south, although the lake post did remain a center for western commerce. Each summer several hundred wandering traders gathered there, French and British, many who had been in the Indian country from twelve to thirty years and differed little from the natives except in color, bearding and degree of addiction to vice. French traders, their number augmented by some from the Mississippi (but who never appeared at the post) were supplied with goods by Frenchmen holding licenses at Michilimackinac. All were supplied with rum and the Indians were becoming so debauched that they neglected the hunting, particularly with the beaver scarce.

The story of Michilimackinac was not the whole picture of western commerce from Montreal. Some of the traders with Indian blood, gone to help in the war, had returned west before Rogers took over at the lake post. In 1768 James Finlay, a Scotsman, a stout forerunner of his kind, by-passed the troublesome post on his way to the Saskatchewan, where he later established Finlay House. When the Hudson's Bay men ordered him out of their territory, which ran from the Bay to the Pacific, he insisted that he had a right to trade within fifty leagues of the company forts and that not fifty men could hinder him. Apparently the Bay officials valued peace over complete supremacy, particularly if it meant a fight with a Scotsman. Perhaps they recalled some troubles with an Irishman, one named Dobbs.

Finlay with boldness offered twenty-five pounds per annum and the passage to the St. Lawrence to some of the Hudson's Bay men, adding his business address and that of his London connections. In 1773 he took in a young Englishman, John Gregory, and for ten years they sent long strings of canoes west every spring. When Finlay retired from the field, Gregory went into partnership with Alex McLeod. It was under them that the young Alexander Mackenzie, the explorer-trader, served his apprenticeship. But there were Finlays in the fur trade for several energetic generations, the mixed-bloods penetrating much of the Rocky Mountain region above the Missouri headwaters; a later one, François, discovered the hard gold of western Montana but suppressed the information as men almost a hundred years earlier had done, knowing that such news would start a rush to the region, a Spanish-French rush run north in the 1700's, an American one in the 1840's. Either would have ruined the fur harvest of the region, destroyed the soft gold of the beaver.

Another Scot, Corry, went out to Cedar Lake, near the lower Saskatchewan, for Todd, that Montreal merchant with his eyes on the far horizon. The trade was so rich that Corry returned for another winter and although he lost two of his men to the Bay company he made so much money he never went out again. Such success by an illiterate trader struck east Canada like a chinook sweeping over the winter Plains. By 1773 goods from the adventuresome new Montreal traders were spreading along the old Indian trails down to the upper Missouri, sometimes past the blue flower of the voyageurs' coffee chicory, "the bloom of the white man's tracks" as the Indians called it. That summer of 1773 the old-timer Franceway reached Finlay House with fifteen canoes, to winter, and the Frobisher brothers also came. In 1772 the Pedlars of Quebec had cut so deeply into the Hudson's Bay trade that Cocking, second, in command at York, was sent out to the forks of the Saskatchewan and overland to the Blackfeet, to measure the invasion of Bay territory. He met a poor forlorn Frenchman, with the Indians some years, but he saw no white traders. Later he heard that forty-five pedlar canoes came up the next year.

Alarmed, the Bay company hurried Samuel Hearne, an official, out to found Cumberland House on the Saskatchewan and to undersell the Scottish competition. He reported upwards of sixty canoes coming inland from Grand Portage in 1774, and twenty or thirty gone south, out of the company's trading region.

Cumberland House seemed surrounded by Montreal traders, who took out furs valued at £15,000 in 1774. Frobisher and some others went up the Hudson's Bay trails and waterways to intercept the Indians on their way to the company. Frobisher offered to buy all the furs of the parties he saw but they refused, their furs promised to the Bay mer-

chants who had advanced their provisions and hunting supplies. The determined Frobisher kept raising the price until
the Indians yielded. It was said he made $50,000 clear profit.

This news, coming soon after the Corry success,
stirred the Scotsmen like a horn from the hills and aroused a
little hope even in the defeated French of Canada, secretly
cheered by the rising rebellion of the colonies. True, putting
down the rebels would be a temporary handicap to the St.
Lawrence region too, but a real conflict might end—who
could say where? Perhaps there might be another reversal
like the one after Quebec was taken in 1629, and then could
not be held. With such a hope, even unspoken, it was no
wonder that Canadian officials warned that the French at the
outposts were not trustworthy.

"Most traders are rebels at heart," was the common
verdict, one often expressed long ago by French officials and
by the Jesuits.

The hope was strengthened when France joined in
the war on the side of the colonies. Traitors might sprout up
like puffballs on the prairie after a rain now. Even some of
the Scots discussed the possibility of taking Canada over to
the side of the revolutionaries and the French, but if the
colonies succeeded, the Navigation Acts would then keep
them out of the English markets and with Paris subordinated
to London in the beaver trade, the whole fur business of
Canada would be ruined.

Several groups of the Scottish traders had formed a
loose sort of partnership of convenience when they first invaded the Bay company territory, Peter Pond, from the
colonies, one of the most aggressive. Then suddenly, with the
start of the American Revolution, the lakes were closed to all
shipping except the Crown's, apparently until the colonies
were subdued. Sitting sourly on the rise overlooking their
warehouses full of goods, some of the Montreal traders could
not help but see that this necessity was favoring the Hudson's
Bay men against the river competition, eliminating the Scots

and their French bush lopers and voyageurs. The few traders who could get goods used all the sharp practices and tricks of the Indian barter. Detroit was particularly blamed. It seemed that the beaver pound kept growing there, the powder and shot decreasing to a half, and the silver ornaments turning to brass before the Indians were around the bend. Rum grew in importance, with more and more of the burn the comparatively harmless red pepper, the cups holding less and less as the layers of lead in the bottoms grew.

Closing the lakes did send more furs north to Hudson's Bay but many more went down to New Orleans, helping to spread French and Spanish influence farther into the beaver regions. New posts were built along the Mississippi and out into the Missouri country, starting St. Louis on her great future. Even the garrisons were reinforced. Americans were welcomed but when Ducharme, Montreal merchant, managed to get up the Missouri with a large cargo of goods about 1778, and started to trade for beaver, the Spaniards captured him and took his pelts and supplies worth between four and five thousand dollars. He tried again in 1780 and failed once more.

Up north there were the unhampered Bay men. Back as early as 1768 when it became clear to many British what alcohol was doing to the Indians, a memorial from the merchants and traders of Montreal to the Lords of Trade had requested that the strong liquor of each canoe for the posts including Mackinac (Michilimackinac) be limited to four barrels or kegs of eight or nine gallons each unless the trader was going north, obviously into Bay competition. Then double the quantity was to be permitted. Several Indian tribes asked for rigid control of the liquor business, but they too, were unheard.

Now, with the lakes ordered closed, alcohol was probably the easiest and surely the most effective item of trade to smuggle past Carleton's guards. Besides it was obtainable, for a price, at practically every post and vessel, with the British service man legally entitled to his daily portion of rum. Alcohol, that prime permeator, also seeped in around south of the lakes, and up the Mississippi and through the Missouri country. The Bay men used the same weapon in the areas of competition. The result was a growing drunkenness, fast approaching that of the 1600's at Quebec, Montreal and out around the posts and missions, with most of the governors, the bishops and missionaries complaining.

The nomadic Assiniboins were less experienced with firewater than the tribes that lived around the posts and settlements, and not as hopeless and defeated. When one of their men died from alcohol, they attacked two forts and killed three Canadians. There is no telling how far the raids and violence might have gone if tragedy in a more immediate form had not struck the tribe. A war party had recently returned with scalps from the upper Missouri country, scalps easily taken, it was discovered later, because a new epidemic of smallpox had swept up the Plains. It came, an enemy, from the direction that should bring only good—the springtime, the soft winds, the geese and swans and ducks, the birds that sing as they rise into the sun and the great buffalo herds. Twice now this stinking spotted disease had come up the ladder of rivers, following at the heels of the white man like a hungry wolf but going around him like the arrow that goes around the white buffalo, and then striking the Indian down. The scalps that brought the sickness were said to be Mandan but they could have come from almost any western tribe.

The disease ran through the Assiniboins as it had the eastern peoples almost a hundred fifty years ago, and many, many tribes since. Scarcely an Indian struck by smallpox lived. It was said that the white man made a strong medicine against it with small cuts, not like the large scarring ones of the Indian in the sun dance and in sorrow. It was probably just another foolish story but the pale-skinned ones did not sicken. The Assiniboin healers tried every cure known, every herb, chant, dance and drumming, every paint mark, sacred sign and song, working desperately, often until they too, fell before this powerful enemy whose throat none could grasp.

Suddenly the Indians began to run from the stink and the dead, whipping their horses until they fell, to lie among those who rolled from the sick travois. Dark bundles like old rags marked the trails for many sleeps. The snows came and passed before those left alive could go back to find the skeletons and bind them on scaffolds or into tree forks or to gather up the scattered bones where wolves had fed, the loose skulls taken to sacred spots and arranged in circles on the beautiful prairie, where years later mourners might still come to sit and smoke and throw their minds back to the time before the spotted disease.

The traders reported that the epidemic of 1780 killed three-fourths of the Assiniboin nation within a few moons. Trade was ruined and for two years Montreal received practically no furs from the whole northwest.* Most of the traders left the Saskatchewan and waited around Mackinac, beginning to quarrel, fight, even kill. In 1780 the Spaniards sent out an expedition led by former French officers, some of them well known around the lakes. With a long pack train of mules they crossed the Plains and appeared at Prairie du Chien on the upper Mississippi; well supplied and free with their gifts, they sought allegiance, and trade, from the Indians.

Langlade of Green Bay, who had led a large party of breeds and western Indians to the Lake Champlain region in 1757, had taken a similar force east once more, this time to help Burgoyne, but returned before the general's surrender. In 1780, with his 1200 men Langlade moved to capture Illinois. He took the lead mines and appeared outside of Spanish St. Louis, sending fear of the scalp knife and the fire stick through the hearts of the timid. In the meantime the St. Louis traders had not been blind to the opportunity offered by the blockade of the lakes. Auguste Chouteau and his halfbrother Pierre went to the headwaters of the Yellowstone and the mountain valleys to spy out the beaver wealth and to

* The Wintercount of Battiste Good, Brule Sioux, lists: "1779-80, Smallpox-Used-Them-Up Winter" with the same for 1780-81. The disease struck across the mountains, killing many among the Nez Perce and leaving the breed boy of the French trader among them a pox-marked one, a "Rough-Face," still described so when he came to the 1851 conference at Ft. Laramie, with later descendants among the South Dakota Sioux.

capitalize on the Indian affection for Frenchmen, built up by
early bush lopers.

There was no beaver man among the American negotiators of 1782-83 for the Treaties of Paris and Versailles.
The former, which was to create a new nation, was largely
dependent upon the maneuverings and the warring back-
drop involved in the latter. England and Spain had their
American empires to consider and France still nursed some
ambitions there besides her war alliance with the victorious
colonies. All three had large European hopes and plans.
Among Bourbon Spain's was her siege of Gibraltar and
France had many wants, including money to ease the unrest
at home, and even such matters of pride and commerce as
the restoration of Dunkirk as a fortification and harbor, both
destroyed seventy years before at British demand. Yet it was
plain that the cleverest diplomats of these two courts
planned to confine the new American nation within the nar-
rowest of bounds, preferably to stagnate behind the Alleghenies, to remain dependent upon Europe, under European
control.

Franklin's provisional draft of the Anglo-American
treaty, completed the fall of 1782, was not to be finally considered until the various agreements between the three European nations had been settled. His four "necessary" points
were: independence for his country, access to the eastern
fisheries, the western boundary at the Mississippi, and open
navigation on the river for American shipping. Franklin and
the most determined, most suspicious John Jay held out
against not only the European negotiators but against the
instructions of their own Congress, dictated by the minister
of France. True, Franklin's insistence on the region east of
the Mississippi was without a look toward the beaver regions
that might lie beyond. He wanted the area for settlement and
a military buffer. He also suggested that Canada be ceded to
the United States as of no value to England except for its fur
trade, and that unimportant. Perhaps this opinion was based
upon the Montreal export figures during the lake blockade
years, when the furs were turned north to Hudson's Bay or

to Spanish St. Louis. More probably his attitude and that of Congress was an early manifestation of the parasitic seaboard contempt for the rest of the nation whose resources were to furnish so much of the livelihood and the power of wealth to that strip east of the Alleghenies.

The treaties were signed September 3, 1783 but despite the "free and open" navigation on the Mississippi River, only the British enjoyed these rights, insured to them from Spain in 1763. The only Americans free to use the river into 1795 were traders from Spanish St. Louis. That year the United States signed a treaty with Spain securing free navigation of the river and the right of deposit at New Orleans.

By now Mackinac had recovered from the Rogers frauds. Montreal merchants, dependent upon beaver, had forgiven the debts of the bankrupt fur men and with the lakes open once more, they divided the west among the traders, gave them credit, fixed prices and arranged for transportation and storage of the furs at Montreal and the final shipment to England. The nine main groups of traders out of Mackinac had formed a loose sort of one-year agreement in 1779 and in 1783-84 completed the organization vaguely considered since 1776—the North West Company of Montreal.

The new firm included not only traders but some of the most powerful merchants of the city. Because some of them, like McTavish, the Frobishers, McGillivray and Henry had worked at the far posts, the agreement gave the officers out in the wilderness, the wintering partners, an interest in the profits. This was an impetus to expansion lacked by the Hudson's Bay men, who were all employees, all except the directors far across the sea.

Occasional fur traders did go to Montreal to live, as the heads of the new North West outfit had, but generally they were a distinct class from the merchants, preferring to remain at the frontier posts and with the Indians, rough, independent men, often contentious. The main problem remained, and grew—the need for fresh beaver territory. The trade beyond Grand Portage, on upper Superior, brought in £25,000 a year and prospects were good for more, with the upper reaches of the Saskatchewan and the Missouri and the country beyond the mountains barely tapped, although Spain claimed much of the lower regions, and the Americans were stirring to reach a long arm westward. Montreal was shipping fine furs worth a million dollars a year and would continue forever. "It is hoped forever," some said privately, "at least as long as the beaver lasts." Publicly the beaver was eternal and like the earth, to be manured back to original fertility any time.

Pond was not consulted when the North West was formed and later, when asked to come in, refused for a while. Pangman, another American, had been overlooked and so joined Pond. With Gregory, McLeod, Mackenzie and the son of Finlay, starting as a lowly clerk now, but to rise fast, they formed a competing outfit.

From the start the North West group led Montreal into a revival of its romantic period, Scottish version. The head offices were in Beaver Hall, up on the rise overlooking the river, and in 1785 the hardy adventurers organized a dining group called The Beaver Club. The charter members, according to *Northwest Treasury,* included eight who were French-speaking; three, all Frobishers, Englishmen; six Scots; and two, Alexander Henry and Peter Pond, from the States, which makes nineteen instead of the seventeen or eighteen usually given. Pond was probably not actually a charter member. Simon McTavish was excluded because he had never spent a winter in the Indian country, a prime prerequisite. Later, about 1792, after the company had been thoroughly reorganized, he was admitted.

There was no evidence that any creature of the earth, including man, ever worked seriously to improve itself even physically, as man improved certain breeds of dogs and cattle and, outstandingly, the Arab horse. Somehow the 18th century, after the intolerance and violence of the 17th, became a time of hope not only for the physical but for the economic, social, intellectual and philosophical improvement of the human race. Some idealists even believed that it was possible for man to establish a society that led toward perfection, and started utopias in various free land regions of the world. But a coarser and more urgent ferment was working in the great masses living under grinding and airless oppression, to explode its sour brew in the faces of the privileged, first in the successful rebellion of the American colonies and then in the French Revolution. Louis XVI, failing to overcome the economic and moral arrears left by his grandfather, was confronted with a rising anger among his miserable subjects. The hated Bastille, symbol of absolutism, went down like a child's tipi in a windstorm. The Reign of Terror brought Louis and his queen to the falling knife. There was the swift declaration of war from the new French Republic against Britain and her George III, who was teetering into intervals of insanity. Napoleon overthrew the French Directory and the revolution was lost under his spectacular career, with even inland America shaken a bit by the desperate convulsions of Europe.

Louisiana, shifted to Spain during the decline of France in America, had become a sort of battleground. French hatters and furriers were forced to get their beaver through London, usually an enemy capital, or New Orleans, where the trade was also slipping into British control through their freedom of the Mississippi River. The merchants received almost as much for their furs at New Orleans as at far-off London but the Indians considered French goods inferior to the British in all except mirrors, beads and other trinkets. The Spanish authorities, with taxes to collect on exports from Louisiana, tried to stop this commerce from the river to the sea. They captured some British vessels along the Mississippi and forbade their colonists to trade with boats on the river or from the Illinois side, a ban difficult to enforce. Soon French furriers were finding London pelts, direct or through other nationals, cheaper than the

Spanish and in better condition, less exposed to heat. Further, Spain, whose relation with her Indians had been largely that of master and slave, produced almost no trade goods acceptable to the free tribes.

Laclede, builder of much of the trade of the vast region centered on his St. Louis, suffered severe losses through his New Orleans partners and the Spanish authorities. The Chouteaus, his son and stepson, successors to Laclede's business, frankly turned to Montreal. French traders like Robidoux, the Perraults, Papins, Sarpys and Labbadies of the St. Louis region became rich through their northern connections, as did Cerré and Gratiot from east of the river. Clamorgan, the Welshman from the West Indies, concerned himself as little with Spanish loyalties as the rest. Even Benito Vasquez, the one Spaniard in the trade, was married to a Papin. The dealers in the nearby towns also used the St. Louis warehouses, the fur all going to Mackinac and on to Montreal, the British merchandise making the long and difficult journey back.

Louisiana traders were supposed to have Spanish licenses, but no one was much concerned with the restrictions, particularly the ban on brandy and rum, and evidently less about the export tax. There were angry charges that the traders met the British at wilderness points to exchange their finest furs for good English merchandise, without tax. As a sort of afterthought from the nation that had annihilated the great American civilizations and stolen shiploads of their art and gold, the Spaniards accused the traders of cheating the Indians.

Commerce, under such conditions, entailed bribery and soon Gratiot, a wealthy man when he crossed the river to St. Louis, found his fortune depleted. He joined the Chouteaus, who traded through Schneider and Company, London brokers. The fur market collapsed during the uprising in France and the swift coalition of nations to quarantine, to destroy, that focal point of revolutionary infection obviously carried across the sea by men like Paine and Franklin. It seems that in these years Schneider couldn't collect for the goods sent to St. Louis, not until the debts were taken over years later by Astor.

The ridiculous reports from the wilderness were not confined to those of the feverish search for the south sea. D'Eglise, back from up the Missouri in 1790, said he found Indians never seen by white men. This must have been deliberately misleading or was another example of the Indian's unwillingness to consider anyone married into the tribe as anything but Indian. Surely D'Eglise knew that traders from New France had fanned down the Plains and out as far as Santa Fe, that the British from over at the lakes and down from the north had been appearing at the Platte for generations and that Frenchmen had lived with the Pawnees over a hundred years. Certainly the Spaniards would have recalled that seventy years ago Villasur found a good supply of French guns, French military strategy and, it was claimed, French participants among the Pawnees up the Platte.

And the Missouri the great highway—

Lieutenant-Governor Trudeau of Louisiana was to preserve the peace and harmony with both the English and the Americans, although the latter were plainly more dangerous. He was not, however, to permit foreign traders, not even the English, on the territory of His Catholic Majesty, the King of Spain, even though 2500 miles of the Missouri, half of the Mississippi and the whole nebulous northern boundary would be difficult to guard. Although drawn into the coalition with England and the others against France, there were Spaniards who realized the weakness of Carlos IV and particularly the weakness in America, with the English threat very close to the rich southwest and the Pacific coast. They feared an easy, almost overnight conquest of all of Louisiana.

In the meantime the merchants of St. Louis were complaining. The British corrupted the Indians with an abundance of merchandise and at prices the Spanish regulations and taxes prohibited. Sometimes Governor-general Carondelet seemed almost ready to act, to send troops for that chain of forts needed along the Missouri, but there was never any money, never any national drive. Let those ambitious

St. Louis merchants see to the defense themselves. He granted some relief, including price control, preference of white employees over Negro, Indian or breed, monopoly trade rights above the Niobrara and the expulsion of foreigners, meaning the British. Now all that the St. Louis complainers needed to do was throw the British out, except that they were allies in that coalition against France, where the bloody head of Louis XVI had been followed by a most unseemly number of others, making his end vulgarly common.

With encouragement from the governor the Company of Explorers of the Upper Missouri, called the Missouri Company, was organized late in 1793 in St. Louis, and promised $10,000 toward expenses. In addition there was to be a prize of $2000, later $3000, for the Spanish subject who discovered the South Sea by way of the Missouri. Robidoux and Vasquez and lesser merchants joined but important men like the Chouteaus, Cerré and Gratiot stood aloof. Clamorgan, the director, resenting the holdouts, moved as rapidly as possible. June 1794 he sent Truteau, an adventuresome schoolteacher, out to the upper river. He was to build a fort at the Mandan villages, establish an agency, fix prices, regulate trade, wean the Indians away from the British and find the route to the Pacific, a considerable undertaking for one man with one pirogue and eight voyageurs to push it up the wild Missouri.

Truteau and the trader D'Eglise both ran into trouble growing out of tribal wars and the fattening avarice of the chiefs, their fondness for bribes, fostered, the St. Louis merchants insisted, by the British, who paid the Indians to harass and delay the men from Louisana.

The Arikaras, relatives of the Pawnees, refused to let D'Eglise take his powder and guns past them to their enemies, and so held him up until the river froze over, which meant all winter. Truteau was stopped by the Teton, the Plains, Sioux, who helped themselves to his goods. Caching what was left, he struck overland to bypass the troublesome river tribes, but he found the Arikara, the Ree, village gone, driven out by constant raiding. Retreating down the river to the Omahas, he built winter quarters near other St. Louis traders and made a second attempt to fulfill his commitments in the spring. Failing once more, he sent letters to Menard and Jusseaume with the Mandans and the Hidatsas, telling them to get out, that Spain would supply the necessaries of life to all the nations of the upper Missouri. There must have been some lusty laughter around the North West Company post up there, and from the Hudson's Bay trader, as well as from all the relatives of those first bearded men to reach the village above the Old Crossing.

The Missouri Company sent out another expedition, the leader to consult with Truteau, surely with his depot established among the Mandans by now. They carried instructions ordering them, if fortunate enough to arrive at the depot before severe cold, "to go overland to the Rocky Chain (Mountains) . . . without delay in order to reach, if possible, by next spring, 1796, the shores of the Sea of the West."

Although this second expedition cost nearly 97,000 pesos it was even less successful than Truteau's one pirogue. It never got farther than the Poncas, where the leader managed to get himself "captured" and, within a short space of time, had acquired two wives and wasted a great deal of the company goods. The information received in return was less than any free trader wandering in and out of the wilderness brought to St. Louis, confirming the English post on the Missouri and trade up there not only with the Canadians but with the Spaniards from the southwest.

Disgusted with the first two expeditions, Lieutenant-Governor Trudeau wrote to Carondelet that since there was no native around with sufficient intelligence to be intrusted with the important discoveries desired, the Missouri Company suggested a Mr. Mackay, a Scotchman.

Perhaps he would have the initiative of his old employers, the men of the North West Company.

CHAPTER V

THE FIVE VILLAGES—
INTERNATIONAL PREY

JAMES MACKAY, recently naturalized Spaniard, was to succeed for the Missouri Company where their own men had failed. No one waited for the slow grind of official action. Six months before the appointment was approved, Mackay left St. Louis for the Five Villages, lumped together as Mandan. In 1787 the North West Company had sent him there, to be carried to the chief's house on a robe by four husky painted warriors, as was customary for visiting dignitaries or representatives of men and organizations long honored.

But this time he was going as a competitor for the trade there and, on the larger field, for the passage to the Western Sea.

Mackay planned his expedition with Scottish realism: four pirogues loaded with merchandise, one to get him past the Rees, one for the Sioux, one for the Mandan and Hidatsa villages, and the fourth to pay his way to the Rocky Chain and overland to the sea. For this he carried a six-year passport, the probable time required. At the cost of 104,000 pesos, and with thirty-three men, Mackay started up the low, snag-bristling Missouri in August 1795, to discover all the unknown parts of His Catholic Majesty's Dominions clear to the Pacific, and to construct such forts as he deemed necessary to protect Spanish trade and territory. When they reached the

Oto village near the mouth of the Platte, the Missouri valley was golden with fall. Crowds of shouting, branch-whipping village children guarded the cornfields against flocks of geese and chattering ducks during the day. After sunset young warriors took their places at the fields against not only wild fowl but deer, bear, even raccoons, as well as parties of marauding Indians.

Complaining of the guns against them now, sold to their enemies, the Otos demanded protection and Mackay built a little fort, promising to mount swivel guns at the corners later, little cannons that could be swung around as the arm swings, to send balls of lead flying upon any attackers, the roar so powerful it would echo against the bluffs standing in a torn wall far off to the east, beyond the river.

Leaving traders with the Oto post to lure the Indians from their dependence on British goods, Mackay went on to erect a fort for the Omahas, who could have no less than their neighbors. He showed the shrewd and calculating Black Bird where cannons would be set on the walls to cut down his enemies, and got a promise from the chief to escort him to the Rees when the Missouri thawed in the spring. In the meantime Black Bird was to send emissaries to the Sioux and other tribes, calling the chiefs to visit Mackay about peace and free passage up the river.

All this was at a price. Black Bird always got his choice of the goods that passed his village overlooking the Missouri, the first selection of everything from guns to trinkets. Not satisfied with the presents brought to him this time, he compelled Mackay to send a boat down to St. Louis "to get the things which he (Black Bird) needed," Clamorgan complained to Carondelet, April 1796. These were sent in a *voiture* armed with nine men "which adds a very cruel sum to our expenses." And there would have to be more presents next fall.

Before this time the cautious Mackay had sent some of his own men out across the winter plains to insure friendly relationships up the river. The leader, John Evans, was a Welshman come to America three years before seeking out a

rumored tribe of Welsh Indians, who, some said, lived in the
west. His party was driven back by the Sioux without making contact. Mackay sent the customary presents of tobacco
and the best woolen cloth he had to the Sioux chiefs and
started Evans out once more, with orders to keep two journals. One was to be a record of the route and distances,
weather and winds—all the scientific data; the other a record
of events and observations on nature, the flora and fauna,
backed by any unusual wild creatures he could capture, alive
if possible, particularly the animal with the one horn in the
forehead, said to live in the mountains. In addition Evans
was to gather data on all the different Indian nations, their
characteristics, their manner of living. If ink ran out through
the months and perhaps years, there was the ink powder, and
if that failed there were the juices of wild fruits. Apparently
Mackay forgot to suggest blood as a usable ink, or a bullet or
any piece of lead as a fair writing instrument in the wilderness. Very important too, Evans was to inscribe the name of
the king of Spain and the Missouri Company on stones and
trees all the way to the ocean, but to cease this if he struck
Russian settlements at the Pacific. From there he was to return immediately to Mackay, whether with the Mandans,
the Omahas or wherever.

Perhaps because Mackay knew the upper Missouri
country he set out to explore and map some of the less familiar territory lower down—the stretch westward from the
mouth of the Rapid, the Niobrara, River, and the sand hills
lying to the south, crossed, it seemed, by a main trail of enemy traders. He had heard that a British party with twelve
pack horses recently headed through the region to the Platte
and that another outfit was going farther on, to strike between the headwaters of the Colorado and the Arkansas,
practically within bow shot of the leisurely plaza at Santa Fe.

It was rumored in St. Louis that the British had
planned a post at the Omaha village before Mackay anticipated them. Or perhaps the place was already there; perhaps

Mackay and Evans were British spies and traitors working at the expense of the Missouri Company but building posts against their employers, Evans searching out an English Missouri route to the sea and to the old but unprotected Spanish possessions there.

News of Spain's declaration of war against England in 1796 did not reach the west for months but the officials in Louisiana understood some of the provocation: the British everywhere, with their contraband trade and particularly the outposts on the shores of the Missouri, spearheads to the South Sea and Santa Fe. In the meantime at St. Louis Clamorgan was making his futile plea to Carondelet for swivel guns for the new Spanish posts up the river. "A fort without canon is a body without a soul."

Many, however, began to look with sharp suspicion after the government pesos gone up the Missouri with no tangible return. Eventually they would have Evans' journal, recording some of his difficulties, even when past the Sioux. The Rees had held him up, but finally permitted him to go on to the Mandans and Hidatsas and their relatives the Wattassoons, but with only a small amount of goods. He gave the chiefs the medals and banners that Mackay had sent and some small presents, bestowed "in the name of their Great Father the Spaniard." September 28, 1796, he took possession of "the English forts" belonging to the Canadian traders and hoisted the Spanish flag "which seemed very much to please the Indians—"

In October several more northerners appeared with pack horses. Evans wrote that he had too few men to oppose them or take their goods but that he "hindered them" and finally forced them out of the territory with orders to stay out of Spanish domain. In March Jossum (Jusseaume) and several engagés arrived, bringing presents from the English for the headmen of the Five Villages. Evidently there was trouble. Evans reported that Jusseaume and others bribed the Indians to enter his house, kill him and take his goods. Some of the loyal chiefs came to inform Evans of the plot and to guard him, saying they refused the presents but others ac-

cepted them. Apparently they were rewarded. A few days
later Jusseaume arrived with some of his men and tried to
discharge a pistol loaded with deer shot at the back of Evans'
head. The interpreter stopped him, and the Indians dragged
the man out to kill him. Evans interfered, and some time
later the culprit left for the north.

It was a properly lurid story, if not too convincing, of a
man known to have an Indian family among the Five Villages, but even more interesting would have been some indication of the opinion the old chiefs held of these traders,
whether of Hudson's Bay, the North West or the new Missouri Company, but there was no one to write that down.
Indian legends and recorded stories deal with personalities
and events, seldom with opinions. While Evans never got to
the Pacific or near it, his journal speaks of the wonders of the
Missouri, with only one fall in all its great course, and that
far up, it seemed, beyond the first, the eastern, chain of the
Rocky Mountains. He reported a curious animal from the
Rocky region, one about the height of an elk, with hair like a
fallow deer, horns like a ram but spiraled like a trumpet
and immense. The creature was short-lived, Evans wrote, because the horns keep growing until the tips stick so far past
the mouth that the animal cannot reach grass and dies of
starvation. The Indians made spoons of these horns, some
large enough, filled once, to satisfy the appetite of four men
at a meal.

Evans doubtlessly meant men like himself. Hungry
Indians, like the voyageurs who ate eight, ten pounds of meat
a day, could empty one of these spoons alone. Evans had
some complaints of the Indians. Those who had frequent
communication with the whites appeared to have contracted
their vices and not their virtues.

Letters back and forth between the border posts of
the two British companies and Evans were usually a little
more diplomatic than his journal, which had to justify his
employment. October 8, 1796, Grant of the North West Company wrote thanking Evans for past kindnesses and that he
wished to withdraw "what little property the N.W. Co." had

there, the very day that the Welshman's journal recorded the arrival of British traders and that he "hindered them" and forced them out. February 26 McDonnell of the North West wrote Evans in a tone to be expected between commercial rivals from nations at war:

> "British subjects are not to be tried by Spanish laws, nor do I look upon you as an officer commissioned to apprehend oth[er] people's servants, if you serve a chartered Comy. why not show the Spanish Governors Orders, declarations, denounciations or manifestoes, prohibiting others from frequenting that country—Then shall we leave you in peace—"

Sutherland at Brandon House, Hudson's Bay Company, recorded in his journal late in February 1797 that some men back from the Missouri villages reported Evans in a wretched state but insisting that all trade go through his hands. April 15 news came in that the Indians of Five Villages had plenty of fur, particularly the Hidatsas, and that Evans was almost at fisticuffs with the Canadians, trying to prevent their trade although he had no goods. The Indians, angered at this interference with their barter, compelled Evans and his men to set off down the river, "the Indians threatening to kill them if they refused."

Apparently Evans had lost his interest in red-skinned Welshmen.

Matters were not good in St. Louis either. Clamorgan was accused of making personal profit from his management of the Missouri Company although the firm was failing. There was some trade. In May 1797 Auguste Chouteau wrote to Grant at Mackinac, asking him "to sell among the Sioux" the two boatloads of fur which he was directing there and to send down 2000 pounds of maple sugar.

Selling "among the Sioux" was one way of marketing furs for Montreal in spite of the Spanish war with England.

.   .   .

The fall of 1797 the North West Company sent their new explorer and geographer to the Missouri villages. David Thompson, another Welshman carrying out Scottish orders, had been apprenticed to the Bay Company from a London charity school at fourteen. Within a year or two he got the usual equipment for a Bay man headed to the wilderness: a trunk, a handkerchief, shoes, shirts, a gun, powder and a tin cup, and was sent out with forty-six others to build posts up the north Saskatchewan. At seventeen he spent a winter in the tipi of a Piegan chief near the present Calgary and the next summer he was transferred to the Crees and Assiniboins, where he broke his leg, which was badly set and troubled him for years. At nineteen he was stationed at Cumberland House to prevent the Indians from selling furs to Frobisher and other non-Bay men. By now the young trader was making notes and maps wherever he went, and keeping a meteorological journal.

In 1797, after thirteen years with the Bay outfit, he left and walked seventy-five miles to a post of the North Westers, who were more interested in his scientific findings. By now, at twenty-seven, David Thompson was a short, compact man, his black hair long all around, and cut straight across at the eyebrows, his nose short, his skin the ruddy brown of the wilderness, his mind penetrating as a Bay dag in the hand of a Sioux warrior, but creative, making everyone see through his writings and his talk. He was pious ever since the charity-school days, with "Thank good Providence" a common phrase from his pen and his tongue. He opposed alcohol anywhere and read from the Bible to his men, usually missionary Catholic.

November 28, 1797, Thompson started down to the Mandan country. His guide and interpreter was René Jusseaume, eight years with the Missouri villages, and accused by Evans of trying to kill him last year. In addition Thompson had Hugh McCracken, often weeks and months with the Mandans, and seven French Canadian free traders, a hearty lot who ate eight pounds of fresh meat per man a day. Thompson lectured them a little on this, but searched out buffaloes with his telescope. The trade stock was on credit from McDonnell, each man provided with goods and trinkets worth forty to sixty beaver plews, all drawn on fifteen flat runnerless sleds, two dogs to each, dogs from the Assiniboins —half wolf. Thompson had two horses, Jusseaume one.

It was late in the season to cross the high, open, practically treeless prairie, covered with three inches of snow. The little brigade started southward, winding up the Souris, the Mouse River, with Thompson carefully recording weather, region and events.

By the first of December the thermometer dropped to 37 degrees below zero, with everyone crowded into the one tipi, full of smoke blown back down the center hole by the high wind. The next day, one degree warmer, a man pushed out to kill a buffalo cow, almost frozen before the carcass could be cut up. With milder weather they went on to a small camp of Assiniboins who welcomed the traders but protested the trip to the Missouri now, with the Sioux on the warpath and their scouts out everywhere, probably already planning an attack at Dog Tent Hill, a high butte overlooking the farthest prairie some distance along the old trail.

December 5 brought 13 below zero again, and a rising grayness around the horizon. Uneasy, the guide took the party closer to Turtle Mountain, but with no wood around either. Thompson scanned the country with his telescope until he located a small grove of aspens about four miles south. He and some of the party started for the timber as the storm closed down, some of the others questioning the compass as a guide on land, perhaps because the needle did not point directly to the north star here. When the storm turned to a howling blizzard the dubious ones decided to follow Thompson, the snow frozen fine as buffalo gnats in the summer and stinging in the wind that blinded the eyes and swept the breath away. The men drew themselves together inside their heavy capotes and whipped the dogs along, the three horses fighting the bits to turn tail to the storm, strike out for some canyon. Night came, white and desolate in the roar of the blizzard. Thompson, who had wintered as far as

Churchill on the Bay and on the North Saskatchewan, had
never seen such storming as this. He tried to keep the men,
all wilderness hardened, in a single file, close enough together to feel out the tracks before they were blown over,
keep the dogs sensing those ahead now that the side wind
tore the shout from the frozen lips. At last they reached the
aspen grove, winter-naked and bowed, but with dead wood
for fire and tree trunks to anchor the tipi.

During the next two days they managed to get as far
as Ash House, an old trading post in ash timber, deserted before the increasing Sioux attacks but with shelter for the
worn dogs and men. By the tenth the dogs were rested and
Thompson started again, and once more a storm struck, starting with rain, turning to that frozen dry snow sharp as Bay
needles in the wind, and so thick that Thompson, bent low
in the saddle, could barely see the head of his horse. All the
men except one, and one sled with its dogs, found the clump
of oak saplings the guide was searching out by the Plains
sense that rises out of the primitive layerings of some men.
A great fire was built up in the protection of a thicket and
the piled-up sleds while several men stumbled back on the
trail, shouting, the sound carried away by the storm. They
found the lost man not far off but down in the snow. He had
caught one glimpse of the fire in a lull, but was too worn to
stand and was crawling through the drifts, crying aloud as
long as he could. He was carried to camp and thawed out but
the dogs with the sled did not come in. The owner offered
half the goods to anyone rescuing them, but no one would
go out into the storm again. Each trader agreed to give the
man trade stuff to the value of two beavers, Thompson and
a couple of the others doubling their share.

By now the party had to leave such shelter as Turtle
Mountain afforded, and cross the plain to the valley of the
Mouse again. The wind was powerful but at their backs for
a while. They killed a buffalo cow and packed the meat
along. Dog Tent (or Tipi) Hill, the Sioux lookout, was not
far ahead and realizing that it would be difficult to stand off
a mounted warrior charge with their dog sleds, Thompson

took the advice that the Assiniboins had offered. Packing dried aspen along for fires, the traders left the ancient trail that led from water to water, wood to wood, taking a chance with blizzard and Indians on the open prairie.

For two days there was more storming, with no chance to move, although the hunters got a couple of buffaloes, very nearby, or they could not have managed to get the meat back to camp in the face of the wind. When the air quieted a little they left the elbow of Mouse River and struck southward through a ground blizzard that blew the snow thick across the unbroken white plain but only waist high, the sun gleaming above it, and Dog Tent Hill off in the distance standing plain above the moving sea of whiteness.

By early afternoon they were so close that Thompson could detect the dark points of horsemen on the snowy top of the butte with his glass. He motioned the men flat into the drifts and waited, cold and freezing, until he saw the riders go down the west side of the lookout and away. Evidently the delay from the cold and the storming had discouraged the Sioux so they gave up and went home.

On the 29th of December Thompson picked out a rising white ridge through his telescope.

"It is the last edge of *Le Grande Coteau du Missouri*," Jusseaume said.

The timber of the frozen river bottoms lay full of snow, with a scattering of buffaloes warming themselves on the south slopes of the breaks. The men shot some and discovered two Fall Indians, as Thompson called the Hidatsas, hunting too. The next day they reached the uppermost of the Five Villages, scattered for ten, eleven miles along the river. The journey, usually ten days in open weather, had taken thirty-three hard ones. There were some old Hidatsas who recalled Verendrye coming in the winter too, sixty years ago, but with less snow and cold on his back.

At that first village a Frenchman called Menoah (probably Menard), with the Indians many years, greeted them. After resting they went down to the Great Village of the tribe, then to the third, with only a few Hidatsa houses and finally saw the last two, the Mandan towns, one on the right bank of the river. The fifth, farthest down the stream, was the largest of all, with 113 houses. All but the uppermost of the Hidatsas were well protected, surrounded by wide, deep ditches and strong stockades, the posts ten to twelve inches in diameter and ten feet high, with many loopholes for arrow and ball. There were two doorways to each, on opposite sides, wide enough for a rider to pass, and closed with heavy logs slid into place. The houses were all earthen domes, much like those that the two Bearded Men saw over a hundred sixty years ago, although that village was gone now, the high point of its location above Old Crossing cut away by the furious spring floods of the Missouri.

The Indians made the traders welcome and brought out a good stock of furs and decorated robes, much corn and dried squash and beans. Thompson, as Jusseaume explained to the chiefs, was not trading but had come to see them and the country. With the interpreter and McCracken, he examined everything, apparently the medicine houses too, one at each village, those of the Hidatsas off some distance, the Mandan in the center of the clustered lodges. Thompson asked many questions but complained in his account that both Jusseaume and McCracken were illiterate. Either they did not understand his scientific queries or the Indian replies, perhaps neither. He did get a count of the Indians, about 1520 Mandans, including 220 warriors and very few children, while just up the river there were many children and 190 warriors among the 1330 Hidatsas.

These were the first earth-house people Thompson had seen and he was interested in everything, including the protection for the horses. The large herds he saw among the Plains people—the Blackfeet divisions (including the Piegans), the Assiniboins and the Sioux, were guarded by warrior herders night and day. At the Five Villages the horses were brought not only into the stockades but into the houses, to separate stalls on the right side of the doorway. Mornings young men took them out to wind-bared knolls for grass and returned them toward evening to feed on a little corn. Obviously there were fewer horses here, far fewer than among the nomadic tribes, who needed them for the buffalo surrounds, to move the lodges, goods and people from camp to camp, and for the fierce warring over hunting grounds. The earth-house people depended less on great hunts or war. They had many spears, the ten-foot shafts headed with flat iron bayonets nine to ten inches long, and four wide at the base, whetted sharp—good defensive weapons for fortified towns. They had many shields and bows and a few guns too, and were eager to add to these, with the tribes around them increasingly aggressive as more and more were pushed westward by the crowding white man. That was apparently one reason that the Hidatsas did not rebuild near their ancient site. Old Crossing had been a sort of peace ground in the early days, with parties camping quietly and safely there when they came to ford the river. Now often whole villages, even whole tribes followed the trails, seeking new homes, fierce because driven from their own regions, and without knowledge of the crossing as ground sacred to peace. Besides, the great buffalo herds that had been fording there in their seasonal migrations for thousands of years now tolled the horse-mounted warrior tribes, both to hunt and to prey on other hunters.

Thompson remarked on the cleanness and orderliness of the Five Villages, the doors always open to any hand and theft consequently a serious crime. The people were courteous, kind, with no loud voices in their towns, no noticeable discord, particularly among the Hidatsas, who had only one term for abuse, mild or extreme. This was "bad"— bad men, bad people.

Thompson was interested in the color of these Indians, much like sunburnt French-Canadians, with brown or black hair, the eyes usually hazel. Other visitors remarked on the fine-looking people of the Five Villages in the early days, the Hidatsas tall, with arched noses, neater than the Mandans. Many important men wore a lock of hair at the temple,

flat and cut off or twisted into a thick knot and ornamented.
Old-timers still wore the loose hair and almost all the men
were tattooed, often down one side, perhaps to the hand.

Like most visitors to the Mandans, Thompson mentioned their dancing women, twenty-four of them, in fine
whitened and ornamented deerskin. They danced in two
rows about three feet apart, up toward the music played by
the men, and back again, and then forward once more and
back, over and over, apparently with enticement that was
deliberate, and accepted. There were rumors that chastity
was almost unknown among the Mandans, and some complaint that this was not true before the white men came,
long ago, with their fine presents.

Although both tribes of the Five Villages were Siouan,
the language varied greatly through long periods of separa-
tion from the parent stock and from each other. Early accounts put the Hidatsas far north. Thompson heard they
once lived at the Rapids of the Saskatchewan northward of
Eagle Hills, which put them between the North Fork and the
South, the latter often called the River of the Gros Ventres,
one of the several names the French used for these people,
although there was another small tribe they called Gros
Ventres, a little farther west and south of the old Canadian
Hidatsas, and of Algonquin stock. In those northern days,
long before the horse came, the Hidatsas had lived in skin
lodges and moved with pack and travois dogs on that event-
ful path through the Souris, the Mouse River region. Some
stopped near Star Mound for a while; some went to the
Devils Lake country, but the largest group headed south to
the Missouri.

Perhaps one heritage of those nomadic days was the
strict chastity of the Hidatsa women, with adultery punish-
able, as Thompson reported. Certainly the women found life
at the river much easier, with the fields, the fish, water fowl
and other creatures as well as the upland game. It had been
less dangerous too, even for the men, safer for the warriors
fighting off attack on the women and children in fortified

villages instead of skin lodges that accepted every arrow and spear and later the white man's lead ball. More men survived and so few had two women.

Thompson recorded the position of the Five Villages, the uppermost of the Hidatsas at 47° 25' 11", the lowest of the Mandans at 47° 17' 22". Disappointed at his inability to discover more of the life and the organization of the tribes, he was pleased with what his eyes could see. February 3, 1798, his party was back on the Assiniboine, at the post of the North West Company. The traders had apparently only one real complaint: the two tribes were still disinterested in killing the many beavers around them, plentiful in the streams with groves of giant cottonwood for food.

Others were trying to tempt those Indians to make beaver, newcomers to the region. Several American traders had already slipped in across the Mississippi and westward as far as the upper Missouri, and more would come. Back in 1793 Thomas Jefferson informed the botanist André Michaux that "sundry persons" had subscribed money for his expedition to explore "the country along the Missouri and thence westward to the Pacific." Unfortunately the finances were still lacking when Spain, fearing a British invasion of Louisiana, secretly returned the region to France in 1800, giving Napoleon, the conqueror, a toehold in America. When this was discovered Jefferson and many others felt it was time to act, and in this the American traders agreed with the government, but with a different concern, a concern for the shrinking furs.

David Thompson, always pushing off into the wilderness to establish new posts, seek out new beaver grounds, must have been reminded many times of one of his early reports, one back in 1794, when he wrote about meeting a relative of the Nipissings and Algonquins:

> We came to an aged Indian, his arms folded across his breast with a pensive countenance, looking at the beavers swimming in the water and carrying their win-

ter provisions to their houses. . . . "We are now killing the beaver without labour; we are now rich, but shall soon be poor, for when the beaver are destroyed we have nothing to depend on to purchase what we want for our families; strangers now overrun our country with their iron traps and we and they shall soon be poor."

BOOK III

THE FIERCER RIVALRIES

CHAPTER I

VOYAGEURS OF THE PLAINS

THE beaver varied little from Nova Scotia to the western sea. Some might be darker, or larger, or with softer, denser furring, but there seemed few deviations from the usual pattern of life, or his protection against the enemy— the trapper and hunter. With man it was sometimes different. The native bush loper or voyageur following the beaver westward was often reluctant to take the first steps out of the shielding brakes and timber that had lain around his shoulder like a warm and protecting robe; yet when he did, often more than the physical darkness around him might fall away. If the man could make himself stand out plain and clear under the bright sun or from his pool of black shadow on the wide moonlit prairie without fleeing back to the sheltering brush, other horizons besides the one where the earth melted might draw back.

Most of the voyageurs were French mixed-bloods and usually they had had some contact with the religion of their fathers or grandfathers, enough so, as Roderic McKenzie observed in 1785, they stopped to drop a jingling piece of money into the box "at St. Ann's church" on their way west, to secure the protection of *La Bonne Sainte Anne* during their absence. They were always aware of danger, even if not from hostile Indians. Lake water can be whipped into a

storm very rapidly, and forty-below-zero winter can kill
gently with its drowsy warmth. Often the missionary's purga-
tory and the devil and demons of hell from his preaching
were added to the Indian's mythical monsters: the giant
beavers, the Folly of the Woods that stole men's minds, or,
perhaps, the most pervasive and certainly one of the most
enduring, the windigo,* for which there were many defini-
tions and many stories. Some said this was a spirit condemned to wander the wilderness forever, others believed
that the windigo was a desperate outcast who had tasted
human flesh, an idea that perhaps grew out of the horror of
the periodic starvation times that brought cannibalism to the
northeast Indians in both Canada and the United States.
Whatever the origin, the windigo remained near water, eter-
nally prowling the nights for victims away from the camp
fires, particularly on lake or stream. Many voyageurs would
not travel after dark by water or by land, perhaps recalling
the windigo song they had shouted out so boldly in the
brightness of day:

> He feeds on the bodies
> Of unfortunate men,
> On unlucky travelers
> And mariners late,
> —Caught in the night on the river.

To many the windigo was a horrible forest demon,
twenty, thirty feet tall, a giant naked of clothing, with a
sinister hissing cry so loud and eerie that voyageurs for whom
it was intended could hear him for miles. His menacing
mouth had no more lip than a snapping turtle, but it was full
of great jagged teeth, and his eyes protruded like a great
frog's, rolling in blood that dripped when they spied out a
victim. The feet were almost a meter in length, with only
one toe, greatly nailed, and pointed at the heel, the hands

---

* See "A Study of a Relationship between Belief and Behavior among the
Indians in Northeastern Canada," by Dr. Morton I. Teichner, a report on
twenty cases of windigo psychosis, including a group panic in 1950.—*Proceedings*, American Ethnological Society, 1960.

like giant claws. The windigo fed on rotten wood, swamp moss and stump mushrooms but mostly on human flesh. He could be destroyed only by fire and even then the heart of ice remained, and, some believed, restored the whole body around it if not pounded to very small pieces as a lump of frozen flesh could be broken with patience and a stone. Then the small bits were to be burned in a very hot fire.

Anyone who saw a windigo without killing him, and there seem to be very few stories of windigos destroyed, became one in human form. When this happened there was only one remedy: fire and stone. The human windigo had to be stunned with a thrown rock or ancient stone hammer, and then burned with all his possessions.

Many eastern Algonquins and their French descendants believed that anyone who tasted human flesh became a windigo, and so sometimes resisted even the symbolic body and blood of Christ offered in communion services, or were terrified, if, after partaking, the meaning was discovered.

The will to believe in the fabulous, so deep in the voyageurs from Quebec westward across the lakes and even down the Mississippi, seems to have weakened very rapidly when they began to work the Missouri, with the vast sweeps of sky and bright, open prairie country on both sides of the river. Perhaps the will to believe the fantastic took other forms and rooted itself in higher places out west, for as late as 1819 the St. Louis newspapers referred seriously to a government plan to portage steamboats over the Rocky Mountains to the headwaters of the Columbia, and mentioned the unicorn that lived in those regions.

By 1790 the path of goods for the beaver trade, whether from Hudson's Bay, Montreal or St. Louis, was still largely by water, the burdens moved by the muscle and song of that unique, independent and bold man of the fur canoe, the voyageur. He was usually gaudy in clothing, often with the mercurial temperament of his French father, his Indian mother contributing moodiness and susceptibility to wind and weather and a thousand unidentified factors. The work, whether down from the cold blue expanses of the Bay or up

from the steamy lower Mississippi, was much the same except
for the difference in the waters, the rapids and falls to portage, the placid lake shores and streams taken by the steady
cut of the paddle, the roaring floods of spring that demanded
the furiously bent back, or the later snags and shallows and
sand bars of the west for the cordelle rope.

The goods and provisions headed out to the trader,
the furs for the return were put up in packs of about 100
pounds. A strong man, an able voyageur, usually carried two
of these on his back at the portages, strap over his forehead
or across his chest, singing and joking as he went. The slings
were of strong cowhide, very soon of buffalo cow, tanned to
preserve the natural bit of elasticity, the give. The structure
of these slings varied some but often they were very simple:
the head piece or center section was four inches wide and
fifteen long, with an inch-wide thong or strap about six feet
in length sewed firmly to each end. The wide section was
fitted across the forehead of the carrier, the ends tied together to hold a bale, box or keg resting just below the
small of the man's back. A second package or bale was set on
top of the first and under this load the carrier was off at a
dog trot to the end of the portage. If this exceeded half or
three-quarters of a mile there was a short rest half way, and
at slightly shorter intervals on long portages. Many carried
four pieces, including the dead weight of shot and ball, for
half a mile. Some could pack six pieces up to that distance or
more, according to the stories, the brags, heard around the
campfires and the dances at the trading posts and the so-
called civilized villages. Such men were pointed out and eyed
warmly by the Indian and breed girls dancing to the saw of
some Frenchman's fiddle or the squeeze of his musette, his
bagpipe—in later years, some Scotsman's pipes.

In the rivers the voyageurs paddled against any current except the roaring white saults, and at rare times might
be carried by wind and sail for some short lucky distances
across lakes, particularly in boats or larger canoes. Usually
the fur brigade was out before daylight, worked two hours,

rested for breakfast, and then went on without midday food to the big meal at night. The food problem was important but simple in game country. In the Hudson's Bay region or where wild geese nested, the ration for a voyageur was one goose a day; on the Plains ten pounds of fresh buffalo, out at Athabasca eight pounds of moose meat, on large rivers three big white fish and west of the Rockies, where game might be scarce, eight rabbits or, if in season, one salmon. The Hudson's Bay Company invoiced much Schouschong tea because the Indians in their region had become passionately fond of it as those farther down, in the French country, craved coffee, often with chicory, the roasted root of that tall, sprangly, blue-flowered plant that escaped the garden plots of the farther posts and followed every trail, even roads where no fur trader's foot had ever passed.

After a trying portage or desperate pull against current and wind, the big kettles were put on and the voyageur's tin cup filled with boiling tea or coffee, the men with their "*Sacré démon!*" cursing the scalding liquid and the hard life, made a little more endurable by the comforting cup. They took comfort too in their pipes, perhaps the small clay ones of the eastern Frenchmen; those largely Indian or from life among some tribe, carried the long fire bags, fringed and quilled or beaded, containing the fire tools: flint and steel and often the small pipe and the tobacco. However the voyageur carried these, they were always with him.

Usually the brigades going out started early in the first barren days of spring. Gradually rushes and arrowheads sprang up along the water's edge, the grasses and the flowers. Ducks, geese and swan, elegant beside the untidy, gulping pelicans and other water birds, squabbled or floated serenely among their young. Loons laughed in the night as the men slept under the upturned canoes or at their edges. Although frail birchback and light, the white man's improvements developed canoes that held great loads and rode best when settled deep in the water. The large ones, the *canotes de naitre*, required four men to carry them empty, and fourteen or sixteen to paddle them well; the smaller northwestern and western canoes could be taken over the portages by two men without hardship.

In the later days some of the voyageurs remaining along the St. Lawrence hired out to settlers moving westward, seeking homes where once beaver were sought. They ascended the Ottawa and other rivers in small boats called batteaux, barks built at Lachine and capable of carrying four or five families each, with five men in the boat, four to row, one to steer. Twelve barks constituted a brigade, each brigade under a conductor who was often an experienced oldtimer from the fur flotillas, as later homeseekers in covered wagons on the Overland Trails were often captained by old beaver hunters, old mountain men.

Sometimes at the rapids part of the boats were left behind, to be brought up later, the advance group doublemanned, each drawn along by ropes, cordelles, fastened to the bows. The men pulled from the bank or perhaps were compelled to wade out into the water on jagged rock or to avoid brush and timber while those in the boats helped with long poles pushing the craft onward, keeping it off rocks and out of the more furious saults.

On the Missouri there was no real portaging; the transports, often pirogues—hollowed-out cottonwood logs— were stouter against the jolts and snags of the powerful river than birchbark, much sturdier, although somewhat heavier, the extra weight of little importance. Pirogues, with firmer tie-ons, were better for cordelling, often required with the river sometimes too strong in flood to face with paddles alone, the current perhaps choked by piles of uprooted trees and old stumps and brush, the river forced through a narrowed passage or boiling over the obstacle. At such places the voyageurs sweated, frantically trying to force one pirogue after another against the plunge of water like a salmon clinging to the rapids of the Columbia. Perhaps the current forced a boat broadside and swept it over, or it was struck by some tree or log shooting the flood, goods and even men lost. Often the voyageurs worked a whole day or more to clear out a passage near one bank or the other to draw the boats up by ropes of buffalo bull hide, arduous but safer. Later, in the broadening shallows, there were often stretches with too little water to move except by the pull of the men on the cordelle path.

As the fur trade moved out upon the broad and largely shallow streams like the Yellowstone and the Athabasca and particularly the summer Missouri, the keelboat became the chief carrier of cargo. The ones used on the Missouri were usually from fifty to seventy-five feet long, with fifteen- to twenty-foot beam. They were staunch vessels, capable of withstanding violent thrusts by angry waters upon snags and buried sawyers lifting and falling in the flood. The keelboats were well-modeled, with sharp bow and stern, built by skilled workmen. Such a boat had a capacity of ten to twenty tons, a draft of thirty inches when light, and usually cost between two and three thousand dollars. The cabin, amidship, extended four or five feet above the hull and its cargo. Along each side of the boat was a narrow board path, often cleated for the moccasins of the boatmen pushing up the river, thrusting their long poles deep into the bottom at the bow and walking with hard, toe-thrusting steps, one man behind the other, toward the stern, and passing quickly to the bow again, the poles thrust down once more.

"I walked them damn boats from St. Louie up the Yellowstone for fifteen years," one old voyageur bragged to his cowpuncher grandsons up in the Dakotas when he was ninety.

Along a few swifter, wilder sections of the Missouri, without a pry base for the poles, and too much power in flood for oars, there was soon a deep cordelle path, the men bending into the heavy buffalo-hide ropes reaching from boat to bank and divided there into five to ten tails, each with a cordeller pulling against a wide leather band over his shoulder and upper arm on the side away from the river. Often the men sang to keep the step, one, *two,* one, *two,* perhaps about

Old Joe with the Wart on His Nose, the Three Little Ducks,
The Black-eyed Marie whose Skirts Fly up, *toutes seules,* and,
when in trouble, the plea to Ste. Anne, whose flowing garments were security from even the almost forgotten windigo.

The Missouri Company had requested 10,000 pesos
annually to help drive the English out of upper Louisiana and
keep them out, with, it was hoped, one or two galliots carrying six two-pound cannons, some swivel guns and twenty
soldiers to patrol the Missouri, also some flags—a good supply of flags. But nothing had been done and the anger around
St. Louis grew until Vasquez, a Spaniard, was arrested and
held thirty-five days for making improper remarks about
Governor-general Carondelet, while under the influence of
"wine." To the new governor Gayoso de Lemos, Vasquez
complained that Carondelet had promised him the Pani
trade and after contracting heavy debts to undertake this,
he found it awarded elsewhere.

By the fall of 1798 Gayoso had other problems. With
the Missouri Company failing, he knew that Mackay and
Evans, "valuable subjects," would be obliged to seek employment where it could be offered—among the Canadian
companies "to our great loss," and so he sent Mackay as
commandant to a little post at the mouth of the Missouri
and later to the Omaha trade, "to take care of him." Gayoso
kept Evans in his own house, at his expense, but was finally
compelled to write Mackay that the man was very ill, "the
strength of liquor has deranged his head," but it was hoped
that he would soon be strong enough to be sent back to his
own country. Apparently no Welsh Indians had been discovered.

The shaking fear of a British attack on Louisiana and
even wealthy New Mexico was not relieved by the gesture of
Carlos IV or rather the hands that had taken all power from
him. The return of Louisiana to the protection of France
brought little security. Napoleon seemed too busy reorgan-
izing Europe to cast even a frowning glance toward America.

The fur market of war-disturbed Europe was naturally very bad and the British penetration of the beaver country was so great that St. Louis traders, once very prosperous, or so it seemed to them now, were losing money. In 1801 the receipts did not even cover the expenses of the wintering places. With so little to quarrel over and nothing but the fluttering held-over Spaniards to govern the region, the quarreling grew hot, particularly between Clamorgan of the Missouri Company and the independent traders, generally spear-pointed if not actually headed by Manuel Lisa. Both sides attacked, with alternate flattery and abuse, the Spanish authorities who had about the power if not the legal stature they had had under Spain—practically none. Clamorgan was still soliciting pay for the 100 militia men, in arrears since June 1796, and the trade monopolies were doled out with curious indecision.

Early in 1801 Clamorgan was promised the Pani (Pawnee) Republic trade but then all the Pani nations were given to Chauvin. The award of the Poncas and Omahas to Sanguinet was rescinded in favor of Clamorgan, with exclusive rights above the Kansas and the Platte River after February 1802, including all the tribes of the Missouri country except the Osages and some Pani. Apparently notice of this change did not reach St. Louis before Sarpy and Vasquez had gone to their trade regions, Sarpy to the Kansas and Vasquez to the Loup-Pani, so nothing could be done about Clamorgan's blanket monopoly until next year, or much about the hundred other conflicts and confusions.

Delassus, lieutenant-governor of Louisiana because France had not taken over, had one hard fact to face: small-pox among the Omahas, Iowas and some adjacent tribes had destroyed their harvest of furs and robes. Immediate precautions must be taken to prevent spreading the disease so fatal to trade. Besides, the Omaha chiefs had been gathered to a council at Prairie du Chien in April by the British, on American soil, and now they refused to let the Spaniards pass through their region on the Missouri. All their convoys and trade for the upper river would have to be routed by the

Platte, the goods shifted from voyageurs to pack horsemen, at least until the Omahas could be bribed back from the British and who was to pay for this in Napoleon's Louisiana?

Loisel, who had been permitted to build a post at Cedar Island in the Missouri above Smoky Earth (White) River, was entering a partnership with Heney, for which Auguste Chouteau, perhaps ambitious to move farther into the northern trade, agreed to advance the capital, on notes. Nothing much came of this. In the meantime Lisa, who had been at San Carlos at the mouth of the Platte for two years, was still protesting, with Sanguinet and others, the Chouteau control of the Osage trade. Moro, a St. Louis merchant, complained to the authorities that those who could buy for cash got their merchandise at least fifty per cent cheaper than those who traded on credit. It seems he was against exclusive trade, at least such as the Chouteaus enjoyed with the Osages for years. He begged for action, now.

"Do not send me incense which turns to smoke when I need food."

Lisa, who worked the political field with the energy he spent in trading, was once more out to gather signatures against Clamorgan, and so abusive, Delassus reported, as to be imprudent and seditious in conduct. Lisa should be reprimanded, but it was admittedly a delicate matter, with members of his family in the post, on the staff of the governor-general.

In spite of the curious evasion of reality during the two years since Louisiana was returned to France, there was as much stir as ever, surface stir, but there was also some more serious investigation. Collot, who spent nine months in America gathering information for the French Republic, tried, in 1801, to acquaint Talleyrand with something of the situation. The Indians of upper Louisiana were once "affectionate to us," he wrote, but had been detached by the intrigues of the English and by time. Now their pleasant memory of the French should be reawakened, and communication opened with the South Sea by way of the Missouri, involving, Collot thought, a portage of some thirty leagues. Besides, there were rich mines in the upper country.

In 1795 Louis Vilemont, traveling North America for His Catholic Majesty, had urged immigration of German, Flemish and Dutch colonists to Louisiana, and that other religions besides Catholicism be permitted. But Spain had refused. Now, June 1802, he was trying to arouse France to the opportunities of her American empire. Although the natives, the Indians, had probably been reduced by wars and alcohol, 120,000 to 130,000 piastres of skins were taken from the upper reaches of Louisiana to Montreal and Quebec. The great goal to be attained, he believed, was the gradual civilization of the Indian villages by the use of agriculture, which was to be introduced among them—as though they hadn't developed some of the great crops, including tobacco, potatoes and corn. It was true, Vilemont agreed, that the Indians retained a tender memory of the French. The village chiefs kept asking "When will the brothers of the great country return? who had left to their red children the province as a hostage and had well promised them to reappear some day in order to live together."

The conduct of the Spanish authorities of Louisiana toward the Indians, except under Galvez, had been "the height of absurdity" all their thirty-six years. Vilemont hoped to raise armies among the natives for France, and to open communication to the South Sea. Rude tales and attestations of several Canadian hunters and Indians indicated that they had often gone afoot from the Missouri to the sea in a northwesterly direction in less than two and a half months. Furs they brought back were such as never found on the known continent but were like those described by Cook as discovered on the coast of Nootka Sound.

To this report Vilemont added a plan for winning over and training the Indians of Louisiana for profit. He pointed out "the audacity till today unpunished of the Canadian Companies who crush underfoot all international law and who have displayed their factors as absolute masters

of all the Spanish possessions from the Falls of St. Anthony to
New Santa Fe and robbed them of all the products." He also
warned of the astonishing increase of the American population and their enterprising genius that excited their ambition and cupidity. Their footsteps were plain on the depend-
encies of Louisiana and New Mexico. Following the example
of the English, they had encroached and would continue to
encroach more and more on both territories.

It was a call loud as the roar of the buffalo bull but
France did not move, nor Spain. December 1802 President
Jefferson had felt out the Spanish representative about a
United States expedition to the Missouri and on to the Pacific. The Spaniard apparently shrugged it off. Many explorations had proved there was no northwest passage, he said,
and was gratified that the President seemed to drop the
idea.

Before many months Jefferson had bought all of Louisiana and by mid-January, 1804, there were rumors that
500 Americans were approaching, apparently growing out of
the Lewis and Clark expedition preparations. Spanish authorities took some comfort from the United States plan to
transfer all her Indians west across the Mississippi, forming
a natural and powerful barrier between these Americans
and New Mexico, to be solidified by the natives of the region,
and the "immense desert which will serve us equally for protection."

Loisel didn't ease the mind of anyone by his letter to
Delassus saying there was only a short portage from the headwaters of Lake Winnipeg's Red River to the James of the
Missouri, the route open down that stream to the Platte
and up the river, with only one small portage from there to
the mountains of Santa Fe and the sources of the Rio Grande.
He was also concerned about the precious metal of the Costa
Negra, the Black Hills, where it was found in nuggets scattered on the ground.

May 1804 the Spanish commandant of the interior
provinces was still protesting the plans of the Captain Merry
(Meriwether Lewis) to penetrate the Missouri River, insist-

ing that the limited forces of New Mexico should be used to restrain "one of the most barbarous nations." He had sent a party of Comanches or other allied Indians to reconnoiter as far as the Missouri to obtain knowledge of the expedition "and even to stop them."

When Lewis and Clark were well on their way Delassus wrote uneasily that other Americans had been informing themselves on routes to Santa Fe and Mexico, and that five traders were starting from St. Louis across the Rio Grande, including two who knew the route. There were rumors too, that Lewis was not aiming for the Pacific at all but was headed around to New Mexico by way of the Missouri. Apparently forgetting all the changes in Louisiana proprietorship, the governor general was still enumerating early Spanish claims to the region and the northwest. He described an expedition he said left Santa Fe at the beginning of the 1700's or some years before—settlers, men and women, with their cattle and beasts of burden, protected by soldiers under the command of an engineer. They sought land and an alliance with the Osages against the enemy tribes. The expedition had failed, but later ones went out.

He might have mentioned the early prospectors and traders up as far as the Yellowstone country, with temporary posts in several places through upper Louisiana. Instead he recalled, with some concern, that the captain he called Merry had presented himself at the post the same time that the United States took possession of Louisiana. Such unseemly precipitation "forces us . . . to hasten . . . to cut off the gigantic steps of our neighbor."

CHAPTER II

AMERICANS TO THE
WESTERN SEA

TO THE echo of the bow gun, and the cheers and shouting of the spectators along the shore, the Lewis and Clark Expedition started west May 14, 1804. It was a showery afternoon but people were scattered far along the Missouri, sightseers in carriages, horseback and afoot, river men, Indians too, stopping to look and then ride on.

There were some jeers, and silent stares under worn muskrat caps, stares and contemptuous spittting from the bearded lips of the western beaver men, perhaps just down with the winter's take from as far as the Yellowstone. Among them were voyageurs who knew every restless bend and bar and snag of the Missouri, at least as these had stood last week, or yesterday.

"*Flotteurs!*" some said scornfully. "Raftsmen!"

It was true that the Lewis and Clark boatmen were Kaskaskians, from the smooth-surfaced Ohio and Mississippi. With these the eastern captains in their tricornes, gold braid and white breeches were arrogantly assailing the wild Missouri and her west, including the Indians, and no one of the expedition able to speak any of the western languages. Drouillard, called the interpreter, was half Shawnee, going into a region largely Siouan in dialect, from the nearby Osages to the remote and warring Assiniboins. Voyageurs fa-

miliar with those western rivers, some carrying Indian blood
from the region, stood watching the expedition go, their
skill and knowledge not ignored, the possibility of their ex-
istence or their importance, their necessity, just never suspected.

Although Jefferson had described his plan for the expedition to the Pacific by way of the Missouri as "for literary
purposes" perhaps he spoke more accurately than he realized.
The innocuous characterization was certainly intended as a
gesture to salve the pride of Carlos' Spain, avoid any necessity of their buckling on the sword, but the plan itself was an
old one with the French and the English, and with Jefferson.
He had been concerned even before he heard rumors of
money being raised, years ago, in London for explorations
between the Mississippi and California, sufficiently concerned
to write "they pretend it is only to promote scientific knol-
ege I am afraid they have thoughts of colonization." In
1783 he tried to interest George Rogers Clark in exploring
the western regions but Clark was busy fighting the Ohio Indians and the British, and involved with the beautiful sister
of the Spanish governor of Louisiana, and with the governor
too—Clark and Wilkinson charged with conspiring to form a
new Spanish province in the Ohio valley, or an entirely new
nation.

Ten years later Jefferson had worked to get Michaux
to undertake the exploratory journey to the Pacific, but instead he found Napoleon bordering on the United States.
Fortunately that conqueror was discovering that success also
costs money and, faced by the threat of renewed war with
England, which would put the world's most powerful navy
between him and his American empire, he sold Louisiana.
He sold what turned out to be the largest practically unbroken pasturable, arable, irrigable region in the world, with
the vast buffalo herds that would, one day, help finance the
railroads needed to cross it. More important to Jefferson, as
to all the nations that looked to America for profit, were the

rivers and their beavers, particularly the great ones that opened in the mountains, near the rivers beyond, also rich in peltry, but flowing in another direction, one that led finally to the Pacific and the China trade. The actual outlay of money for the expedition was to be small, $2500, the soldiers sent along costing no more than their regular pay and keep, perhaps less, out where meat was available for a flintlock's blast.

Jefferson's detailed plans dated back to the spring of 1803, when he wrote that his secretary, Meriwether Lewis, was learning to "shoot the sun," to take bearings. The selection of Lewis was partly, it seems, a sort of gesture to the followers of Washington, and particularly to the memory of the man himself, through his sister, who had married Fielding Lewis, uncle of Meriwether. The co-leader, William Clark, was a younger brother of George Rogers Clark, chosen, perhaps, out of the boyhood friendship of Jefferson and Madison with the Clark brothers at their Grandfather Rogers' estate in Virginia, and later around private school. Their common antagonism to the British strengthened the old ties and determined the purpose and much of the makeup of the expedition, which was to follow largely on the plan projected in 1774 by Carver and Whitworth.

The expedition started under the command of the red-haired William Clark, with York, his Negro servant and slave, coal black and tall, a magnificent figure for the adventure ahead, standing behind him. Captain Lewis, blond, considered a dandy around Washington, precise, studious and engrossed with his health, was not there. He joined Clark several days later, with his dog Scannon, described as "of the Newfoundland type." There seems no real agreement on the number of men with the expedition at any given date. Apparently some voyageurs and soldiers joined at different times and for varying periods. The number is generally put at from forty to forty-seven men although there are more names than that mentioned in the journals and accounts.

Probably a fairly constant number was forty-five, including the two captains. Their boat was masted, with eighteen to twenty oars, equipped with a swivel gun at the prow, two swivel-mounted blunderbusses for the sides and Lewis' novelty, an air gun that fired by compression. There were also two heavily loaded pirogues, and a couple of horses for the hunts and to carry messages over far stretches.

The first camp was six miles up the river, with the curious coming there to see. But later an occasional watcher might stop along the bank, or on some far off bluff; nothing more. The river was crooked and increasingly full of snags as it lowered from the ice flood of spring. The expedition met downriver fur canoes and strings of loaded bull boats, round and spinning a little in the eddies. Now and then they caught sight of an upriver brigade, but most of these were far ahead. On good stretches Clark broke out the sail but this was not the Mississippi or even the Ohio; here a gust of wind could send the boat up on a sand bar, to be worked off painfully, and slow, or against a sawyer, lifting up and down in the current, just under the surface.

Totally unfamiliar with the Missouri, the crew worked under difficulties that the most haphazard engagé once over even part of the river could have avoided. While trying to keep to the narrowed current as it swept upon them from a sharp bend the steersman was suddenly confronted by thick, overhanging timber. The mast went with a crash, the first of several lost. Often the voyageurs couldn't use either the oars or push poles and had to tow the boat, bending under the leather as they plodded along the bank on miles of worn tow paths. Perhaps they had to wade the mud and clamber over driftwood and brush and trash. When the berries along the shore began to ripen, and the deer and turkeys increased, Clark laid over to make spare oars, getting timber out for twenty while the hunters looked for buffalo and brought in venison. The mosquitoes thickened too, and the vast piling thunderheads, beyond anything these men had ever seen, sent their lightning crashing down the skies and shook the earth with their thunder.

Where the bluffs drew together the river swiftened, breaking the tow rope, letting the boat swing around, broadside to the current, the men plunging into the water to hold her from going over. The pirogues were usually luckier, almost as gay as dragon flies skimming the water compared to the ponderous boat that the men called a barge. The black pirogue finally did catch on a sawyer and began to sink, the men shouting as they went into the water, holding the little craft, unloading to make the repairs. Farther on the river widened once more and with the shrinking current, more and more sandbars thrust their backs through the water. One a mile long was covered with a solid mass of driftwood, and no telling how much more ready to rise as the muddy water retreated. Clark, still hoping to make headway by sail, had a temporary mast put in, and the next day a turning wind in swift current swept the boat clear around three times, thrusting it heavily, awkward as a great water-logged duck, upon bars and snags, to the curses and sweat of the men.

Although the crew was a diverse one, the space was so compact that it seemed there could be little opportunity for a sneak theft. When it occurred it was from the whisky stores. Two men were court-martialed and found guilty, one sentenced to fifty lashes on the bare back, the other a hundred. With a crew of the usual independent voyageurs there would certainly have been mutiny.

The morning of the Fourth of July the bow gun was fired over the river, sending swarms of ducks and geese, pelicans, herons and a couple of awkward shitepokes into the air, and deer crashing through the underbrush. Perhaps the roar of the gun angered the snakes. One of the men was bitten on the foot, and got his proper cup of whisky.

"I'd liefer get the lash than the snake bite," one of the whisky snatchers remarked.

Quick work with the knife bled out the poison and left the man with nothing worse than a sore foot and a whisky head the next day.

Those out hunting or manning the tow rope had

seen much ancient beaver sign all the way up the river, and many beaver meadows, where trappers had left the dams deserted, to be swept out by floods, the old ponds growing up in dense sedges and grasses or in brush and young trees. Then finally they saw an occupied house, the first evidence that any beaver remained. By then they were far enough from all settlements, with enough Missouri boating behind them that the expedition was beginning to run on an evener routine. The smooth-water men were becoming hardened, if not yet expert, in the fight with the Big Muddy. It was sail a short distance if the wind was southerly, perhaps to run into a sawyer or submerged stump, with everybody jumping into the brownish water to free the boat and drag it into the shallows if damaged. Perhaps there were downriver fur canoes passing, the paddles cutting the water, the muddy drops sparkling in the sun, the teeth of the younger men white in their dark bearded faces, in half envy, half derision.

After the expedition passed the shoaled mouth of the Platte, the captains prepared for their first Indian council. Two men were sent horseback to call the Otos and Pawnees in while the expedition landed and built a bower of saplings and the sail on the western bluffs, with the flag blowing high over it, plain far up and down the river. Word came that the Indians were off making meat, so Barter, who volunteered the information that he spoke a little Oto, was sent to bring them in. He never returned, but the Indians finally came, many of them showing the bearding, the lighter skin of white blood among them for many generations. There were smokes and feasts and orations. The captains told them of their new Great Father in a place called Washington, and then, by naming six new chiefs, initiated the system of government chieftainships on the Plains, a system by which it was hoped the Indians could be controlled. If not, other men could be put in their places, their cooperation also bought. Now, for the first time in the memory of the oldest legends told, the people had to sit under chiefs they had not selected. But there were gifts, including a can of powder and a little whisky, although not as much as the least trader gave. But there were promises of many, many more gifts later, sometime.

Naming the place Council Bluffs in the report, the expedition went on past the old trading house to the Omahas. The river was noticeably shallower above the Platte, and so full of snags and bends that the boat had to be rowed for long stretches, even eighteen miles once. But there were fine big catfish in the river; deer, elk and small game stood to watch the expedition pass, barely running from the boom of the guns along the bluffs. The earliest of the grapes hung in darkening clusters from the wild arbors in brush and trees, and the barrels filled began to ferment almost at once, promising a fragrant red wine.

The men sent to bring in the deserting Barter, dead or alive, failed even to find the public horse he rode, leaving the expedition with only one. Now a second man vanished, perhaps encouraged by Barter's success or feeling the same call of the Platte River that he did, and that had tolled so many others to slip away from the upriver brigades practically from the first. While pursuers were out after the missing men the expedition reached the grave of Black Bird, the Omaha chief who had managed to squeeze so much tribute from every trader going up the river until the white man's smallpox struck him. Lewis and Clark climbed the hill to put a flag on the pole that had once flown the Indian memorials to their chief. The next day they sailed eighteen miles around a bend that was half a mile across the neck. Beyond lay the old Omaha village of 300 earth lodges, burned and deserted four years ago when smallpox killed almost half the tribe.

Once more the mast had to be replaced, but that night there was fiddling and dancing with some belated Otos coming in. The next day the second deserter was returned, and sentenced to run the gauntlet four times through the party, each man provided with nine switches to punish him, the Oto chiefs watching silently, their robes drawn up about them. The next day there was more counciling, more chiefs made.

Ever since St. Louis there had been steady complaints about the clouds of mosquitoes and the recurring but mild dysentery and colic, laid by some to overeating on fresh game and wild fruit. Then one of the men, Sergeant Floyd, did not recover in a day as the others had, and without a doctor to diagnose his illness or to treat what was called colic, he died and was buried on the east side of the Missouri with war honors, Lewis performing the ceremony, Clark's red hair blazing in the sun.

By now the expedition was nearing the dangerous regions, where, some of the returning traders had warned Clark, there were frequent robberies by warring Indians seeking arms, or to keep the weapons from their enemies. Traders had been ambushed, perhaps by rival fur outfits or river thieves moving west from the Ohio. But most of the losses were to the encroaching British companies and their Frenchmen living with the tribes. The furs going north wore deeper trails every year, and new ones made, reaching down as far as the Platte and below—half a dozen spreading to the trading spots of the upper Missouri and down along the foot of the Rockies to the Snakes and the Black Men, the Utes, and on the other side of the mountains too.

"That is why we are here," Clark had said.

Late in August sixty Sioux of the bad reputation for halting traders, robbing them, came in from their village over on the James River. They came singing and shaking their rattles and were received with two guns from the bow piece and the flag snapping in the perpetual wind. The usual presents of tobacco and small items were given out, with a red-laced coat, a cocked hat, a white shirt and other, lesser gifts for the head chief, including an American flag to fly over his village. The Sioux boys displayed their proficiency with the bow, the young men danced to the drums and rat-

tles, and then the warriors rose, one after the other, to relate
their exploits in the hunts and in war, mostly in war. Afterward more chiefs were made and the headmen invited to
go to visit the Great Father when the expedition returned.
There were many long speeches, apparently interpreted by
Dorion, living with the Sioux over twenty years.

For miles Clark's men had noticed ribbons of clear,
gleaming water winding themselves through the thick and
muddy Missouri.

"The Rapid River, the Running Water," the Sioux
had said, meaning the Niobrara.

Before the expedition reached the river they ran into
the bad weather supposedly common over the region. A roaring windstorm filled the air with sand from the bars and
broke the mast. Finally they got to the mouth of the Niobrara, the swift stream striking the flank of the Missouri
from the west in a handsome wilderness of brush and timber
and game. A new mast was cut and installed here and then
they pushed on, the clumps of trees thinning out, the prairie
thrusting itself against the shallow bluffs on both sides of
the river, which was noticeably shrunken. Progress was difficult even by oar and pole until the boat was turned to the
less broken eastern shore with its worn towpath. A cold rain
began to fall, the boat stuck on a sandbar and swung broadside into the current, so the men had to take to the water
again. When they finally made anchor and camp they welcomed a warming dram.

Some distance back a gray horse loose along the river
had been caught up to replace the one Barter took along.
Placed in the care of a nineteen-year-old private, both
seemed to be lost now. Some argued that the smooth-cheeked
Pennsylvania youth had deserted too, perhaps was heading
home horseback across country; more probably he was drawn
into a buffalo chase and perhaps got lost, if not killed in a
stampede or set afoot by horsethieving Indians. The buffaloes were plentiful now, the herds darkening more and
more of the western prairie, drawing the eyes of the river
men from their work, until after a while buffaloes, even great

moving herds plunging into the Missouri and out the other side were commonplace. Everybody did go on shore to see a "rack of Bones of a verry large fish   the Back bone 45 feet long," as Sergeant Ordway described it in his journal, and marveled at such a great fish* in the Missouri, that was often too shallow to float the barge properly.

Finally the man in charge of the horses got back with only one, the other worn out during the sixteen days of his search for the river and the boat. He had been lost and, out of ammunition, was almost starved.

Each river left behind cost the boatmen extra labor in a lowered Missouri, and they must have welcomed the promise of a stop-over at Cedar Island. Loisel's post out among the cedars seemed proof of the rumored dangers along the upper river. The fort was a sturdy one, sixty-five by seventy feet, surrounded by tree-trunks set deep into the earth, extending thirteen and a half feet above. This was the country of the warring Sioux, with a band of them camped nearby when Clark arrived. The usual conference was called, with all the usual speeches. The captains made more government chiefs and gave out the usual medals and presents, including an American flag, which these Indians unexpectedly treated as casually as any colored cloth.

"They say they have one thirteen, fourteen years ago," the interpreter explained.

"Where from?" he was asked.

The Indians pointed east. Men, probably traders, from the east brought it, and pleased the Sioux so that the wintercounts of three tribal bands named the season of 1790-1791 for the flag.

The conference went well enough on all except talk of peace with their neighbors, but when Clark was ready to go on, there was trouble with the head man. He grabbed the cable of one of the pirogues. Holding it fast, he sat down on the bank to emphasize his refusal to let the expedition go to their enemies up the river. No one dared touch him, even without his warriors pushing up along the bank, suddenly

---

* Probably the fossil remains of a cretaceous reptile.

painted and armed; nor could Clark order the pirogue thrust forward by a mighty dig of the waiting paddles. Jerking the cable from the chief's hands or dragging him into the water would mean a bloody fight and surely the failure of the peace purposes of the expedition.

But something had to be done, and immediately. Loudly Clark ordered the large swivel of the boat loaded with sixteen musket balls before the eyes of the Indians, and the blunderbusses with buckshot. At his command the men swung the guns upon the chief and his warriors. Then firmly Clark announced he was going on, motioning up the river, going on even if he had to cut down all opposition with his cannons.

There was a long moment while the men stood at fire, ready, the Indians perhaps recalling the roar of the gun at the bow in salute the day the expedition arrived. Still they made no move, their faces stony. Clark gestured the guns aimed, the large one directly upon the chief. For a moment the dark Indian eyes stared into the face of the red-haired one. Then slowly his strong brown fingers moved, let the cable slip from them. Calmly he rose and with his blue British blanket drawn in dignity about him, he walked away as from some casual meeting.

Everyone was relieved. The white men had been greatly outnumbered and would probably have been destroyed although many Sioux would have died first from the blasts of the three swivels and the fire of the flintlocks, even if there was never time to reload.

This is the way the Indians said it was, years later. They had known that these white men admired them as a people, that their camps had been the finest Lewis and Clark encountered, the lodges of handsome whitened buffalo hide, painted in bandings, and picturing the exploits of the owners. When the expedition first arrived, the Indians had carried Lewis on a painted buffalo robe to the chief's lodge, feasted all the visitors and at night, under the chilling September stars, they had danced in paint and regalia around great fires. Only one of the many Sioux wintercounts men-

tioned white men with flags for this year, but several counted
it as the time the white man came and danced on his head—
Priv. François Rivet.

Late in October the expedition halted a while at the
three Arikara earthen villages and then at a hunting camp
of the Mandans, where men, women and children were
making meat for the winter. Even there, in the temporary
location, McCracken, North West Company trader, was busy
accumulating robes and hides as the cold nights thickened
them.

October 27 Lewis and Clark reached the Five Villages
of the Upper Missouri, still strung out for about eleven miles
along the river, the two upper ones the Hidatsas, the lower
three Mandan, the lowest of these—about forty earth houses
—with two or three Frenchmen living there, including the
trader Jusseaume and his Indian wife and children, and no
telling how many of the Indians carrying French blood or
for how many generations.

The Americans stopped a couple of hours and went on
to the second Mandan village, with the third one just across
the river, on the south side. Here, 1610 miles out of St. Louis,
the expedition camped and hoisted the flag, with Indians
gathering rapidly from both sides of the Missouri, all hurrying to see, some of the women astonished at the few men
who were still in uniform, the tricornes and gold braid of
the captains.

From this day on there were always Indians around.
The first morning, without official arrangement, some of the
Hidatsa chiefs rode down to greet these white men of whom
they had already heard many things by signal and by mes-
senger. The next day the bow gun called the leaders of all
the villages to a council. They came, the Americans watching
them arrive, with some women and children too, and were
struck by the appearance of the Soulier division of the Hidatsas, who were lightest skinned of all the Five Villages, some
of the children actually fair-haired.

This first council was a day to make friends and to show the marvels, the Indians trailing behind the captains, looking, touching. They were particularly pleased with the air gun and how rapidly and repeatedly Lewis could fire it without reloading and without powder.

Ah-h-h, this could be very useful, some of the chiefs admitted. It was so often their supply of powder that was gone as swiftly as the smoke of it.

With a forty-eight-hour knowledge of the Indians, Lewis and Clark made two new chiefs for each of the villages and added recommendations for two more in each of the Mandan groups, four each for the Hidatsas, although many of the latter were off on war parties, surely some important men. There were careful gradations even in the medals given out, gradations thoroughly explained to the Indians. Those to the first chief of each village carried the impression of President Jefferson, the second of weaving and domestic animals, the third a man sowing wheat. What these pictures meant to the Indians no one inquired, particularly a man sowing in a field—against all the fertility practices of these agrarian people. There were the usual presents and the usual talk of peace among the tribes, peace and safety for their families. Handsome clothing and a flag were sent to Big White, head of the Mandans. In the evening the expedition received a dram all around and afterward the men danced to the violin as had been common on the way up the river. It pleased the young Indians very much but there had been a curious aloofness, an expectancy, among the leading men at the day's council.

The fall days were very windy and before Lewis and Clark were settled, the tenderfoot easterners saw what carelessness with fire on the prairie could do. It seemed the blaze was set by a Mandan youth, perhaps by accident, although the Plains Indian learned about live coals while still a toddler. There were rumors that one of the soldiers had sneaked a little rum to the youth, making him reckless. However the fire started, the wind swept it over the dry fall prairie with such speed that a man and woman, apparently butchering buffaloes, were killed, while another couple and a child were badly burned. A half-white boy came through the fire unhurt because his foresighted mother threw a fresh buffalo hide over him. The prairie fire burned on past the expedition camp in the night, the entire sky aflame.

Before the end of the week Big White sent an invitation stick to Clark. At the chief's lodge the captain was seated in the place of honor beside his host, who threw a handsomely worked robe over his shoulders as a gift. After the usual smoke the Mandan said he was pleased to know that there would be peace so his people could hunt without fear, the women work safely in the fields, and everybody sleep at night "without their moccasins on." Some of the resentment of the last council was cleared up for Clark when the chief told him that the Indians of the neighboring villages were out hunting when the white men came but hearing the news and expecting presents, the hunters quit their task and came back immediately. All were disappointed, some outright dissatisfied.

Clark must have given this some thought. Evidently the Indians did not understand the difference between his expedition and trade. They had learned to expect competing gifts from the fur buyers, whether from St. Louis, the North West Company or Hudson's Bay, all vying for the hides. Perhaps the Indians had expected the gift of liquor for the accustomed "big drink," the competitive intoxication that the traders made, usually the first day and night. No wonder the Indians had hurried home. Later Clark discovered that the taste for liquor had not developed much here. In the meantime Big White agreed to go to see the Great Father, and now, to show his friendly intentions, he had two of the steel traps he said were robbed from the French brought in and laid at Clark's feet. To these he added twelve bushels of corn.

Back at the boat Clark was met by a couple of chiefs from the third village, and then the head chief with whom

he had just visited came too, dressed up in the finery sent to
him. He brought his two small sons, who must see the white
men dance.

So it went, Indians in silent moccasins in the camp
every moment, peering around the boat at sunrise and before, and still there at moonset. In the meantime Lewis
wrote to the North West Company agent at the Assiniboine,
explaining the purposes of the expedition and enclosing
copies of their British passports for the far west end of the
journey. These he sealed with official wax and sent up by
McCracken, the trader from the hunting camp, setting out on
the 150-mile trail.

When feathers of ice edged the morning river and an
occasional skift of snow ran gray along the prairie, Clark and
his men began to shiver. Their blood, thin from the malar-
ial south, told them it was time to get the winter quarters
under way. The boat was moved slowly along the river, Indians lining the bank watching, some crying to them not to
go.

"Stay, white-man friends, stay!" they shouted, seeming almost as concerned that the expedition should not settle
near another village as that it must not depart entirely.

Finally the boat was anchored seven, eight miles below the mouth of Knife River, on the northeast bank of the
Missouri. The task of locating a good winter spot, protected
from storm and near firewood and game, was facilitated by
Graveline, the old Arikara trader who was to stay with the
party all winter and two men from the "Cannon Ball" River,
Degie and Greinyea, in Clark's spelling, probably Grenier.
Later the Canadian Le Page was accepted for enlistment. He
had lived with the Cheyenne Indians for some time and
knew considerable about the Little Missouri country up
ahead. True, these were all fur-company men of varying
status and their joining the explorers might seem a little
suspect, as was Jusseaume's hiring as the Mandan interpreter. He moved his wife and family to a skin lodge set up

outside of the post, where he was joined later by Charbonneau from the Hidatsas. All company men.

The new post was located on a point overlooking the river, in cottonwoods, tall and spreading even in their winter nakedness. The Indians said it was a fine place for horses, perhaps reluctant to lose it. In deepest winter they grazed their herds on any wind-swept slopes during the day and gave each horse a little armful of cottonwood to gnaw in the night. That time was almost here, with the geese flying south before the snow, the Indians said, watching the cabins at the new Fort Mandan go up as fast as Clark's men could work. The timber was large and heavy with greenness to carry by hand, with no horses to drag the big cottonwood and elm logs into place. There was some ash, but small, as was its nature.

Clark could find few uninterrupted hours for his work. By this time he had discovered that Charbonneau, his Hidatsa interpreter, knew only a few trade words of the language and sign talk for "Not good enough," meaning a hide fell below standard. Jusseaume was away much of the time, trading, and yet every sunrise Indians waited at the river bank for the white men to stir, and kept coming all day, some to see, some hoping for presents. There were usually some chiefs among them. One morning Little Raven of the Mandans came striding ahead of his wife who carried about sixty pounds of dried buffalo meat, a robe and the traditional welcoming pot of cooked meal. Clark gave the woman an ax and some trinkets, and the chief the anticipated husband's gift. Such exchange of presents was always a legitimate excuse for visiting the whites, as was news. Some Hidatsas rode down to say that fifty lodges of Assiniboins were arriving to visit and trade, much as they had come with Verendrye in 1738, much as they came at least once a winter and always to the annual summer fair, for the Hidatsas were the traders of the Upper Missouri. The Mandans brought news too, of their antelope hunt, 100 caught in a drive down a large V of brush fencing they had built from far out on the prairie converging on a strong pen.

But most of the Indians just came to watch the strange activities of these whites, the men squatting over their pipes along the new walls in the fall sunshine, the women with children on their backs perhaps working rawhide or sinew or beading, or grinding paint in the little stone cups. Sometimes several settled to a desultory little game of chance, shaking the gourd bowl with marked stones or plum pits, while they kept a diffident eye on all that was going on. And when mess call came, they expected to eat too, for they were guests. Besides, these white men were using the Indian's land, his trees, his river, his game.

One night before the cabins were done Clark was awakened by the sergeant of the night guard. He came out of the deep sleep after a late hour with the Indians, but it was no alarm, no Sioux attack. Instead the sergeant called him out to look at the sky, lit by a great streaming whiteness that rose and fell out of the north and then rose again, long brilliant tongues of cold flame licking out over their heads.

"The snows are lighting a path for themselves," an old Indian spoke in his long-time trader patois. He barely lifted himself from his sleeping robe against a pile of logs not far from the two men standing with the paleness of the sky on their upturned faces.

Along in November three Hudson's Bay men arrived at the villages and sent proper word to Clark that they would come to see him soon. In the meantime Charbonneau brought two young women of the Rocky Mountain people, the Snakes, and four pack horses loaded with pelts and meat to trade.

As the winds became raw, the ice clung to the river edges all day and the swans flew very high overhead, the Mandans began to tell Clark their tribal history, making it last a long time, night after night, beside the fireplaces kept roaring. They had been a powerful tribe before the white man's smallpox came across the country to them, long ago. In those days the neighboring tribes had all been afraid of them, and now they were only one large village and the small ones. They had come to the Missouri lower down and moved up to the Rees a while but got into war with them, and so came up to the Hidatsas and lived in peace with them ever since. Together the Five Villages were strong. They could raise over 1000 good warriors, the Mandans about 350, the two divisions of the Hidatsas the rest. Now they were at war with the Snakes and the Sioux, but large parties of Snakes always came to the trade fair up with the Hidatsas every summer and even small parties visited back and forth with the Sioux, on tribal business, to trade corn and squash and other river products or just to feast and dance.

In mid-November the white men were invited to the ceremony of adoption between the Assiniboins and the Five Villages, including the formal acceptance of prisoners into families. In the west here prisoners were not to be tortured as the Iroquois were before Champlain's eyes 195 years ago. An adopted prisoner could even rise to power in the chiefs' lodges, the women, as wives, with the subtler power of the matrilineal, behind even the greatest chiefs. Seventy lodges of the Assiniboins gathered as guests up at the Hidatsas but they were such expert horse thieves that their hosts had sent the extra horses clear down to the timber near the fort, fourteen, fifteen miles away, and well guarded by warriors, so the herd would still be there when the visitors went home. The Mandans, too, had some uneasiness about their Assiniboin guests. Black Cat came to Clark about this. They had been putting up with insults from both the arrogant Assiniboins and the Crees until the chiefs could discover if the Americans here meant their words of peace between the tribes and intended to see that the peace was kept. His people had been deceived before. The man Evans who had trouble with Jusseaume had come from the south to live among them in 1795 and was made welcome and then fooled them. He gave them none of the protection he promised, and never returned with the guns and ammunition he agreed to bring. The Assiniboins sat across the trader trails from the north, controlling all that came to them from that direction, saying how many guns, how much powder the villages could have. In the south there were the Sioux who said "no" to everything that was to come as far as the Rees.

Clark nodded. He knew about that, recalling the Sioux chief who had sat down with the pirogue cable in his hand.

Now the woman trouble began, or rather reached the stage that could no longer be ignored. There was a noisy fight down at the interpreter lodges, scarcely sixty yards from the post. An Indian had come to kill his wife. Clark hurried down with a little force of men; such conduct could not be tolerated around the expedition headquarters. He was told that the trouble had started earlier, soon after the white men arrived. Then about eight days ago the Indian couple had come to an angry disagreement and the woman fled to the wives of the interpreters. Day before yesterday she had returned to her village but by evening she was back, badly beaten, and stabbed in three places. Now her husband wanted to kill her.

"We Derected that no man of this party have any intercourse with this woman under penalty of Punishment," Clark wrote in his journal, the order provoked by the husband's insistence that one of the sergeants had slept with his wife and if the white man wanted her, he could have her.

Clark ordered Sergeant Ordway to give the husband some presents and told the Indian he believed that no man had "touched his wife except the one he had given the use of her for a nite in his own bed." He assured the man that none of the party should touch his "squar," as Clark wrote it, or the wife of any Indian, "nor do I believe they touch a woman if they knew her to be the wife of another man." He advised the Indian to take his wife home and live happily. The grand chief of the Mandans came to lecture the man and finally the two went off together, but not necessarily satisfied. Certainly Clark knew there would be more such trouble—and the winter not half over.

CHAPTER III

WINTER OF THE EXPLORERS

PRACTICALLY every literate man around the Five Villages and Fort Mandan kept a journal of some sort that winter of 1804-05. This included the North West and Hudson's Bay representatives, who were required to keep detailed journals. In addition to their traders living with the tribes of the Missouri both companies sent fresh supplies of goods down, and some of these men, particularly of the North West, left accounts.

The fall supplies of the North Westers were in charge of Larocque with Charles Mackenzie and a free trader, La France, with their four voyageurs to handle the packhorses. To avoid being stopped by the Assiniboins they left the worn old trail and took a circuitous route over the plains, still mostly aflame or smoldering from the big prairie fire. They saw whole herds of buffaloes with their hair singed, some blinded by the burning of their mop, as the hair hanging over the eyes was called. Half-roasted carcasses were scattered along the route, some piled in gullies or at the feet of steep bluffs where herds plunged over in their terrorized stampedes. The wind whipped up dark clouds of soot, the faces of the men blackened, their lips, nostrils and eyes smarting, with no water or wood or grass left anywhere. They whooped the packhorses along to Dog Lodge (Tent)

217

Butte, the high broken area never totally burned over. They found water here, without the usual Sioux war parties but they did encounter a small group of Assiniboins and had to use guile to escape.

The scouts must have signaled the approach of the traders to the upper villages on the Missouri, for the Hidatsas came swarming out to meet them, wishing them joy, and congratulating themselves on their coming. They made a great feast for them that night, anticipating plenty of fine hot tea with the sugar deep in the drinking gourds. At the village the newcomers found four Hudson's Bay men who had arrived about a week before. A party of Assiniboins had detained them for days, as prisoners, and took handsome tribute for their liberty. With largely diminished trade stock, but anticipating no competition, they had raised their prices, hoping to make up some of the loss. The Indians had been angered, holding back their robes and pelts. Now the welcomed North West men were here among them, and the prices would come down.

Larocque had known about the American expedition here to explore the Pacific in the spring, probably from McCracken and the Lewis communications. Now he heard more, of their way of living, their repeated counciling, particularly with the Mandans, near whom they had located and that they gave out presents for peace and adherence to their Great Father. Most of the presents were refused by the Hidatsa chiefs, they told Larocque, not saying that it might have been because the goods were much less than those of the Mandans, or that they were working for some gifts from the North Westers. Or even because they were known as an independent people.

The coming of so many British traders to the villages, particularly to those up the river, convinced Lewis he must investigate. He went to the Hidatsas with two interpreters and six soldiers. The day after he arrived Lewis complained to Mackenzie that they had not been welcomed very graciously at the upper village. He had sent word ahead to

Horned Weasel, the chief, announcing that he intended to take up quarters in his house.

"He returned for answer that he was not at home," Lewis said in outrage.

Then, again without much tact, he added that he had assumed it was common only with Mackenzie's English lords not to be "at home" when an undesired guest came, not, he implied, among American Indians living in dirt huts. It apparently never occurred to him, former secretary to Jefferson, that his uninvited approach to a Hidatsa chief on the upper Missouri might be as resented as it would have been by the president in his official residence.

After haranguing the Hidatsas and explaining the intention of the expedition to the west, much of it in language, in words, unknown and foreign to the limited interpreters, Lewis gave out some clothing and trinkets. Some of the Indians accepted the gifts and yet could not be reconciled to welcoming these strangers as friends, saying if the white men had come with their hearts good, they would have loaded their great boat with good things. It was true that they brought ammunition but they preferred to shoot it away idly instead of sparing a shot of it for the poor Indians who had trouble getting ammunition against their enemies. Those who had been to the fort admired the gun that fired its forty times from one loading, little lead balls that could be pebbles, and air, nothing more than air. They seemed awed by the magic, but one Hidatsa chief was not awed by anything of the expedition.

"My young men on horses would soon do for them as they do for so many wolves," he said. He had found only two sensible men among them, the worker of iron and the mender of guns.

Lewis took two chiefs and a substantial party of warriors back to council at the fort. The Hidatsas watched these go in concern. The Mandans had told them that the whites would join the Sioux during the winter and cut them all off here. The rumor was aided by the movement of the interpreter families to the shadow of the big guns, and the very

strength of the fort, which none could hope to breach when
the stout pickets across the front were all up. Lewis tried to
contradict these impressions. He had accused LaFrance of
speaking unfavorably of their intentions and reported that he
informed Larocque and Mackenzie that the conduct of their
interpreter was displeasing and would bring consequences if
they did not stop him. Down at the fort the Hidatsa chiefs
and their followers were amused by what they saw, particularly the dancing of the white men, with Rivet dancing on his
head, his feet straight up, keeping time or held close together and wearing his fur cap with more dignity than his
head ever managed.

For several nights the yip and wail of the coyotes rose
thin and high above the coarser howl of the big, whitening
prairie wolves and then one morning the whole valley was
lost in storm. The river fell and before the sun reappeared,
there was a foot of snow. Larocque had gone down to visit
the Mandans and call at the fort. Almost before he could
shake the frost from his white capote in the official quarters,
he was told that he must not make chiefs and give out medals
and flags. Larocque laughed and said he had no such intentions.

The medals and flags of the Americans had been distributed to the chiefs on their promise to give up war except
in defense of the people, yet before long White Wolf of the
Hidatsas went against the Blackfeet to avenge the death of
his brother the fall before. With only fifty warriors he had
trouble finding an enemy party small enough to attack so on
the way home they killed four men from a Canadian canoe
fur brigade, traded their scalps to the Rocky Mountain Indians and then tried to keep it silent.

Finally Lewis and Clark moved into their space, the
buildings set in two rows to form the arms of a V, each hut
with four rooms and a loft of split plank padded thick with
slough grass for warmth and silence. The shed roofs of the
buildings slanted up to the outer wall which was, Sergeant

Gass wrote, about eighteen feet high. The angle of the V held the storerooms. It was really an arc that could defend both walls. Here a sentry watched all night while in the day a sentinel walked the entire post. The opening of the V-shaped post was being filled with high pickets and a sturdy gate, almost cannon proof, Larocque reported.

By now most of the Indians had moved to their smaller, more sheltered winter villages. The fur traders had established themselves and for a few days the Indians crowded into their quarters to see the goods obtainable for their robes and peltry, mostly wolf. In the lull around the fort Clark's men had made a stout elkhide rope to pull the boat up on the bank before the river trapped it with ice. One of the sergeants dislocated his shoulder taking the mast down and four attempts were made before it could be replaced, with no doctor around. The men got their drink of taffe (tafia) and needed it after the cold hard work.

Before these things were settled, the Sioux attacked the Mandan hunting camp and killed a chief's young son. Clark went over to offer his help. He took along twenty-three men in full uniform, paraded them through the village, their colors gay against the piled snow along the paths, and crowning the domed roofs of the houses. Clark knew that 300 lodges of Cheyennes were coming to the Mandans, and because they were recognized as allies of the Sioux, he tried to anticipate possible trouble. He offered the bereaved father any assistance he wanted and went back to settle a little more woman trouble. When one of his soldiers and Drouillard, the Shawnee interpreter, got into a fight over one, it was between Clark's own men and he tried to keep it within the post. Now Jusseaume was aggrieved and jealous over both his wife and his job.

As the cold closed in there were rumors of buffaloes coming, and then one morning the whole plain back from the river was covered by a glistening frost cloud, frost rising from a vast, closely packed night bed of buffaloes. Criers ran through the villages as far off as the upper Hidatsas, and since these clouds were visible for many miles on the horizon,

perhaps through the camps of the Sioux, the Assiniboin and
even the fringes of the Blackfeet and Crees. Great strings of
horsemen rode out, kept in order by established routine and
by smoke and mirror signals. Lewis went too, with fifteen of
his best hunters, they and a few of the traders the only ones
with guns. The Indians shot the buffaloes by riding up along
side, preferably by setting small bunches into circling, the
barebacked hunters on their best buffalo horses keeping the
great shaggy animals on the run into a tightening spin, bringing down the fat cows for the butchers to come later, the
meat to be hauled home on packhorses. Hunting and feasting
became the chief concern. Large parties went out every day
from one village or another, often killing whole sections of
the great herd but taking only the tongues now and the best
of the hides to be tanned to robes for the traders. Some of
the old ones made the signs of foreboding.

"It can bring no good, this wasteful killing when none
is hungry."

But the wolves cleaned up the carcasses, their fighting
and howls keeping the night alive, gorging until they were so
full that they could be overtaken easily the next day, making
hides for the traders but, even more prized, good sport for
the young Indians who rode them down.

These days of the late fall hunts were the happiest
ones for the young men of the villages. The Hidatsas, particularly, had plenty of beaver in their region, beavers considered as friends, as much the playmates of their watching
children as they had been when their upper village was
above Old Crossing, and the two Bearded Men came. But
neither Hidatsas nor Mandans would trouble to kill many
beaver. They told Mackenzie they would like to supply him
with the plew he wished if they could be obtained by a chase
on horseback. Pursuing beaver in the earth to satisfy the
avarice of the whites was very degrading.

"What use are the beavers? do they make gunpowder
of them?" one chief asked. "Do they preserve them from sickness? Do they serve them beyond the grave?"

When Mackenzie said that the northern Indians were

very industrious and great friends of the white people, the chief replied, "Our fathers were not slaves!" It was true that the white man had brought some good things to them but he also carried the smallpox and the evils of liquor in his hand so the Indians were diminishing and no longer happy.

The weather-wise buffaloes sought the upper Missouri where the snow blew off the rises, and with bluffs to protect them from drifting into the freezing blizzards just a few days before the thermometer fell to thirty-eight below zero. Many of Clark's easterners, unused to the deceptive dry cold, were frostbitten, York among them, but so that it became a great joke, particularly when it spread to the Indians. A Sioux, a short-time captive among the Mandans, called the year "The Winter-the-Black-Man-Froze-His-Man-Part."

There was more trouble to take Clark from his plans for next summer, his interviewing western Indians and making maps of their accounts. Once more it came from the interpreter camp. Charbonneau did or did not owe the trader LaFrance a horse. Jusseaume was still discontented, and an Indian came in a jealous rage to one of the interpreters because his wife was being tolled away. What amazed and shocked the soldiers was the sight of a number of men from the Mandan village dressed in women's clothing, come to sell corn at the post for little trinkets and fineries.

With the cold settling in, the Indians took up their winter games, sometimes a wild chase of the snow snakes— light wooden darts—sent flying along the snow or ice, preferably on smooth stretches in the village paths or, larger and noisier, on the glistening Missouri. The usual games of rings and long crosspieced sticks were moved to smooth snow or ice. Several times the soldiers tried to join in but either the games became awkward and formal or the novices were run over in the rush. The children had their games too, some taking up those of the elders, or making snow palisades or playing "Hiding the Tracks." The young Hidatsas spent much time out on the snowy hills sliding down on buffalo-rib sleds, brought to them, it was said, by an early visitor from far off in the country of the rising sun.

As winter settled in there seemed more and more Mandans around the fort, often remaining all night, when the snow crackled and popped with the cold outside. Then one evening they were all sent home. Tomorrow, they were told, was the white man's big medicine day, very big medicine. Such words they could understand. They rose in respectful dignity and drawing their robes about them, the women with children on their backs pulling the blankets up, and went away in grave and decorous step, one behind the other, into the cold that trailed frost behind them.

At the cloudy dawn of Christmas the swivels were fired from the fortifications, the roar echoing over the frozen river and scaring the grouse from the tops of the whitened cottonwoods, followed by a volley, each man firing a round, the stinking smoke hanging blue over the fort. Then the men were given a solid drink of tafia and the best food available. There was a little speech by Lewis and a condolence to the one acknowledged married man with the original force, consoling him for his Christmas away from his home. Afterward some of the men went hunting but there was shooting and capering at the fort until nine at night.

The next day a large party went to the Mandan villages to dance, but the real celebration came on New Year, with moderated weather and a great deal of gun roar and powder smoke. A toast was drunk all around and about nine in the morning, fifteen or sixteen men went to the first village to dance, taking fiddle, tambourine and "soundin'" horns. Outside they fired a round, played their music and reloading, marched to the center space and fired again and then fell into their jigs, shuffles and clogs on the frozen ground. Rivet danced on his head while the others whirled around him, the Indians pushing up to see, even the shiest of the maidens. It seemed that the whites also had the Contrary, the Foolish Ones, those who must by vow or dream do all things backward or upside down.

Then the visitors went from one earth house to

another, dancing there, drawing the Indian girls into the whirling, the most ready to come usually those with white fathers or grandfathers, partly, perhaps, because in their social dances, the Indian girl makes the choice, not the youth or the man. She draws her partner into the flying steps around the fire. Later in the day Clark went up with his servant York who danced for the Indians too, his feet a clatter in his jigs, delight in his broad black face, all his great frame agitated as he patted juba to the sawing of the fiddle. The Indians poured back out into the snow-ringed open space before the winter medicine lodge, the eyes of the women shining to see such a man as surely had never happened before.

Clark left York with the dancers while he went to visit with every man of note in the village except the two who had favored the British traders from the north over the Americans, or perhaps kept aloof for other reasons, in spite of all he and the more eloquent but more chilly Lewis could do. The dancing pleased the Indians so much they kept the white men at it until late, some staying all night.

The next day Captain Lewis, the interpreter and most of the men went to the second Mandan village and frolicked there too, as they called it, so there could be no injured feelings. The men returned in the evening but as usual some stayed. The next day a Hidatsa came after his wife, who had felt abused and fled to the post for protection some time before. Perhaps there was another motive behind both comings, the Hidatsas deciding to take the path that seemed to get attention from the white men. Some had been asking, "Are the Hidatsas then a people of no account, not worth visiting by the white man dancers?"

After the post settled down again, Clark returned to his map making. He got some peace because the nearest Mandan village was preparing for the three-day buffalo-tolling ceremonial. The great herd of early December had gone as suddenly as it came, and with the vast concentration of meat eaters on the upper Missouri, the large tribal visits to the Five Villages that had cleaned out most of the winter's supply of meat and field produce, there must be a hunt. The buffalo must be brought very friendly, with so much of the game killed, and what was left made very wild for the bow after all the gun shooting of the Americans from the fort.

The scouts sent word that the buffaloes were headed toward the villages but seemed to hesitate, seeming to turn their heads away. Now it was time to make the bringing medicine, with everything leading to the final nights when the old men of the ceremonial came to sit in a circle in the dusky medicine lodge, a handful of coals sending fragrant and whitish twists toward the smoke hole above, the red light of the firespot barely touching the faces of those along the walls. Loudly the chanter demanded if there were any young war leaders willing to make the great sacrifice, the greatest this side of the death scaffold, in honor of the cow, the buffalo; to bring her close.

In response to the repeated call, a string of young men entered, bringing their wives wrapped in long robes. When they were lined up at the far end of the earth lodge, the old men rose, dropped their ancient medicine skins and moved forward on their gnarled and bony legs, making pawing motions like buffalo bulls, lowering their heads and roaring.

It seemed that the procedure varied from night to night but apparently it always led to the husbands pleading with the old men to take their wives. Sometimes the young women stroked the arms of the old men of their husband's choice, perhaps opening their robes, showing their nakedness, and then, clutching the robes together again, drew the men outside. In some reports the wives were offered to young men who were to rise and follow the women to the night-dark prairie, while the old men danced around them out there, bellowing and pawing, going through their buffalo dance.

Obviously this seemed a little chilly, at the far-below-zero weather of early January in 1805, but Clark heard the stories and sent a man to the dance the last night. The observer reported that in this final ceremony the young wives drew old men away, some scarcely able to walk from age and decreptitude. If the old man (or a white man invited to take part) returned without accepting the sacrifice, the wife was offered again. Sometimes after two unsuccessful overtures, the husband threw a valuable robe over the reluctant one and begged that he not scorn them further, despise them, publicly. Clark's man came back saying he had been given four girls, to help bring the buffaloes back, but he may have been bragging.

The Hidatsas too were making their annual winter buffalo medicine, returning to their big holy lodge off some distance from the summer village. Inside stood the sacred shrine of the tribe, topped with the skulls of two men who had brought great gifts and power to the people, one of whom, it was said, had given himself to the thunder and died with a hole in his head from a spear of its lightning—to bring the rains on the crops and the prairie, the people believed. Lower down on the shrine lay the sacred buffalo skull, adorned with dangling eagle feathers, the means of much meat. Perhaps the Hidatsa winter ceremonial to the buffalo head was more private, or perhaps the tribe was deliberately slighted; none of Clark's men seem to have been there. Even if it had been recorded, there would have been none to say how much these old Mandan and Hidatsa ceremonials were changed in the shift from a largely agrarian life to the growing dependence upon the great horse-mounted buffalo hunts and the mystical significance of the mass killings. How much was taken over from the old rites to make the earth fertile, and how much was borrowed from visits and adopted captives of the long-time hunters, the Blackfeet, the Assiniboins?

Soon after the buffalo hunt was done, several Indians who had been far west at some time, including a chief of the lower Mandans, came to the post with a sketch map of the Missouri on buckskin. It started up in the Rocky Mountains and showed the Yellowstone too, and its six rivers flowing in from the south. The country out there was hilly, much of it timbered, with many beaver. There were great falls on the Missouri about 800 miles to the west of the fort here, the interpreter said.

By the tenth of January the cold had clamped down again, to forty below zero, yet over across the iron-hard river the Mandans were making war medicine to avenge the chief's son, killed in the fall. Some of Clark's men went over to see that too, with the hoods of their capotes meeting the thick bearding on all but the nineteen-year-old among them, with only a thin curling around his chin, and on the mixed-bloods like Drouillard. Charbonneau and his companion returned from a small Hidatsa camp over near the Little Missouri, their faces frozen. They reported that the North West Company planned to build a post for the upper villages and that the Hudson's Bay men were talking unfavorably about the Americans, the head chief of the Hidatsas also spreading slighting remarks about the expedition. None can say now how much was truth and how much was conspiring by the interpreters, playing one group against the others, like a breed coquette her lovers, and apparently with the same personal advantage.

Clark had other problems now. Several of the men had caught a venereal disease from the Mandan women. He tried to keep the force from further infection and doctored the sick men but a week later his journal mentioned one man who was very bad with the pox.

As the weather warmed a little, some of the Hidatsa headmen rode down. Welcomed, they stayed over night. The next day thirty Mandans, including six chiefs, hastened to the post, aggrieved. Their neighbors stopped on their way home and called them liars, claiming that they had been told by the Mandans that the Americans would kill any Hidatsas who came to the fort. Instead they were well treated, and the whites had danced for them too.

Because Lewis had little talent for peacemaking, Clark tried to soothe the Indians but before they got off the post a Hidatsa chief came with a man who brought his wife to wait on Clark for the night* as a special honor. The

* She was probably a captive from some enemy tribe. A Hidatsa woman could not remain a member of the tribe after adultery without long purification and none was to be passed out to a guest.

woman was handsome and Clark took them out to see the air gun and had two shots fired from the big swivel, which pleased them. The war chief had brought a roll of deerskin with a large map of the Missouri drawn on it and pointed out the route he planned to take against the Snakes in the spring, when the horses were strong for war. This must have surprised Clark. He knew sixteen Snakes had just arrived at the Hidatsa village with word of a couple hundred lodges not far away and coming for their usual late winter trade of horses for corn and beans, and with pack loads of beaver for the fur men. Clark sent an invitation to the Snakes. They came, eager to see the wonders of the post and the men who were to go through their country after the ice broke up. They were feasted, with a finger of sugar in the coffee cup, and a warm place for the night.

Once more the interpreters made trouble. Jusseaume's wife left him. One of Charbonneau's women had been sick and Clark ordered York to give her stewed fruit and tea at various times, raising a storm of gossip and jealousy. More important was the friction with the traders because this involved foreign policy and the thrust of empire, and might, just now, prevent the peaceful passage of the expedition through British territory west of the Rockies. Larocque of the North West asked to join them to the Pacific. Clark refused, and busied himself bleeding several men suffering from pleurisy and dosing them with silver sage tea, bitter and black—the western trapper's remedy for practically everything but a broken leg. Clark even sawed off the toes of an Indian boy whose feet had been badly frozen.

By now the buffalo ceremonials really seemed to be working, bringing more than that little bunch right after they were completed. A large herd came in down the river, toward the Sioux. Clark took a detachment out to make meat for the post, leaving Lewis in charge of the place and its exasperations. Within a few days Lewis wrote that Black Cat, the head chief of the upper Mandans, had more integrity, firmness, intelligence and perspicuity of mind than any other Indian he met here. Fortunately the lower Mandans didn't see his journal, and could not have read it.

Clark returned from the hunt afoot, gaunted under his bushy red beard by the thirty miles on river ice and through snow nearly knee deep. He left the horses with the two sleds to haul the meat home, but a hundred Sioux swooped down, cut them out of the harness and whipped them away, one of the horses belonging to Mackenzie of the North West. Lewis marched a party out after the mounted Sioux and returned, still walking.

In February the chinook struck the western country and water came down the Missouri on top of the ice for a few days. The Americans worked to free the boat, with rollers under it ready for the slide into the stream. Seeing this, the Indians, particularly the women, hurried to bring their old kettles, axes and field tools to the blacksmith for repair, the men too, with their broken guns and traps. They remained to watch the wonderful bellows and hear the soft thud of the hammer on white-hot metal. Clark completed his map of the west country and the notes from the visiting Rocky Mountain Indians—Snakes and others, including captives from where the streams follow the sun. Lewis met with the traders again, repeating the purpose of the expedition. He saw a party come in from the 200 Assiniboin lodges wintering on the forks of the Little Missouri, with extra horses to trade for corn and beans, and bringing such great packs of fine winter peltry that Larocque was compelled tc head north on snowshoes for more goods. These riches of beaver should certainly be kept in the United States but now was not the time to invite trouble, even war.

Water began to stream from the shrinking snow that patched the south slopes and roar down the gullies from the drifted prairie. The river ice cracked with reports sharper than the big swivel, and broke up into vast white blocks and stretches that began to move, crushing, grinding, piling up, and pushing in dirty banks and windrows out over the flooded bottoms. Suddenly most of the Mandans were gone from the post, many busy at the river in the annual sort of harvest. When the first winter storms came sweeping over the Plains, buffaloes and other large animals in great numbers headed for the Yellowstone and the Missouri, seeking protection in the bluffs, the brush and timber. Often the herds were drawn out upon weak ice and broke through, perhaps pushed on by the moving mass behind until thousands had been swept away and frozen into the ice. In the spring the bodies were washed out and scattered along the banks for hundreds of miles, the flesh greenish under the hide, and ready to come alive the first day of warm sun and flies, with a horrible stench that only the buzzards could endure, but until then the meat was so tender it almost fell apart, ripe for those with a taste for it, as the Mandans had, perhaps from the days before the horse, when large supplies of meat were welcomed under almost any circumstances.

By now they were so fond of high meat that they often buried larger, older buffaloes all winter to eat in the spring. This year the Missouri had remained so low that there were fewer carcasses than generally but when they came down with the ice, the Mandans took to the river, the young men leaping from one ice cake to the next, perhaps falling between, to bob up elsewhere, towing carcasses to the bank. The women slipped out of their doeskin dresses and plunged into the icy water too, saving drift wood, for fuel was always scarce and often compelled moving whole villages. There was no shyness about the naked body among the Indians; the floating wood was important, and the ripened meat like the hung game of the English, the hung beef to some Americans, a great delicacy.

With the ice going out Clark put the men to testing his six new pirogues in some clearer backwater. As soon as the stream ran free the expedition must start. Le Borgne, the gigantic Hidatsa chief, came loping down for a last conference with Lewis and was finally given a medal too, and a gorget, arm bands, a shirt, a pouch of trinkets and a two-gun salute. Now that the plans were all made, there was one last difficulty with an interpreter. Charbonneau moved his tent and his wives outside the post, saying he would not go with the expedition on the terms agreed upon long ago. He would not accept his turn at work or guard; he would take along all the provisions he pleased, and return when it suited him.

"Corrupted by the North West men," Clark wrote.

The captains gave Charbonneau one day to return on the original terms. If he didn't, Graveline, a better man in every way, would take his place. There would be no difficulty about horses at the Missouri headwaters. The Snake visitors had assured Clark he could get all the horses he wanted, without any intercession from an unreliable interpreter's wife. So Charbonneau gave in.

By early April the ice of the Missouri was gone but the stench of rotting buffalo carcasses left along the bottoms was enough to drive the men from the post when the wind turned in that direction. The river, gray and sullen, ran deep and free except for an occasional log or clump of brush from some point washed away by the flood. The boat, too big for upriver, was ready to return to St. Louis, loaded, with ten men in charge of Sergeant Warfington, who was trusted with the letters, reports and dispatches, particularly those of Lewis for President Jefferson.

Then, April 7, the string of pirogues pushed out and turned slowly against the gray flood, Indians lining the bank at every village until they were past the upper Hidatsas. With Charbonneau, and his young wife and baby, who would become the romantic interest of the expedition, Lewis and Clark set their faces westward, up the Missouri, the stream "offering, according to the best accounts," as Jefferson told Congress two years before, "a continued navigation from its source, and possibly with a single portage from the Western Ocean. . . ."

CHAPTER IV

FUR FAIR AND
BLACKFEET WALL

THE eagles had flown back up the river, the buffalo calves were growing, and the fawns. The young antelope quivered with fear in the patch of bull tongue cactus where the mother had left him, safe from the soft-padded predators: the coyote, the wolf and the occasional mountain lion.

In the Missouri valley young beavers played on the houses, sleeping a while, then up again, to push each other into the water. Roses fell in pink cascades at the edges of the brush patches, sweetening the air for the women working in their fields and gardens, or busying themselves with the robes of the spring hunt and preparing food and other welcome for the thousands of visitors who would soon be coming, for the Moon of the Trading Fair, June, was almost half over.

The traders of the east and the western version of the bush loper who followed down the foothills of the Rockies and penetrated the farther slopes on both sides of the mountains as far as Santa Fe had found no ancient pattern of trade gatherings to compare to the one at the villages of the Upper Missouri, centered with the Hidatsas. Hunting tribes from far mountain valleys and up toward Hudson's Bay had come, and worn their trails deep. The western people brought the skins and horn of mountain sheep and goat, the fur of marten and lion besides plants and herbs, obsidian for arrow and spear points, and sea shells and walrus ivory from their own trading centers on the farther slopes. From the north came much dried meat, winter wolf, often pipestone and sometimes reindeer horn and white bear and fox. In exchange they took home corn and beans, the lesser products of the agrarian villages, their handsomely worked deerskins and buffalo robes, and always the memory of another pleasant visit to a place where there was a half moon's time of peace for all.

The first journey of the young Indians from the Village of the Bearded Men east to the great fur fair of Montreal and their return with white-man goods had brought a change in the trading here. Gradually the visiting tribes brought the beaver that the far away pale-skinned ones wanted for their knives, axes, awls, iron arrow points and fine beads. Then later even kettles were brought across the lakes, and guns too, but not traded to the enemy. True, by then the Sioux already had some and in the west occasional Spanish merchants sent their men to gather beaver for their iron goods and horses from the Rocky Mountain Indians— from the Snakes, Crows, Bannocks, Flatheads, some Nez Perces and many river Blackfeet.* There were also men down from the Saskatchewan country, some remaining with the Indians as the early ones had stayed with the Hidatsas of the upper Missouri.

In spite of the competition and the growing wars among the crowded tribes, the Hidatsas managed to keep a hand on a good share of the trade through their favored upper-river position, even though they were no longer near the trails of Old Crossing. For years now the goods had been brought right through their gates by the British and by the merchants from down the Missouri, enlarging the importance of the villages as a trading place of peace rivaling the

---

* Early accounts seldom differentiate between the three divisions of the tribe —Piegans, Bloods and Blackfeet. Often aggressions by other tribes, such as the Gros Ventres of the Prairies, were credited to the Blackfeet.

early white-man posts of the lakes, making it like a sort of Grand Portage at rendezvous time, but operated by Indians. Although the traders had penetrated the upper Missouri and beyond for several generations, and there were rumors of permanent British posts to be built out there, so far it was not done, but the Hidatsas felt that their favored position was threatened by the American expedition gone west. Perhaps Clark planned to build trader houses up along the Missouri, forts too strong to knock down, protected by all the holding-guns that the Americans owned, the three that they called swivels and that long-shooting one whose powder was air.

When Larocque of the North West Company returned with his packtrain of goods, the Indian rendezvous was already gathering at the upper villages. A small party of Assiniboins and four Canadian free trappers with packs of beaver were there, and the chiefs, uneasy because the trader had not arrived by then, sent scouts far out to look for him. Later, when Larocque made plans to go on west after the trading was done here, the Mandans particularly rose in anger. They could not permit it. He must return to the North West post on the Assiniboine. If the western tribes obtained more guns they would become independent, insolent and dangerous, too, but Larocque knew that it was the prospective independence that the Mandans feared most, independence from paying profit, paying tribute to the Five Villages for their goods.

When it was clear that Larocque was determined to go, the Indians refused the promise of horses for the journey except at double the price the mountain tribes would demand, and told him stories of great dangers out there. Menard, a trader with the Hidatsas for four years, had gone out and while returning with nine horses, many pelts and two captive women he bought, he was waylaid, robbed of even his clothing and his knife. He returned afoot and so pitiful that the Hidatsas killed several Rocky Mountain Indians to avenge his mistreatment but such killing was bad for peace and for trade.

Larocque went for help from his powerful friend, Le Borgne. The Hidatsa leader lay ill in the sleeping robes but he listened. His adopted son was a chief among the mountain tribes. It would be good to have his trader friend go with the son's people and perhaps this could be managed.

Soon after mid-June, when Lewis and Clark were camped up in the red-bluff region of the Missouri near Portage Creek, in mountain-Indian country, 300 lodges from out there, including twenty of the Snakes, arrived across the river from the Hidatsas. All the lower villagers had gone up to see the handsome sight, the four, five different peoples moving like a great army, riding four to six abreast, the Crows the most numerous. Each tribe was led by its own head chiefs, riding in dignity in fine whitened or moderately painted and beaded buckskin, the simple feather, one or two, of the high office in the braided hair, neatly parted at the forehead or with the upstanding front roach of the Crows. The elegance of these headmen was in their horses, in the snow-patched blacks, bays and yellows, the fiery sun-maned chestnuts, the silver-tailed golden duns. They were escorted by their lesser chieftains and the war leaders in feathered bonnets and painted glory, their buckskin crusted with beadwork and fringed with tresses of horsehair symbolic of the scalps taken and the coups counted. Their horses might be painted too, the feathers and scalps at jaw and foretop blowing in the wind, the tails streaming out. They carried their most elaborate accouterments: painted and feathered shields; long bows or perhaps great lances, adorned with flying bands and feathers; war clubs swinging at the wrists of the men; here and there a gun rubbed to shining balanced across the withers of a war horse.

Behind the fighting men rode the women, the older in heavy elk-tooth or shell-adorned dresses, the young handsome in ocher and vermilion, necklaces heavy over their beaded doeskin dresses, the fringes of their elaborate saddle trappings hanging almost to the ground.

There were children too, many, the smallest in skin bags slung to the round pummels of the women's saddles, those a little older riding alone, perhaps tied into their seats, the youths whipping their horses in a run along the edges of the Indian parade, showing off to the girls. In the center of the moving tribes were the packhorses and those drawing the travois with the old people, some with small children and pets in willow cages so none fell out, other travois mares dragging the rolled-up lodges and the baggage along—over two thousand people, like a migrating population.

The visitors halted on high ground behind the village and slowly formed a great circle to the trilling of welcome from their gathered hosts. The leading chief of the visitors addressed his warriors and then led them in a whooping charge through the Hidatsa village, scattering dogs, raising the dust, his long string of men all over and under and behind their horses or clinging to the sides, with a toe over the back and a hand hold in the mane, sliding over, striking the ground with a swift moccasin on one side and then on the other. Mackenzie and Larocque, who had seen many good northern riders among the Blackfeet and Assiniboins, decided these were the finest horsemen in the world.

Finally the Indians camped and in an unbelievably short time all was orderly, blue smoke rising from the fires, women bent over their cooking, children running out over the prairie or to the river.

The next day the Indians from the villages, dressed in their best, returned the parading with a similar show. They had more white-man goods, more finery, more arms, and looked more warlike but they were poorer horsemen. Afterward, in the evening circle of chiefs, Le Borgne introduced Larocque and Mackenzie to the mountain chief Red Calf. He spoke favorably of the men of the North West Company but had no praise for the Americans who had gone up through the country of the Snakes and Crows and Blackfeet, where some here had seen them pass. Then Larocque had his gifts brought out, a large collection, from big and small hatchets to knives and armfuls of twist tobacco; from tinder boxes to dozens of awls, rings, and pounds of vermilion; from several kinds of beads by the package and the hank to 1000 bullets and a caddy of powder. Then he offered the big pipe, the calumet of peace and friendship, with the best of tobacco. Each man took a few whiffs and Larocque rose to say that he and his two men were going back with them, with goods they would need during the summer, in payment for help and beaver, otter and bear. He promised that there would be men out among them so long as they treated them peacefully, as brothers. During the summer he hoped to select a place for a trading post out there, for all the tribes.

Then Larocque gave Red Calf a flag, a Canadian one, and other special gifts. In return he was adopted as father by the rising young chief.

The Hidatsas offered the pipe to the visitors and laid their presents before them: 200 guns, 100 rounds of ammunition for each; 100 bushels of corn and some merchandise—kettles, axes, knives, clothing and finery. Afterward the Rocky Mountain Indians led out 250 fine horses, large bales of buffalo robes, leggings and shirts of the bighorn sheep, for this too, was a kind of trading, a kind of competition in generosity. Afterward there was much feasting and storytelling and the long, long dances in the summer night, the very young eyeing each other, shy or bold.

The visiting Rocky Mountain tribes went through about the same formalities with the Mandans. In the meantime the traders in the villages worked to make a little profit beyond the gift robes and pelts received from the hosts and passed on for goods. Mackenzie accepted some beaver from the Crows but their plews were badly dressed, split up the back instead of the belly, cutting the best section in two, damaging the finest fur. These Indians were arrogant, hard to deal with because, Larocque decided, they were afraid of being cheated, of paying four times the value of anything.

The Indians began to scatter; the traders baled their pelts for the packhorses. The night before the Crows moved out, Le Borgne sent for Larocque to get his two helpers ready to go along. Afterward a crowd of the boldest Hidatsa warriors pushed into Larocque's quarters, threatening his life if he dared go west. Someone had run for Le Borgne. The great chief entered with his war ax raised. Staring around him in the firelight with an imperious air, he demanded in a thundering voice why so many Indians were gathered here.

They had come to bid the whites good-by because they would never see them again, now that they were going into the dangerous western country.

Le Borgne roared them down and harangued them, his voice so powerful that chunks of earth fell upon them from the roof, the protesting Indians suddenly without voice, slipping silently out into the darkness. But there was also disapproval in the visiting camps. "Where are you going, white men?" some of the young Crows demanded.

"Return, go home," others, older ones, advised when they saw that Larocque was determined to join the moving people. "We do not wish for your company; some of our young men have no discretion. We are afraid," meaning afraid of what might be done to the whites.

But Larocque did not hesitate, not even when one of his voyageurs backed out. He called the man a coward and then ignored the abusive response. Many Indians had collected around them, and Le Borgne, there to escort his guests on their way, rose to shame the protesting Crows. They were over a thousand, the white men three. Let the women be kind to these strangers, help them with the camps and the food, for they were generous and would repay every goodness toward them. The white men wanted beaver, for what purpose he did not know, but they would pay for the pelts in guns, ammunition and other useful things.

He received a quiet reply from an old chief. The fear was not of the whites themselves but that they might be bad medicine, bring misfortune and tribal conflict. Their people

were of two factions, led by Red Calf, who received favors
from the white men, and Red Fish, who would receive none,
and was raising objections, threatening trouble.

Larocque knew the Crows had once been a part of
the Hidatsas and had split off over a foolish quarrel, over the
division of a buffalo paunch or something equally trivial.
Yet he must go on, to report on the beaver and to select a
spot for the North West post. He knew that the Hudson's
Bay traders were powerful with their favored mountain
chiefs, and so were the men from Montreal who had come
among these people long ago.

With Le Borgne and an escort of Hidatsa warriors
riding beside their chiefs, the Rocky Mountain Indians
strung out up Knife River in late June, and it was already
plain that some of the escort would remain with the visitors,
drawn by the handsome young women. Before the escort
turned back, a herd of buffaloes was discovered and a good
little hunt made, so it seemed that the white men were
not to be bad medicine, in spite of the talk of those who
were receiving gifts from the Bay traders. The warrior who
tried to steal Larocque's gun may have been merely covetous.

There was thunder and rain for the grass, rain in the
Moon of Cherries Ripening, here where so little fell even in
the spring. Then, past the bad lands of the Little Missouri,
the scouts reported more buffaloes, a big herd, and so the
hunt was carefully planned, the guns counted, 204 without
those of the white men, so none could be sneaked out and
fired to scare the herd. Larocque apparently added one or
two more guns and a substantial amount of ammunition.
Afterward, when colic appeared among the children at the
big meat-drying camp, Larocque doled out drops that relieved the sickness. Now the women made him welcome,
even those whose men still turned dark faces against him.

Much of the Little Missouri country had been
trapped by the Assiniboins but farther up there were some
beavers and Larocque coaxed the Indians to catch a few
and prepare the hides as he wished—summer hides, practically worthless, but he bought them as an encouragement.

The Powder River was more promising, full of beaver dams, with many of the yellow (grizzly) bears, the plains above the deep canyon dark with buffaloes—a rich river, rich in four-footed gold.

Gradually bands broke off, the central camp smaller, the problem of grass and wood simpler. By the fifth of July they had climbed close enough to the mountains so Larocque bought two buffalo robes against the cold nights. The Big Horns stood in a granite wall ahead, and the Indians, remembering that the trader was going as far as the mountains, began to protest his departure. Without an interpreter it was difficult to explain that he was going along to the Yellowstone, their usual home, so he would know where to find them when he returned with more goods. He enjoyed the reluctance to let him go now, even if only because there were still presents in his packs.

At the Tongue River bears were so thick in the choke-cherry patches that the droppings were like stable manure, many of the tall trees broken down by them, those remaining so full of shining black cherries that there seemed no leaves at all.

Apparently this was the customary time for the women to disappear with their lovers into the mountains. Even the chief who led the moving camp lost his wife, and wanted to swerve off after her. When fear of an enemy attack came, everyone sat up past dawn, ready to flee, the horses loaded, the children sleeping in sacks tied to the saddles, for with all the helpless ones along, the best the warriors could hope to do was hold the enemy back a while, but they never came.

One evening a Snake rode in from a band that had been trading with the Spaniards so Larocque knew they were still competition here. On the Yellowstone they met a small party of Arapaho Gros Ventres who had traded with Crooked Arm McDonald last winter. But in spite of all this penetration, the country was still full of beaver, and so, after promising to meet the Crows in their own country next fall, Larocque and his men started back to the Hidatsas.

There, October 10, he heard that fourteen small boats of American traders were below the Five Villages and while this proved true before he left for the fort on the Assiniboine, Larocque was pleased to hear that the North West Company had managed to buy out the XY competition—another aggregation of energetic Montreal Scots. The Hudson's Bay outfit and now the Americans with their open highway, the Missouri River, were competition enough.

Lewis and Clark reached the Pacific in November 1805. They passed Indians who had guns and other white-man goods a long time, and heard rumors of a Boston trading vessel out at the mouth of the Columbia. Clark built a little fort near the Clatsop Indians but the situation was different than back at Fort Mandan, the Indians here so poverty-stricken that there were no traders in the region and little of the amusement or the friendly anticipation of last winter with the Five Villages. On their return the party divided, Clark to Three Forks and across to the Yellowstone. Lewis left their outward path at Bitterroot Valley and turned north to the Blackfoot River, across Lewis and Clark Pass and into Black-feet country, where he fought the first skirmish with the tribe that was to stand like a wall across the path of the American fur men for a long time. At the Missouri he re-joined Clark for the trip to St. Louis.

There was little new information from the expedition but some of the suggestions were interesting. The explorers emphasized the importance of the Marias River, abounding "in animals of the fur kind" and which "more probably furnishes a safe and direct communication to that productive country of furs exclusively enjoyed at present by the subjects of his Britanic Majesty." Their report on the Yellowstone duplicated Larocque's findings for the North West, as also rich in animals bearing fur and that the river "will afford a lucrative fur trade & will hold in check the N W Co on the upper Missouri which we believe it is their intention to monopolize if in their power." They considered the higher stretches of the Missouri waters richer in otter and beaver than any other country on earth and recommended forts on both the Yellowstone and the Marias to control all the commerce of the Missouri and its affluents, and believed that the trade from these two posts could be carried to the East Indies by way of the Columbia much cheaper than by any other route. The expedition reports expressed fear of the combination of the XY and the North West Company, which must be kept off American soil. Both Lewis and Clark knew that Hudson's Bay men had been draining furs out a much longer time than the North Westers, and that they were everywhere; they had seen them. The explorers did, however, understand that the Indians had to be won over and posts established to draw their trade from the Canadians. Traders must be sent to the Cheyennes, Crows, Snakes and other western Indians.

Not that anybody was waiting for the journals and reports of the expedition for this information. All of it and more had been available at the St. Louis waterfront for years. Besides, Americans had been coming straight across the Mississippi a long time, and lately up the Missouri. James Wilkinson, of Spanish intrigue, now governor of Upper Louisiana and commander of the areal troops, apparently felt secure enough in Jefferson's mood for expansion to enter into an agreement with Aaron Burr to conquer the Mexican provinces while Lewis and Clark were spying out the British hold on the Columbia drainage system. True, Wilkinson was also receiving a pension from Spain, on and off.

One of the purposes of the expedition had been to lure the Indian chiefs to American allegiance, and on the way down Lewis and Clark had stopped to gather up those willing to go to Washington. At the Hidatsas they gave Le Borgne the big swivel gun as evidence that the Americans intended to protect his people, and to help wean him from the Canadians. They stopped at the Mandans, and picked up Big White and made promises of many presents to come for those with half-white babies in the cradleboard or under the buckskin dress. As Dorion, a mixed-blood himself, said, "The

white man scatters his seed like the cottonwood, blown on
every careless wind."

Farther down the Missouri Lewis and Clark met traders from the Cheyenne country headed for the mountain regions. Colter wanted to join them and was given his release,
to turn his feet toward more adventure than the whole expedition had encountered or would, from St. Louis to the
sea and back.

After a winter in the Yellowstone region the daring
Colter started down the Missouri in a canoe alone. At the
mouth of the Platte he met Manuel Lisa and a large, well-
equipped brigade financed with the help of William Morrison and Pierre Menard, brother-in-law of Pierre Chouteau.
Drouillard, the Shawnee breed who had been with Lewis
and Clark, but a good sign talker by now, went as Lisa's
lieutenant. Colter was persuaded to turn back once more,
as the only man who would know the region and the Indians. Lisa's trade goods were in a keelboat, hard to drag up
the river, but with two swivel guns to reinforce his talent at
conciliating Indians, gently or severely, as seemed prudent,
although his enemies did accuse him of going beyond diplo-
macy in shifting danger from himself to his competitors.

The brigade got past the Sioux and was stopped by
the Rees, with 200 to 300 warriors along the bank firing a
volley across Lisa's bow. He turned ashore and women came
hurrying down with big skin sacks of corn to trade but a
warrior sprang forward and slashed the sacks with his sheath
knife so the grain poured out over the ground. The women
fled as Lisa ordered his men to their guns and turned his
two swivels on the Rees along the bank. They retreated some
distance and after a while the chiefs came holding their
pipe before them in peaceful overture. Lisa let them approach and accepted their apologies with his Spanish face
darkened in scorn.

Even the Mandans were threatening now, perhaps
through loyalty to the British, but Lisa got past by leaving
the boats and walking boldly through the villages, interesting the Indians, probably by talk of presents. Some distance

above the Mandans he came upon between four and five thousand Assiniboins in ceremonial camp. This required a bolder policy. When the swivels were heavily loaded, and every man's musket prepared for a fight, Lisa steered the keelboat straight across the river toward the Indians, ordered all the guns aimed where none could be hurt, and fired. The Indians, mostly northerners, were so appalled at the spitting fire and smoke, the roaring in the river bluffs, that they fell over each other in their run for the hills. A few chiefs and warriors stayed and asked to smoke a peace pipe. Lisa sat with them a while, gave out a few presents and went on.

Although he had planned to trade with the Blackfeet, he went to the country of their Crow enemies, up the Yellowstone, and located his post at the mouth of the Bighorn, enough to arouse jealousy and outrage among the Blackfeet —the Americans siding with their enemy, and a weak one, which meant a great loss of face to the powerful tribe. It was probably done on the advice of Colter, who thought of the beaver riches of the Yellowstone country and bothered little about Indian politics or prestige. Manuel's Fort, as it was called, to distinguish it from Lisa's post far down the Missouri, was the first building in the upper river country, if the stories of an early Spanish post are discounted.

Late in November, when the streams were frozen and trapping had to wait, Lisa sent Colter out to map the region and bring in the Blackfeet and other Indians. Apparently few except Crows came; no Blackfeet, but Colter traveled over a wide expanse of country and his descriptions of hot springs, geysers and brimstone lakes earned the name of Colter's Hell for a whole region and the reputation as a great liar for him.

The next summer, according to his stories, Colter went to the Three Forks of the Missouri and got several hundred Flatheads started to Lisa's post. Not far above the mouth of the Gallatin they were attacked by their ancient enemies, the Blackfeet, the number varying in accounts, up to an improbable 1500. The fight was apparently a desper-

ate one. Colter, wounded in the leg, crawled into a small
thicket and loaded and fired from there on the ground, trying to move each time from the betraying blue puff of smoke.
The whooping and gunfire and the rising cloud of dust and
smoke brought a nearby party of Crows charging up. Even
so, the defenders were still outnumbered but so many men
were being killed on both sides that toward evening the
Blackfeet withdrew, quiet and orderly, as was customary
with Plains Indians, who did little fighting after sundown.
They took their wounded along, and apparently the body of
an important war leader, leaving the rest to mark the battleground with their bones.

Big White, the Mandan chief, and the interpreter
Jusseaume with their wives and one child each had accompanied Lewis and Clark to Washington. The spring of 1807
they were ready to go home, escorted by Ensign Nathaniel
Pryor and some soldiers. There was also a party of Sioux at
St. Louis, eighteen with some children, in charge of troops;
two trading outfits—Pierre Chouteau and thirty-two men for
the Mandans; young Dorion with ten for the Sioux—and
some extra hunters and trappers, all headed up river. The
seventy-two men, besides the Indians, started together late in
May, not far behind Lisa's brigade that had picked up
Colter.

The combined party reached the lower Sioux without
difficulty. Those going on, fifty men and the Mandan chief,
arrived at the first Ree village the morning of September 9.
To the surprise of everyone, the Indians fired several guns
toward the boats. Dorion, the interpreter, demanded the
reason. The Indians ordered the party ashore, to get provisions, they said. Pryor had seen Lewis and Clark treated well
here and so he had the boats anchored and then discovered
that the Rees were at war with the Mandans and apparently
hungry to capture their head man. Besides, several upper
Sioux bands now allied with the Rees were in the village.

A Mandan woman, captive here for years, came

aboard to warn the chief. When Lisa was ready to leave for the upper country in the spring, he had been asked to wait for Pryor's party escorting Big White home. Lisa refused, hurried on ahead and when the Rees tried to stop him he said a large party was coming behind him, bringing the Mandan chief and a great deal of useful and fancy goods. In addition he gave the Indians many presents, including guns and ammunition so they let him go, probably because no alarming reports must reach Pryor's bigger party, perhaps scare them back or bring too many soldiers, with cannons.

Dismayed by the story, and certain to have heard of Lisa's refusal to wait at St. Louis, Pryor ordered the Mandan chief to barricade himself in his cabin against any swift, overwhelming rush, and prepared his men for action. Then he called a parley and tried to explain the purpose of the journey, gave the Ree chief a medal and somehow got away from the lower town, although the Indians were still in bad humor. The two interpreters, Dorion and Jusseaume, went by land through the upper villages and although the Rees were clearly hostile there too, Pryor was determined to land to take on the interpreters and confer with the chiefs. He was told the boats would be detained, that Lisa had promised this party would remain to trade with them. The warriors grabbed the cable of Chouteau's barge, without soldiers, and motioned Pryor on. He refused to go, and urged Chouteau to make some concessions, which must have been resented by the trader, the brother-in-law of Menard, one of the financers of Lisa. Finally Chouteau did agree to leave a man and half his goods with them but now the Indians wanted everything, including the Mandan chief.

Pryor must have remembered the old Sioux who sat on the bank holding back one of the Clark pirogues, and the loaded swivels that were turned on the Indians. But Pryor was not equipped for such a maneuver and besides, he was responsible for an Indian chief, for, perhaps, the peace of the whole Indian country. The warriors were lashing themselves into a fury now, dancing, whooping, crowding up close, the leaders demanding that all the powder and arms be left here. When this was refused too, the chief went into a loud harangue and threw his new medal on the ground. One of Chouteau's men was struck down with a gun barrel, and then the firing began, against the boat and Chouteau, with soldiers sending a scattering of lead in return, Pryor answering with a volley. The Indians retreated to a fringe of willows along the bank about fifty yards off, more concealing than protecting. But the white men were hopelessly outnumbered by the swarming tribe from everywhere, and so Pryor ordered a retreat down the river. Unfortunately, by now Chouteau's barge was stuck on a sand bar and the men had to get out to drag it away under balls spitting up water and sand around them.

Finally all the craft was afloat and moving, the Indians running along the bank, keeping up the fight for an hour, until the boats neared a point where the current passed almost within touch of the waiting Indians. The leader was a Sioux chief with a white band around his head. He had to be stopped, so one of Pryor's sharpshooters took careful rest-aim with his Pennsylvania-Kentucky rifle and killed him instantly. This move must have been suggested by someone who knew Indian warfare, the Mandan chief, perhaps. Inevitably, with a good man dead and the evening upon them, the Indians gathered up the fallen chief and started slowly, solemnly back up the river.

Three of Chouteau's men were dead, seven wounded, one mortally. Pryor had three wounded, including Jusseaume. He suggested to Big White that they try to reach the Mandan villages overland, traveling well out on the prairie, but the chief objected. The wounded Jusseaume and the women and children would be helpless in attack. It was as well that Pryor was overruled. The party would certainly have been detected by the scouts, always out. So Chouteau and the rest all returned to St. Louis, Pryor reporting that it would take 400 armed men to get the Mandan home. It was the first summer of real aggression from the Rees, the start of twenty years of trouble.

.   .   .

Lisa returned to St. Louis in 1808 with glowing reports and enough handsome prime beaver to lure some of the
leading businessmen of the city into a new ten-man organization, with him and his partner. This included the sly
Chouteaus, despite Pierre's experience with the Rees after
Lisa went through, Benjamin Wilkinson, Sylvester Labaddie,
Andrew Henry, William Clark and Reuben Lewis, brother
of Meriwether, the governor who, it was said, also invested.
The purpose of the St. Louis Missouri Fur Company was
trade at the headwaters of the big river, Lisa and Wilkinson
to manage the posts.

Their first expedition prepared to leave St. Louis
June 1809. Big White was still to be returned to his people,
who must have decided by now that their chief was a prisoner of the Great Father, although word had been sent to
them of the Ree attack. Still, they saw American traders go
up and down the river, past everybody, and must have believed what seemed most reasonable. They knew the rumors
too, about Lisa sacrificing Pryor and their chief to save himself and prevent the traders and trappers with the government expedition from getting past into the upper Missouri
country that Lisa considered his private beaver preserve.

Now the Missouri Company had a $7000 contract to
get the Mandan chief home, and an agreement with Governor Meriwether Lewis that no one would be authorized to
start for the upper Missouri until after the company's date
for departure. They were to raise 125 men as the Missouri
Territorial Militia under Col. Pierre Chouteau to go as far
as the Mandans and then be added to the company employees. The expedition was the largest to move up the Missouri, 300, some say 350 men, half experienced voyageurs
—French Canadians and creoles from Kaskaskia, St. Louis
and Detroit—and half American adventurers on the promise of subsistence to the beaver grounds in return for work
with the boats. Arrived there, each of the leaders was to be

furnished with a good rifle, sufficient ammunition, six good beaver traps and the assistance of four Frenchmen for three years, the leader to divide a fourth of the profit with his four men.

Thomas James enlisted as a seasoned rifleman with the expedition, to continue as leader of a small band of trappers, the equipment and compensation guaranteed by his contract signed at St. Louis. The party started on time, with thirteen barges and keelboats. James was captain of one of the barges, manned by twenty-four Americans, with Dr. Thomas, the surgeon of the company, and Reuben Lewis, brother of the governor, along. They rowed, push-poled, cordelled, warped and sailed their way up the river, the flotilla usually out soon after daybreak and going until late at night under Lisa's relentless drive. They ran out of provisions not far above the Platte, the Americans eating boiled corn without salt while they hauled barrels of pork and such luxuries as dried fruit, sugar and liquor over the sand and mud bars and saw the owners feast on venison with wine and cigars and a little music. Even the voyageurs, accustomed to thin fare, little but meat, were treated better than the Americans, who now began to disappear, two, three here, a couple more there, so by the time they reached the Mandans, James recalled years later, there were scarcely a dozen American boatmen left. Some found their way back to St. Louis in a few weeks, others wandered the plains and mountains for years, some to fall unheralded to Indians, or rival furmen in unrecorded places.

At the Mandan village the Indians came hurrying out to the barge in their bull boats on a day so windy that the river was whipped into waves. They paid no attention to the whites but were excited over their chief, back as from the death scaffold. When the government presents were given out, the Indians took them but their eyes still followed Big White and his family and soon their moccasins were hard on the chief's tracks.

James considered the Hidatsas, fifteen miles up the river by water, the opposite of the Mandans, a manly, independent, warlike and big-hearted people. He reported that there were four or five Hudson's Bay men among them, probably lumping all the British traders together, and that they crossed the river at sight of the flotilla and set off northeast. They were suspected of inciting the Blackfeet against the Americans and had been gathering the tribe, with other Indians, to a regular summer trading up at the Missouri falls, trade that included arms.

Lisa built a fort near the Hidatsas, unloaded the larger boats and started them back before the ice came. The post, on the west bank of the river, was a square blockhouse, the lower section a room for trade, the upper part the living quarters for Reuben Lewis and the hunters. There were small outbuildings, all surrounded by a fifteen-foot stockade with space for a garden that was tended faithfully in the pattern of Lisa's more permanent posts, which were set up for comfortable living, with barnyard animals and fruitful gardens.

In November the Missouri *Gazette* reported the return of two men from the Mandan party bringing word of the chief's safe delivery and news of the British influence among the Blackfeet, with trading houses on the Yellowstone and elsewhere. Ramsay Crooks, Miller and McClellan, who had permission to start to the headwaters of the Missouri after Lisa's party was gone, had been stopped by the Teton Sioux, where Lisa had paused on his way up for a dog feast. Some angrily tied the two incidents together.

Pierre Chouteau, his sons and the doctor returned to St. Louis, Lisa too, leaving the ten Americans who remained of the expedition denouncing him, claiming they had been cheated, demanding the traps, guns, ammunition and men of the contracts. The traps that they were finally offered were old and worthless and so refused, most of the men set afoot in the wilderness without gun or ammunition. James finally bought a set of beaver traps from Colter for $120, a pound and a half of powder for $6 and a gun for $40.

Most of the trappers and traders arrived at the Bighorn post late that fall. Menard was in charge, a high-minded, honorable gentleman, the favorite of all the com-

pany. Planning to establish a little post at Three Forks, he
sent two men with a chief of the Snakes and his family ahead
to kill meat and to scout the early spring route. Thirty or
thirty-two men under Menard and Henry followed, to find
the Indian lodge stripped, the bodies of a woman and a boy
nearby, their heads split open. The chief and his younger
wife had escaped horseback. The white men were not
harmed but surely this was a warning, to the Indian allies of
the trappers and perhaps to all Americans.

With Colter as guide the party went on to the conflu-
ence of the three rivers that head the Missouri. Although
they marched fast, Colter found time to talk about the skulk-
ing, murdering Blackfeet around here and how he outwitted
them when he was in the region a couple of years ago.
He and a man named Potts had gone up the Jefferson (or
some creek joining the river, Colter's stories seemed to differ
on this) for beaver, each in a canoe. Suddenly about 800
Blackfeet appeared on the bank, ordering the white men to
shore. Colter, thinking only of robbery, dropped his traps
into the shallow water on the far side of the canoe and
paddled over. The Indians disarmed and stripped him and
motioned Potts to come in too. He shouted he might as well
die where he was, and got a shot that crippled him. Firing
back he killed an Indian and was instantly stopped by a
hundred bullets,* Colter said.

Potts' body was dragged out upon the bank, cut to
pieces, the entrails, heart and lungs thrown in Colter's face.
(Perhaps he and James who related this had been reading
the usual atrocity stories. Indians, Africans, or any other people resisting invaders are always pictured as reacting the
same way.) Relatives of the Indian that Potts had killed
tried to get at Colter with their tomahawks but they were
held back while he was motioned away out upon the prairie.
He started to walk, and was urged on, to run. When young
men began to drop their blankets and leggings and came
after him, shaking their spears, Colter ran, heading for the
Madison, which, he says, was about five miles off. Halfway

* Riddled by arrows, according to Bradbury, *Thwaites*, Vol. V.

his strength failed and blood began to gush from his nose. He was well ahead of all the Indians but one, who came on, his blanket streaming out behind. Suddenly the Blackfeet let the blanket go, and charged with the spear in both hands. Colter grabbed it, twisted the handle and broke it off in the Indian's hand and killed him with the iron-pointed end. With that and the blanket he set out running again, the Indians whooping behind him. At the Madison he dove in and came up inside a beaver house* to a dry resting place. The opening must have been mighty easy to discover, at least for Colter. The Indians thrashed around the brush, the bank and the water and stood on the house over him, looking around. Toward night they gave up, but Colter still had to climb snow-capped mountains out of the valley because the Indians would certainly be watching the only pass through to open country.

This is tall-tale stuff, particularly in the James version. There is no such place where the Madison and Jefferson are only five miles apart, besides, the river would have flowed in as well as out of such a valley, which makes at least two outlets or passes. When he reached Lisa's fort at the mouth of the Bighorn, about 300 miles away after eleven days of travel, he said he still had the spear and the blanket but his beard was long.†

With the post at Three Forks started, Menard remained to finish it and trade with any Indians coming in while the hunters went out to get beaver so long as the hide was still prime enough. Planning to cover all the Missouri above the falls, eighteen men started up the Jefferson and four went down the river to trap it out. The four lost a canoe with the cargo and after eluding a small band of Indians they got back to the fort overland. In the meantime the

* Under a lodging of driftwood according to Bradbury.
† Growing a long beard in eleven days is a tall tale in keeping with the stories of unicorns in the Rockies; a transcontinental water route; the 300 Crow warriors Liver-eating Johnson supposedly killed, practically the entire force of young men, and while living peacefully among them with a Crow wife; the 2500 Red Cloud warriors killed at the Wagon Box Fight in 1867; or the publicity-produced derring-do of the western Long Hairs.

eighteen on the Jefferson were attacked the third day out, two killed, three apparently never heard from again, and all the goods, furs and equipment lost. The remaining thirteen straggled back in groups to Menard. A party was sent out to bury the dead and make a gesture toward pursuit, but prudently returned early and helped prepare for an anticipated attack on the post.

When no Indians came near, either with bullet or beaver, the men started to go out on short hunts and trap runs, getting more grizzlies than castor but aware from the nervousness of the game that there were Indians around. Finally the men began to break up into small parties, trapping the lesser streams, then one morning Drouillard, the part-Shawnee, was found dead and horribly mutilated, with the bodies of two other hunters nearby. The rest hurried to the fort, which by now seemed hopeless as a center for trapping or trade. Leaving Henry and some of the men there, Menard led a party, with Colter guiding, across the divide to the Yellowstone and Lisa's post, bringing thirty packs of beaver along, a small harvest for all the work, the goods lost and the men dead.

Some of the furs and goods stolen from Menard's party reached the British posts through the Gros Ventres of the Prairie—beaver skins marked with the names of Vallé and Immell, and even some New Jersey banknotes. But not all the profit of the Missouri Company was lost in Blackfeet country, no matter who did the marketing. Down in the Missouri the Cedar Island post that Lewis and Clark had found so stoutly built was burned, with furs valued at $15,-000. Perhaps a more permanent calamity was the drop in beaver, from a normal price of $4 a pound on the market to $2.50 and apparently to go lower.

Henry remained at Three Forks for a short time, still hoping to open trade with some of the Indians. At last he gave up, abandoned the post and crossed the mountains to the north fork of the Snake River, Henry's Fork, and built the first American post west of the Continental Divide. He and his men spent a winter there, with peaceful but very poor Indians around. Game was so scarce that the hunters were finally down to horse meat. By that time the men were deserting, some sifting back to the Missouri, some to New Mexico, some probably to the Indians. The spring of 1811 Henry and his few remaining followers struck across the country for Lisa's post and down the Yellowstone and the Missouri. The post on the Bighorn was given up too, the richest beaver region left on earth closed to the very exclusive St. Louis Missouri Fur Company, already tottering, the initial investment of $50,000 gone like a sandbar in a Missouri flood. The whole country above the Five Villages was closed to the Americans, at least for a while, by the Blackfeet wall.

CHAPTER V

PURSUIT OF THE
ETERNAL REMNANT

"A worn field may be manured and again made fertile; but the beaver, once destroyed cannot be replaced."

—David Thompson

THERE were still those who believed that the beaver would return as the migrating geese and the buffaloes, but others saw that the beaver regions had been drawing in upon themselves ever since the first iron was offered for peltry to perhaps the Micmacs of Nova Scotia. Now it seemed that the gentle creature once named for its soft, defenseless belly was at last hiding himself, keeping to the rougher, less accessible country. No longer was a day, a week or a month of paddle and portage from the markets enough to reach the beaver fields. Instead there were months of struggle against the sullen Missouri and, beyond the river-heads, as well as everywhere else, vast overland areas to cross, buffalo country perhaps, with streams far apart, and often stretches that even the prairie herds scorned—badlands and torn foothills and finally the mountains. There, where the rocky streams flowed clear and cold, the banks of many of the marshes and ponds still lay free of bones left bleaching in defilement and unnatural shaming, with no scrap of fur to cling to them anywhere.

But now more of the new trap-carrying enemies penetrated these remote regions, enemies from whom a dive into the depths of dark water was futile, and a scuttling into the washes dug deep into the banks too often ended in a trap set at the outlet. These enemies were coming like a three-pronged spear, the Hudson's Bay men from above, the North Westers in the middle and the Americans from the southeast.

The Americans too, had home competition; nothing as ruthless as the rivalry between the Bay men and the North Westers sometimes became, but one that they worked hard to destroy. It had started with President Washington, who was eager for good relations with the Indians, and to drive the British and the Spaniards out of the trade in the south. After five years he persuaded Congress to appropriate $50,-000 for goods to sell to the Indians at cost. The next year, 1796, he won approval for his factory system, with an appropriation of $150,000 for "liberal trade with the Indians." Factories, trading houses, were to be located at various places, mostly east of the Mississippi. The idea was sound but instead of holding the field to itself, as in the coinage of money or the mail service, the government granted trading licenses to private parties, without enforcing official standards and so found itself reduced to competing with a horde of irresponsible and conniving, even lawless, rivals.

The government plan was to let the Indians do the hunting and trapping in their country, neither hampered nor degraded by white men living among them, and by the white man's alcohol. This would have helped preserve the western animals from ruthless slaughter. The Indians were to be independent, free men gleaning furs for their wants, bringing their harvest to the factories where they would receive a reasonable return in reasonably priced goods. Unfortunately the factors were not permitted to extend any credit to the Indians, who were always a year behind, as was natural with most trappers, whatever their color. The tribes went where they could get traps, ammunition and supplies on time, and the traders sent men out among them to collect the furs practically as fast as they were caught. Even in the trade goods the government was handicapped by the rule compelling the patronizing of home industries, not yet producing the best grade in many items and often none at all of some that the Indians were accustomed to and liked. The traders hired men whom the Indians knew and understood, perhaps members of one or more tribes by marriage; the government trader was a salaried man, frequently a political appointee, a stranger to Indian ways and languages. Nor was the factor permitted to carry out the system of gifts and tribute to important chiefs that the fur companies had built up during the years, and usually he understood little of the courtesies and formalities so important to Indians.

Even more fatal, in some regions, was the ban on government trade in whisky, while the private trader smuggled it in. So, in spite of the cheaper goods at the government houses, and the honest trade rating given the furs and robes, the Indians went where they had been going, trading in the old way. If the private buyer had been excluded none of the government handicaps would have mattered; further, the large outfits were using pressure in Congress, crying out against government competition, although by 1800 only two federal houses had been established. Yet the system was denounced as infamous, with the charge made that "Even the Indians would despise the government for peddling."

Back in 1804, Congress, while providing a government for Louisiana, had included federal acts "to regulate trade and intercourse with the Indians" and to establish and maintain trading houses in the region. Before the legislation could be put into effect, Auguste Chouteau appeared to ask Jefferson for power over all the "Indian trading licenses and the direction and all the profits of the trade carried on by the government with all the Indians of Louisiana, replacing all the capital." Apparently the government and everybody but Auguste Chouteau were to get out of the trade.

Jefferson pronounced this inadmissible but "as he may be either useful or dangerous," Chouteau was given licenses for extensive trade and grew wealthy. While Wilkinson was governor of Upper Louisiana and with the power of Indian agent, he joined Chouteau in the trade with the Osages and the Indians of the Mississippi and the Missouri, and was unscrupulous enough to withhold licenses from other traders.

The most active antagonist of the government system was John Jacob Astor. At sixteen the German youth had gone to England, seeking a fortune in his brother's musical-instrument business. Hoping to do better in America he came over with a small stock, fell in with a fur dealer and traded his instruments for pelts in New York, which he sold well in London. After a study of the European fur markets, late in 1784, at twenty-one, he was back and by 1800 he was a power in the Montreal trade, avoiding the tariff against the United States by shipping to London from there, although he was the leading fur merchant of the States too, in spite of Auguste Chouteau's efforts to keep him down by shutting the St. Louis trade to him.

Worth perhaps half a million by now, with ships reaching the farthest China markets, Astor moved more and more of his business headquarters to New York as the British tariffs went down. Hearing of the riches of the Northwest, he was eager to have Spain and the Russians driven from the Pacific coast, and went to Washington, seeking a charter for the American Fur Company, an organization that would "embrace in the course of 4 or 5 years the whole of the fur trade" and extend to the western ocean, with a range of posts or trading houses on the route of Lewis and Clark. He hoped for a monopoly of the fur trade in Louisiana and all the Missouri country. A permanent company would insure the good will of the natives, not like independent traders, here and gone, and caring little how they cheated the Indians. He took up these aspects with Jefferson, without mentioning the monopoly but stressing his desire to exclude the Canadians from the American fur trade, with control of the northwest by American fur men. Jefferson liked Astor's plan as it was presented to him and wrote favorably to Meriwether Lewis, then governor of Missouri.

Astor got his company chartered in New York, and moved into the northwest to harvest the sea otter and other fur bearers. Unable to get government force against Russia and Spain, he suggested an agreement to supply the Russo-American Company with trade goods to the Russian ambassador, and thought much progress had been made.

Astor was unwilling to risk his new company in the northwest venture or to seek help from St. Louis, so he turned to the North West Company and, according to his friend and admirer, Washington Irving, offered them a third interest in the Columbia River trade. But their Mackenzie had crossed the continent to the Pacific long before the Louisiana Purchase, and many employees of the company had penetrated much of the Columbia River region long before Mackenzie's exploit. Apparently the North Westers believed they could win what was left of the Pacific northwest trade alone. Perhaps Astor's offer was merely a polite gesture before he approached company men dissatisfied with their shares and positions since the reorganization with the XY outfit. Three of North West's veteran traders, Alex McKee, Donald McKenzie and Duncan McDougall, did join Astor, followed by the two Stuarts. Astor's associate, the St. Louis merchant Wilson P. Hunt, brought in Ramsay Crooks and Robert McClellan, the two traders who were driven back down the Missouri by the Indians in 1807, and blamed Lisa for it.

June 1810 Astor's Pacific Fur Company was organized, with fifty of the 100 shares going to him because he advanced the capital and was to bear the losses for five years, the profits to be divided according to the shares. With typical energy Astor immediately planned two expeditions for the mouth of the Columbia to establish Astoria. The first one, by sea, arrived March 1811, not far ahead of North West's David Thompson. Hunt, appointed coast agent for five years, led the overland Astorians out March 14 of that year, going by way of the Missouri, the number varying from perhaps sixty to sixty-five and more, including the wife and two small sons of Dorion, the interpreter, and John Bradbury, the Scottish naturalist. Hunt started with four boats, sailing when they could, rowing, poling and cordelling when they had to, the voyageurs singing, often responsively from bow to stern, or the steersman carrying the lyrics, the men bringing in the chorus, in their French, singing perhaps of the river, the windigo, or repeating some old folk ballad whose elements they barely understood:

> Behind our house there is a pond,
>   Fal lal de ra.
> There came three ducks to swim thereon
> All along the river clear,
> Lightly, my shepherdess dear,
>   Lightly, fal de ra.

One may wonder what "shepherdess" could have meant to the bush loper's mixed-blood great-grandson, a voyageur whose idea of a sheep was the creature that grew the big horn spoons of the western tribes, and a pond the work of beavers.

Hunt had no experience in the west but being a sensible and cautious man, he had selected the best assistants and engagés he could hire; he had talked for some time to Colter and had the Missouri traders Crooks and McClellan along. An early start gave him good depth of water over the old sawyers and stumps and snags, but there was a swift current, and great piles of flood-borne brush and uprooted trees lodged in the bends and at the points, great floats of current-choking driftwood, the narrowed stream roaring through with such power that every foot gained for the boats took sweat and panting curses. In the meantime Bradbury wandered along the banks, marveling at the size of the great old cottonwoods, and the progress of the bees across America, brought by early immigrants and gone wild, now already found in old hollow trees along the Missouri. He noted the bears, examined the rocks and the flowers, watched the Indians, and listened to many stories verging on the tall tale.

By the time the Astorians were breakfasting at the mouth of the Platte, April 28, it was very clear to Hunt that he would need a good supply of oars and poles for the long stretches without timber ahead, as well as keep an eye out for mast replacements. There was a great deal of cold, driving rain but Hunt knew he must keep going, with the winter waiting to meet him in the mountains.

The failure of Lisa and his brigade to crack the Blackfeet wall and the forced retreat from the upper forks of the Missouri, all the region above the Hidatsa post, put his company into a desperate situation, and with no word from Andrew Henry and his men who went west across the mountains from Three Rivers. By the spring of 1811 it was decided that Lisa, as the most experienced and energetic member of the Missouri Company, was to make a last attempt to stave off bankruptcy, at least to discover what became of Henry and his party. Lisa was taking Charbonneau along, and Sacajawea, sickly in the south, and anxious to see her own country once more before she died.

A young Missouri author and lawyer, Henry Brackenridge, son of a leader in the Whisky Rebellion of 1794, had been easily persuaded to join the party. They left St. Charles April 2, in apparently the best barge, the best keelboat, ever to face the Missouri. There were twenty oars, a good mast with main and topsail, a swivel gun at the bow and two brass blunderbusses in the cabin, one over Lisa's berth, the other over Brackenridge's. Most of the merchandise—strouding, blankets, lead, powder, tobacco, knives, guns and beads—was in a false cabin, as perhaps less detectable by a boarding party.

There had been the usual trouble collecting the contracted rivermen who were always having one last carousal and drink with friends. Lisa, after all his river experience, had selected the youngest, hardiest men without the need to consider familiarity with the Missouri. The second day out they made substantial headway and by the fifth of April found some good sailing, but with the hard spring rains, the current rose and the piles and rafts of brush and driftwood in the river began to float again—a great trouble, with the water too deep for poling. Already the men had to pull the boat along the best they could, past sawyers and hidden snags, the black-browed Lisa driving everyone, including himself. He was at the helm one moment, then with the grappling iron at the bow and often at the push poles, his presence, his voice, his orders, his cheering exclamations and personalities drawing new energy, a further effort, from the men in what turned out to be an attempt to overtake Hunt, already three weeks ahead.

No one knew better than Lisa that one boat and twenty-five men could scarcely hope to get very far on the upper Missouri now, perhaps not even past the first Sioux party, but added to the sixty of Hunt the prospects were good. Further, Lisa seemed to fear that the leader of the Astorians might secure his own passage from the Sioux by promising that their old friend of the Missouri Company was coming just behind, bringing all the goods that they liked, and thereby inviting them to hold him, perhaps rob him if he tried to go on, as he must, for the beaver that the company needed so desperately, and for news of Henry, if that was possible. Perhaps Lisa was remembering how he had maneuvered the attack on Pryor's party with the Mandan chief four years ago, and on Crooks and McClellan the same time. The two traders, with a supply of goods, were with Hunt now and must not beat Lisa to the valuable furs. Besides, some men bringing down the winter catch told him that the Sioux were not going out upon the prairie for their usual spring buffalo surround this year but were waiting for the upriver traders with new supplies to plunder.

Lisa pushed on from daylight to darkness whenever possible, despite the spring storms, with the sails drooping wet and useless or worse, driving the boat upon sawyers, piles of driftwood or into the bank. The few times when it was absolutely necessary to lay out a storm, Lisa read Brackenridge's copy of *Don Quixote* in Spanish, but more often he led the fight against the river, perhaps attempting ripples —swift, shallow current over sandbars—four or five times before they finally got through by pole and cordelle.

By the end of April Lisa had gained five days on Hunt, according to the news from the downriver fur-loaded craft, but he knew they had to do better, and drove the men more and more, even when they turned surly and mutinous. Desperately he sent Charbonneau ahead with a letter to Hunt, asking him to wait, on the assumption that he would be pleased to add Lisa's keelboat and twenty-five men to his force to get past the Sioux and the rest. Charbonneau and his companion reached Hunt just below the Ponca village. Hunt did stop, but only long enough to trade about two dollars' worth of tobacco for around 1000 pounds of dried buffalo meat with the Indians, and then pushed on. At breakfast May 26, above the mouth of the Niobrara, someone noticed two small canoes hugging the far side of the river, keeping hidden as well as possible—three men coming down alone, a mighty daring venture. Hunt hailed them with a gunshot. They crossed over; Hoback, Rezner and Robinson from Henry's party. They told of the Blackfeet harrying, and the starvation winter at Henry's Fork. The oldest, Robinson, sixty-five, wore a bandanna knotted at the corners over his head because he had been scalped, not by the Blackfeet but long ago, in early Kentucky.

The men had ominous news of the tribes gathering not very far up the river, bragging that no traders would get up past them this year. To Hunt's inquiries they said that the Lewis and Clark route to the Pacific was far from the best, and with the Blackfeet angered since the Lewis fight, the most dangerous one. On their way back from the head-waters of the Snake they had cut across overland and avoided not only the high mountains but the Blackfeet wall. With the glow of that far country still upon them as they talked, it took little to induce the three men, even old Robinson, to return to the wilderness to guide Hunt back up their route from the Snake to the Grand draining into the Missouri.

Sioux emissaries came to warn Hunt that they were at war with the Rees and the Five Villages above and that no traders could be permitted to reach them. Farther on Hunt found the river bank lined with Sioux warriors in paint and arms, ready to stop him. He had the swivel and the two howitzers set with powder only and fired, and then drove in as heavy charges of lead as they could stand, ready, the guns of his men loaded too. At 100 yards the boats were stationed, the men seized their arms and rose up to fire. The Indians were doubtful in the face of so much power, and pulling their robes out open before them, moved the skins from side to side, requesting a peaceful parley, the interpreter said.

While Hunt held his fire, waiting, fourteen chiefs walked forward in a slow, stately file and settled in an open circle on the sandy river bank. Reluctantly Hunt, without experience, started to meet the Indians, flanked by three men on each side, including Crooks, McClellan and Bradbury, leaving the men at the boats standing over the cannons and the arms, ready.

The conference moved with the usual slow formality from smoke through orations and gifts. In the end there was handshaking all around and after several days of short travel and interruptions and threats, and a great deal of firmness, Hunt got his boats through.

By then Lisa appeared, apparently passing the Sioux villages in the wake of the effective determination left behind by Hunt, and the impression of almost ninety well-armed men within the region. Not that Lisa was spared all uneasiness. He had been moving as quietly as possible, forbidding all shooting at game, cordelling when necessary without shout or song. They passed the place where Hunt's party had been stopped by very many Indians, and were slipping on when three buffaloes came swimming toward the boat. It was too much for those who had never seen this, or perhaps ever seen a buffalo. Guns began to roar and as expected, an Indian appeared on a bluff, looking under his shading hand. The next daylight shots boomed across the river just ahead of Lisa, and an American flag whipped out on the bank, with Indians signaling. Knowing there was no escape now, the trader turned his boat toward the shore, his men preparing for defense, each oarsman with his gun in reach.

A row of Indians were waiting on an old log, but Lisa

knew there must be more in the brush, many more. By sign talk he told them he was their trader but unlucky, as they knew. All his furs had burned last year at Cedar Island. Now he was very poor and on his way to save his young men left in the upper country. But he would return and build another post for them on Cedar. Brackenridge was impressed by the fine appearance of the chief and his handsome young warriors, painted, with red fox tails trailing at their moccasin heels.

Knowing that they were not yet past the most dangerous gatherings possible, Lisa welcomed a little luck. A swift summer storm brought a heavy downpour of rain that not only helped obscure them and kept the Indians in their lodges, but filled the sail and sent the boat running.

The next morning they saw Hunt's outfit up ahead, with many Indians that turned out to be Rees, not so arrogant now that they were at war with the Sioux again and needed white-man arms if not help. The boats all went on to the Five Villages, where far tribes were just leaving belatedly from the summer fur rendezvous of the Indians. Hunt traded for more dried meat and added some horses to those from the Rees and more from Lisa in exchange for the boats. In one of these, loaded with furs, Bradbury and Brackenridge returned to St. Louis.

August 6 Hunt struck overland up Grand River, heading across the Little Missouri and the Little Powder, through the Wind River Range to the Green and finally to Henry's Fork of the Snake. It was a hard route for Dorion's wife and small children but a safe way past the Blackfeet wall. Dropping a party of trappers to gather beaver, Hunt went on. Unfortunately he gave in to the clamor of his men and deserted the horses in favor of fifteen canoes although no one with him knew anything of the water run from there to the mouth of the Columbia. Still, it was late October, with winter already upon them in the mountains, and speed looked very important. Evidently there was no notice of possible Indian information about the Snake. Almost at once the canoes began to break up in the wild canyon and with them went much of the provisions. Several caches were made; the cold bore down upon the party and game grew scarce. In desperation the expedition began to divide, separate, break up almost as swiftly as the canoes in the Snake canyon. Through cold and starvation they tried to push westward. One party reached Astoria at the mouth of the Columbia January 12, 1812, with Hunt arriving almost a month later. From then on stragglers came in at intervals, reporting this one dead, and that one. The last seven stumbled in January 15, 1813, over a year after the first ones. By then Hunt had been sent on Astor's *Beaver* to trade with the Russian Fur Company and eventually reached the Sandwich Islands where he waited for the ship's return from Canton, China.

The invoice of merchandise shipped to the northwest on the *Beaver* October 1811 showed a cost of $22,342.38 in New York, and included 1085 gallons of brandy; 1082 rum; 605 4th-proof gin and 496 gallons of London Particular Tennerife wine. How much of this was intended for the Indians is not clear but the Astor who, it was said, discovered that his profit was much greater if he added liquor to the flutes he traded to the tribes of upper York state had never forgotten the value of alcohol. He used it copiously in his trade among both the Indians and the Cantonese.

With the goods left after the *Beaver* sailed on, a large party of around sixty men started for the interior June 1812. David Stuart was to build a post on the Okanogan and spend the winter with the Indians; John Clarke, with four clerks, went to establish a central base at the Spokane, in opposition to the North West house there, and to send subordinate traders out among the surrounding tribes. Donald McKenzie intended to start a post on the Snake for the Nez Perce and secure some of the cached merchandise, mostly stolen, while Robert Stuart with a small party headed back overland with dispatches for New York.

Suddenly now the region west of the Missouri Rockies, with North West men entrenched, seemed full of Astorians too. Clarke, on his way to the Spokane, left his canoes in the care of a friendly chief of the Catatouch, a division of the Nez Perce, the tribe that had befriended McKenzie's party on their way to Astoria the winter before. The next spring Clarke returned and found his canoes safe. He gave the chief a present of ammunition and tobacco and, while unpacking the canoes, showed him a pair of silver goblets, talked big of the importance of those who drank from such vessels, and poured a little wine into one for the chief to drink. The Indian was pleased with the goblet, turned it over in his hands and passed it around the circle like a pipe. Next morning it was missing. Furious, Clarke demanded it of the whole camp. The goblet was located and brought by all the people together, the thief along too, confident and safe, now that the cup was being returned. Clarke hanged him.

The Indians were enraged and perhaps a little stunned. At least they let Clarke and his men jump into their loaded canoes and push off into the swift stream.

That July the large John Reed party left Astoria for the Snake River country, to trap through the winter and collect horses for the overland expedition back to St. Louis the next spring. They were joined by those hardy mountain men, Robinson, Hoback and Rezner, and located on the present Boise River. There was trouble from the first. One man vanished, probably picked off by Indians, another fell from a horse and died, a third was lost to the King's Evil. Then in January the desperately wounded Giles Leclerc came staggering back from a trapping campaign and told Dorion's wife that Pierre and all the rest had been killed by Indians. The woman caught up two horses, put the dying Leclerc* on one and riding the other with her two sons, whipped for Reed's headquarters, but everyone was dead there too, so she started for the Columbia River. She managed to ford the icy, roaring Snake but couldn't cross the winter mountains and so she

---

* The story as told by the descendants of Louis Dorion, son of Pierre, suggests that Leclerc was helped to the back of a horse and died on the way to Reed's post. Franchere says that he died in a few moments after reaching Dorion's lodge.

camped and somehow survived to spring by eating the two horses until starvation drove her with the boys on to Walla Walla, where some Indians cared for them and took them to North West Company canoes coming up the Columbia.

The killing was considered the retaliation for very severe treatment of the Indians by the Pacific Fur Company men, particularly Clarke's hanging of the Catatouch tribesman for the theft of the goblet the previous spring. Whatever the reason, the Dorion woman remains one of the heroines of the years of the beaver men.

Robert Stuart's party, headed for St. Louis with the dispatches for Astor, had grown to seven, but even with Crooks and McClellan along, they managed to wander around in some befuddlement, much as though the compass had never been invented and none among them remembered that the sun rose in the east or that they had followed the Snake to the Columbia the year before. Although they recognized the Snake they went back down it for a considerable distance before they broke from this umbilical that a river can become to man, and set out eastward once more. With such confusion and the desperate trials and escapes, it is no wonder that their exact path is still disputed, particularly whether they actually came through South Pass on their way to the Sweetwater, the Platte and down to the Otos, who knew Crooks and McClellan well and gave the party their first sense of reality, of security. Here also the men first heard of the war against Britain.

With Hunt, Crooks and McClellan all away from Astoria, McKenzie and McDougall, both former North Westers, were in charge. By now they considered the whole Pacific venture an impracticable and unprofitable mistake, even before they knew of the war and that a British naval vessel was expected any day to take possession of the post. There were North West men all around, men offering to pay the overdue wages of the Pacific Fur Company employees, to be deducted from the merchandise and furs—from all there was to show for Astor's investment in the company, by agreement "up to $400,000," including the lost *Tonquin*. They sold, by some reports for $80,500, to the North Westers although the amount actually paid for Astoria, to be called Fort George, and the interior posts and their contents, seems to have been about $58,300, of which $14,000 went to employees. Astor put the value at closer to $200,000 than the $40,-000 he apparently received in bills on Montreal. Many of the Pacific outfit, with old ties to Canada, joined or rejoined North West. Hunt returned from his voyage in time to regret the sale, and to start word of it to Astor.

So the American colors came down from the nation's first precarious grasp at a Pacific empire.

Once more the only creature, man or animal, in North America to profit from war was the beaver, and not even he in regions convenient to the British companies. Although the war hawks in Washington had planned to grab West Florida and particularly Canada immediately after the declaration of hostilities, they actually got little more than blockaded ports on top of the earlier Embargo and Non-intercourse Acts. Americans on the Missouri ran into more and more trouble, with little trade above Manuel Lisa's post near the Council Bluffs of Lewis and Clark, and even there a Shawnee and a Santee Sioux brought news of the scalps, prisoners and booty taken by the Indians in the lake country, and below, as allies of the British in the war. Now was the time to strike all along the Missouri, from St. Louis up.

The men from Hudson's Bay and the North West Company had little competition for the beaver south of the boundary from new Fort George to the Platte, but the Napoleonic wars had impoverished Europe, particularly fashionable Europe. In addition nutria from South America was suggested to the cheaper felting markets as a substitute and the fine woolens of England were making some headway against fur in garments. In 1812 the North West had to see the company exports fall to £30,000 from the £81,400 of 1808, and rise no higher than £47,000 by 1817.

This decrease in business was not due to lack of effort, particularly in the west. Alexander Henry, the Younger, who had built up the trade at Pembina was transferred to Fort George, and was drowned in 1814. He had started large brigades working the upper country and establishing posts but after four years the system was dropped. Sparse furs in the mountains and deserts of the Columbia basin made wandering parties more profitable than permanent posts, less expensive and more successful in gathering up scattered pockets of beaver and in locating new fields. These wanderers swept over the region like the Mormon crickets of later years —as far east as the Green, deep into Utah and Spanish territory, and up along the coast toward the Russian traders.

"They went everywhere, but with live water sometimes a hundred miles apart and beaver wood mighty scarce, there was no profit," the breed grandson of one of the trappers said, ninety years later.

The real threat to the energetic Scots of North West in the region of the 49th parallel and south was not so much scarcity of beaver or the Americans as the Hudson's Bay Company. Although the Bay men were without the thrust or the daring and imagination of their Scottish competitors, they had long-range financial backing and practically absolute territorial control of most of outer or upper Canada by charter and assumption. Even when operating on American soil, the North West Company had that long narrow trade corridor to Montreal that made them as vulnerable as any beaver colony on a stream that could be turned aside with the cut of a shovel. In 1810 Lord Selkirk became a power in the Hudson's Bay Company and proposed a settlement of dispossessed Highlanders in Canada. After some stout opposition he was given 116,000 square miles of territory in the fork of the Red and the Assiniboine, directly astride the North

West route, cutting off the one life stream of the western trade to Fort William and the sea as surely as the shovel cut off the water from the beaver pond.

The man selected to establish the Selkirk colony was Miles MacDonell, born in New York, his family Loyalists, one of those angry groups who, having fled from a revolution, dedicate themselves to a return, to the destruction of the successful with whatever terrorism is in fashion. Apparently North West was looked upon as a successful revolutionary too. Early in 1814 MacDonell confiscated their pemmican and other supplies stored near the Souris. In return the North West ordered him out and tried to induce the Red River colonists to move to what was described as "better agricultural lands." They refused, and left. Selkirk refounded his settlement and sent soldiers to destroy Fort Gibraltar and recover the arms and goods taken. In March 1816 the sheriff of the settlement forced his way into Pembina. Next the North West attacked a force under Semple, governor of the colony, at Seven Oaks, killed him and twenty of his men and drove the Highlanders out again.

Selkirk arrived with more settlers and an armed guard. He seized Fort William, headquarters of the North West Company, and under his authority as justice of the peace of Upper Canada, arrested some of the men and stopped all North West traffic west and south. His men crossed down into the United States and added Grant of Fond du Lac and William Morrison to their prisoners and sent them to Montreal for trial. The North West sued. Once more the long years of Bay monopoly were contested in Parliament and the courts.

In 1816 Congress outlawed alien fur dealers on U.S. territory, not the voyageurs, interpreters and clerks, important to domestic traders, but outside merchandisers. It was an optimistic move, even with the 49th parallel established as the international boundary from Lake of the Woods to the Rockies. As for the traders, all those married to Indian women south of the border were, by matrilinear pattern, members of the tribes and belonging to the country. Others came in for the richer market times and for such events as the Hidatsa trade rendezvous. Many tribes still carried their furs north by packhorse, the beaver of the Blackfeet more often the result of raids on others than from their own catch and cure.

In the meantime Canada could not tolerate this private war. A committee was appointed to bring peace between the two fur companies, and failed, but the ruinous and violent competition was destroying both outfits and particularly the Indians through the rivaling floods of alcohol, and scattering bare beaver carcasses over the farthest wilderness for the wolves and the buzzards. Under some pressure North West approached Selkirk with the idea of combining. He hardened, determined to crush the company. More and more duplicating posts stared across streams and inlets at each other, sometimes with relatives, such as the McLoughlins, on both sides. There was bloodshed between their agents, even dueling, the Indians playing one side against the other for price and present, with increased drinking competitions to open trade. Selkirk was making preposterous charges, claiming that before the North West came in, the Hudson's Bay Company kept its posts on the Bay, although everyone knew they had been forced to send buyers out among the Indians by the competition of the Montreal men long before the birth of the rival company in 1784, and that some of the experienced traders who organized the North West came from the far posts of the Bay outfit. Radisson, the chief organizer of the Hudson's Bay, was one of the most aggressive traders among far Indians.

Selkirk also accused the North Westers of sending hunters to compete with the Indians in beaver fur, thereby angering the tribes and exterminating the animals. There was truth in this, but many North West men had learned not only the trade but the hunt while working for the Bay company, and before them stood the precedent of the early French, who depended almost entirely on white and then breed hunters. Nowhere did the North West debauch the Indians as much as the French and the British of the 17th and 18th centuries.

In the end North West obtained damages from Selkirk. With his health and most of his fortune gone, Selkirk died in 1820. The area of his settlement returned to the control of the Bay Company. Before now the government had begun to examine the old files of the 1749 investigation into the Hudson's Bay charter and the questioned Kelsey journal. Perhaps the cancellation that failed then could succeed now. This threat chilled the hearts of the directors in London like a blizzard wind from the prairies. In the meantime the wintering partners of the North West Company were told that their financial straits had become desperate. With Selkirk, the most relentless enemy of any merger, dead, a coalition was agreed upon and completed rather hastily in 1821, under the older name—The Hudson's Bay Company. There was, however, less stress upon the gentleman adventurers and more upon the North West treatment of the men out in the trade. The practice of sharing profits with the winter partners, the officers out at the posts and with the brigades was adopted.

The push of the Scots added a new vitality to the Bay Company and in 1826 the territory was reorganized under George Simpson, who became, with the now unchallenged expanse and power of the company charter, head of an empire prepared to battle the Russian fur men and particularly those Americans south of his border. He approached the task with the vigor of a poor boy of illegitimate birth on his way to a knighting, some of his chief opponents the Chouteaus, largely compelled by circumstance to bear the mother's name instead of the father's. It was ambition against ambition, hard as granite and steel.

Down on the Missouri the Americans had already entertained Prince Paul of Württemberg, who, if not the first of the exalted visitors to the region, was at least the first journal keeper of that long string of romantic princes and nobles somehow drawn to the shrinking domain of the Indian and the animals.

ROMANTIC BUCKSKIN TO THE LAST BOISSON

WITH the Blackfeet country still rich in beaver, southern hunters tried to slip in and out, but as fast as
possible, usually leaving no camp sites to be detected, not
even the slightest trace of smoke from a bit of aspen fire to
search out the sharp Indian nose. Small parties, a man or two,
tried setting trap lines, running them early the next morning,
pulling them and never returning, the long, unexpected
moves made without track or sign, perhaps down the freezing
waters of a rocky creek or slipping out in the darkness to
make dry camp on the upland somewhere.

Another and even more dangerous method of taking
pelts in the Blackfeet country was the spring beaver hunt.
When the snow was going, the ice about to break up in the
tributaries of the Yellowstone and the Missouri, a selected
region was scouted very carefully by two or four men who
knew the country and the ways of the Indians. They worked
far from known winter camps not only of the Blackfeet but
the other tribes too, and before new grass strengthened the
ponies for move or for war.

The fur-capped, tangle-bearded hunters watched the
sky, peering along the edge of the open hand held over the
sun, peering as close to the blazing rim as possible, for there
lay the secret of the weather of the next moon. There and in

the movements of the snowy owls, the magpies, the sage hens and in the set of animal ears—moose or rabbit. With warming weather ahead, and cracking ice, the men slipped up some good beaver stream, prepared their canoes, more often skin boats, or merely a buffalo bull hide laced boat-shaped between two old logs that would seem driftwood from far off.

When the ice began to rise on the flooding waters that roared in from the melted snows above, the men pushed out into the broken floe, preferably two in a boat, one with a gun in his hands, a second loaded beside him, the paddler with a long crook-ended pole handy to catch the dead or wounded animal before he went down. Most of the beavers were flooded out and huddled together, the young too, on the top of the houses, or washed off, swam frantically along the edges of the flood, easy to pick off. Sometimes hundreds were killed by a single party in a day, slaughtered like the helpless antelope in the surrounds. Often not half of the bodies were rescued, perhaps only one in five or even nine or ten. With poor marksmanship and many cripplings, or with a slow hooker, the rate of recovery among the floating ice and driftwood was even less. Carcasses of sunken beaver were usually lost until the bloating of warm weather brought the bodies to the top, the fur slipping and worthless, the beaver wasted.

Gunfire was dangerous in Blackfeet country and had to be managed carefully, after a wide and thorough reconnaissance and consideration of the wind that would carry the report. Sometimes the hunters worked with the Shawnee and Iroquois hunters drifting west since their home regions were taken by the whites, their hunting grounds gone or impoverished. Most of those who came had some white blood, perhaps far back, a long time ago, but still there, so with the teaching of the preachers and the missionaries they could deny their natural religious abhorrence of this waste of nature's food supply, this indignity of death brought upon a brother creature when none needed to eat.

That a new era was opening seemed plain in the streets and the finest old houses of St. Louis. Cerré, the last

of the old regime, clung to his satin small clothes and silver
buckles, but down at the Mississippi River there were new
clanking, splashing, smoking monsters to haul freight, nor
were these keeping to the Mississippi. November 13, 1818,
the Missouri *Gazette* quoted from a letter going the rounds,
saying that the government was fitting out an expedition to
the Rocky Mountains and the northwest coast:

> "A steam boat (*Western Engineer*) is now building at
> Pittsburg for this expedition, and which it is expected
> will be able to proceed up the Missouri to its source. It
> is ascertained that *there is a passage through the Rocky
> Mountains, and at the distance of about five miles after
> you pass the mountains, a branch of the Columbia com-
> mences running to the Pacific Ocean!!!* It is intended
> to take the steam boat to pieces at the mountains and re-
> build her in this river. The expedition is to traverse the
> continent by water, and to be absent about two years.
> —It will pass the first winter on this side of the Rocky
> Mountains! ! !"

The three-hundred-year-old talk of a passage to China
had really been changed very little by the experiences of
hundreds of men, north and south of the Canadian boundary,
not by Lewis and Clark, not by the Astorians, not by the hundred men at the waterfront of St. Louis who must have
roared through their beards at this curious notion of those
glaciated heights that stood between the Missouri and the
headwaters of the Columbia. The men who had been with
Hunt, or knew the Snake canyon and the lives lost there,
must have wondered at this fantasy. Talk of the unicorn living in the Rockies started again but this was not as convincing as the giant-beaver legends of the Great Lakes or the
windigo of the voyageurs had been around the dark woods
and hungry marshes.

There was anxiety, angry denunciation and some
amusement the winter of 1818-19 over the plans for this Yellowstone Expedition going against the Blackfeet and to the
northwest against the British. General Atkinson finally got

his force of over a thousand men and their supplies on four large steamboats built expressly to buck the Missouri current. The engines blew pistons, the boats sprang leaks, and caught on snags and sawyers. Two never got into the Missouri at all, and only one made it to the mouth of the Kansas River, and stopped, the first alarm of the Indians turning to whoops and laughter when the fiery monster pounded and roared like a great crippled bug dying in the water.

Atkinson shifted to keelboats with man-driven wheels and if these failed, there was always the final degradation for an expedition publicized with such great talk—the tow path. American troops might learn the rhythm of the pull but they would never have the colorful clothing of the voyageurs, or the songs.

The fifth steamboat, the *Western Engineer,* planned, according to the newspapers, for portage over the Rockies had been built with an eye on some of the difficulties of Missouri navigation. The seventy-five-foot craft was only thirteen wide at the beam and drew only nineteen inches of water. The wheeling was at the stern, to avoid snags and sawyers. The purpose of the *Engineer* was scientific, to fix a site for a military post at or near the mouth of the Yellowstone, study the history, trading capacity and genius of the Indian tribes, make a correct military survey of all the Missouri and obtain a thorough knowledge of the country, soil, mineral and curiosities to where the Rocky Mountains met the international boundary. Among the men under Maj. Stephen H. Long were Jessup, the mineralogist; Say, botanist and geologist; Baldwin, zoologist and physicist, and Peale and Seymour, landscape artists and ornithologists. The boat was well protected by artillery under Maj. John Biddle, brother of Commodore James Biddle, joint administrator of Oregon with the British, and brother of Anne, wife of Wilkinson, accused of treason and for a while governor of Upper Louisiana. Indian agent with Long was Benjamin O'Fallon, nephew of William Clark, who controlled all that went in and came out of the Indian country.

The *Western Engineer* started after Atkinson's troops

and churned steadily along under Peale's elegant flag picturing a white man with a sword and an Indian with the calumet of peace shaking hands. The St. Louis *Enquirer* carried a further description:

> "The bow of the vessel exhibits the form of a huge serpent, black and scaly, rising out of the water from under the boat, his head high as the deck, darting forward, his mouth open, vomiting smoke, and apparently carrying the boat on his back. From under the boat at its stern, issues a stream of foaming water, dashing violently along. All the machinery is hid. . . . Neither wind nor human hands are seen to help her; and to the eye of ignorance, the illusion is complete that a monster of the deep carries her on his back. . . ."

Indians and white men too, stood on rises in wonder, perhaps to recall, in old, old age, the day that changed the Missouri. Farther on Indians would have fled or fallen down in terror at this fire-breathing serpent swimming their river if the progress had not been so slow and painful, so wavering and uncertain, stopping here and there, to back with an angry roar and complaint, perhaps turn, make ponderous lunges at obstructions, helped over at the last shaking, pounding moment by angry shouts and the sweat of the pole men. As the river fell, sometimes the boat was ripped by some great jag of mud-anchored stump of giant cottonwood under the roily water. Then there was a shout of orders, the wheel paddles pounding desperately to push the boat to the shallows before sinking. Regularly Major Long tied up somewhere for a ringing of axes to replenish the long rick of wood for the firebox while a party of scientists and artists went overland afoot, cautiously, for even here, among the tamest of Indians, there was contempt for any so newly sun-blistered, so plainly outsiders.

At Fort Lisa Long was welcomed by a wide gathering of Indians who had heard of the fiery serpent by word or signal, and several parties of river whites. The swivel gun boomed along the Missouri bluffs in triumph even though the boat was still practically a thousand river miles from the Yellowstone and an incalculable distance from that optimistic portage to the waters flowing westward. They were ten weeks out of St. Louis and some of the cottonwoods on the bottoms were beginning to yellow, the runs of sumac along the bluff tops red as warrior blood. Soon the river would be frozen, frozen so solid that whole buffalo herds could cross.

Long turned the serpent head of his *Engineer* toward the shore half a mile or so above Lisa's trading post. There he set the men to cutting logs for winter huts and then headed his pirogue down river on his way to Washington. By November all but one of Atkinson's keelboats with his army and supplies, his officers and their families had dragged to anchor above the *Western Engineer,* up near Council Bluffs. This wasn't the Yellowstone but Atkinson laid out substantial winter quarters on top of the bluffs, establishing the post later named for him—the first military establishment in the Indian country of the Missouri, and of all ever built, the most idyllic, the area to be characterized long afterward as the Elysian Fields of the Fighting Sixth.

The first winter of the U. S. Army in the Missouri country was the last of the region's most daring trader —Manuel Lisa, the only Spaniard to reach prominence through all the years of Spanish claim. Since 1815 Lisa had tried to spread his little trading houses up the Missouri again, stopping well short of trouble, short of the Blackfeet wall. Each post was still equipped like a small farm, with livestock, poultry and gardens. His first white wife died in 1817. He married again the next year and brought his bride to Fort Lisa, sending word ahead that his Omaha wife, Mitain, be given generous presents and sent away. Lisa, like many of his French acquaintances who fathered mixed-blood families, wanted his Indian children to have the opportunities he could give his white ones. He had already taken Mitain's small daughter away to St. Louis and left the mother with her skin slashed, her clothing torn, and ashes in her hair as for one dead. Now at his command she took her infant son away to the Omaha village, but soon slipped back to squat against the wall of the fort in the evening shadows, the boy on her back, her shawl drawn over them both.

Lisa and his charming second wife, who spoke only English to his Spanish and poor French, welcomed their new white neighbors, particularly the families of Atkinson's post. Everyone knew Mitain's story, and with her son seeming old enough to take to St. Louis, Lisa sent for her. She finally came, and placed the boy in his father's arms, begging to go along, to live in any corner or hut just to be near her children. Lisa refused, promising her and her people many fine presents. She was not consoled, and the anger among the Omahas at this taking both children from the mother, to whom they belonged by matrilinear right, brought protests from both the chiefs and the government men. Lisa, always a cagey trader, decided to leave the son with the mother. He died in 1820, leaving provision for the education of both Indian children.

Before the year was well along, it became known nationally that Johnson, the inept and tricky contractor of Atkinson's wood-burning hen-coops, as the steamboats were called, had managed the first graft from public funds to touch, if only by intention, the upper Missouri country. For years it was the largest. The denunciation was greatest where the promise of a steamboat portage over the Rockies had been most readily accepted. Enemies of Calhoun, Secretary of War, abused him for trusting the expedition to the crazy fad—steam—and on the wild Missouri. Calhoun protested that he had obtained the approval of Atkinson, the quartermaster general, and President Monroe, and was reminded scornfully that Monroe had a personal stake in the west. He has studied law under Jefferson, sided with him against both Washington and the Federalists, had helped sneak through the purchase of Louisiana and was a particular friend of William Clark, Superintendent of Indian Affairs, who ran the Indian country with his relatives so closely it was called Clark's Preserve. Then it leaked out that Monroe had advanced more money to Johnson than Calhoun anticipated, and still the hen-coops didn't work.

By spring the exaggerated plans, the scandals and mammoth expense of the expedition for the insignificant accomplishment were under congressional investigation. Atkinson's appropriations were cut. There would be no swift passage to the Pacific, no hindrance to British penetration, not even a Yellowstone fort. Some of the blame was put on the Missouri River, but mostly in a bragging tone.

"Too thick for soup and too thin to plow," was the complaint. Yet apparently the river wasn't a proper marching route for the U. S. Army either, not quite solid under foot.

Major Long's appropriations for his scientific expedition were also slashed, and after the learned men and the artists had practically wasted a winter in the wilderness. Seymour did produce many sketches and paintings, including several large canvases added to during the summer. As art his work was perhaps disappointing but historically the paintings are of tremendous importance. Unfortunately all but a few of the roll of western canvases said to have been large as a barrel were misplaced, lost.

Instead of the well-equipped and manned *Western Engineer* for gleaning scientific data on the upper Missouri to Canada, the best Long could manage was funds for a short survey. He could take perhaps twenty men, scientists, the two artists and seven soldiers, but only six horses or mules from government funds, and a mean little stock of goods to trade to the Indians for necessities and to make a few presents, mighty shabby presents as the chiefs quickly let Long know. Instead of a far exploration through new wilderness, he had to set out to find the source of the Platte River and then swing around through the Arkansas and Red River valleys, practically on Pike's much earlier route.

"It's always easier to bait the Spaniards a little than to confront the perfidious Albion," one of Long's men wrote home. Besides, the west was furious about the treaty of 1819, which gave up all claim to Texas and now a revolution boiling among the Mexicans, with no telling what opportunities that might bring.

With Lisa dead before he could lead the younger men of the new Missouri Fur Company up through Blackfeet country, Joshua Pilcher, now president, delayed sending out an expedition through that lack persistently dogging the men of St. Louis—shortage of capital. This was aggravated by news of a congressional frown on the Yellowstone Expedition, which was to have blown a hole wide as the horizon in the British-armed Blackfeet wall. In 1821 Pilcher did get as far as the Bighorn and built a post near Lisa's deserted fort but named it Benton* for the new senator from Missouri. In 1822 Pilcher with 300 men on the upper river and the Yellowstone brought down furs valued at $25,000, perhaps because the Hudson's Bay Company was still less energetic than the North Westers it was absorbing.

Confident, perhaps anxious to carry out Lisa's plans, or to succeed where he had failed, Pilcher decided to take over the Blackfeet trade and sent a party with Jones and Immell to the dangerous Three Forks. Immell had been driven out there with Henry but the beaver drew him back. The trapping was rich and on their return to Fort Benton with apparently twenty packs of their catch they met some Blackfeet. They camped together, cautiously, but made friendly talk about building a post for the tribe below the falls of the Missouri. Two weeks later on the way down the Yellowstone, they were struck by Blackfeet, the two leaders and five others killed, and all the furs, equipment and horses lost, the value estimated at $15,000.

So the Blackfeet wall was still solid as the granite mountains, all the company hopes of expanding into the far northwest dead, another post at the mouth of the Bighorn closed, the working capital of the company lost. Pilcher re-

* Fort Benton at the head of steam navigation of the Missouri was located in 1846.

treated as Lisa had done—to the thin trade of the lower Missouri.

In the meantime Andrew Henry had been remembering the wealth of beaver gold in the headwaters of the Missouri too, particularly after Pilcher's first harvest came down. With William H. Ashley, a business man of St. Louis, he put a notice in the Missouri *Republican* calling for "one hundred young men to ascend the Missouri to its source." Their party included names that were to settle into the maps of the west, and the stories: Jedediah Smith, William and Milton Sublette, Robert Campbell, Etienne Provost, James Clyman, David Jackson, Jim Bridger and Thomas Fitzpatrick, the start of the Rocky Mountain Fur Company but not formally organized until 1830. Early in 1822 Indian Agent O'Fallon, nephew and protegé of William Clark, Superintendent of Indian Affairs and a partner in the reorganized Missouri Fur Company, protested to the Secretary of War about the trading license issued to Ashley and Henry. He objected to the trapping but ignored such activities by the Missouri Company men.

Henry had taken a preliminary expedition to the mouth of the Yellowstone, set up headquarters and sent parties out to trap and trade, but the country was so nearly stripped to beaver bones that he started for the rich fields he remembered at the headwaters of the Missouri. The Blackfeet struck him near the falls, killed four of his men and drove the rest back.

Early the spring of 1823 Ashley started up the river with two keelboats. He had already lost a keel with merchandise worth $10,000 to the mud of the lower Missouri and news of the Blackfeet attacks on Henry's men was still to reach him. In May he approached the Ree villages, the tribe long unpredictable, barring passage to some, robbing some, motioning others on after extracting generous tribute. This year they were sly and aggressive, perhaps seeing the success of the Blackfeet and encouraged by the British, although Pilcher and his men may have been trying a Lisa trick where O'Fallon failed, hoping to keep this powerful new competition out of the region they intended to reoccupy by setting the Indians against the new brigade.

Although company men had been attacked, the Rees seemed friendly when Ashley first stopped with gifts and goods to barter for a pack string and saddle horses. His interpreter was Edward Rose, of Indian blood too, as well as Negro and white, and with years of life among the Crows. Rose suspected that the Indians were breeding trouble and advised Ashley against leaving his boats moored overnight up beside the village, and his horse party camped with the stock on the shore nearby. In the night the Rees attacked, ostensibly over a white man found among them and killed. The onslaught was silent at first, and then exploded into the flaming fire of British fusils. There was no way to rescue anyone or even move the boats because the rivermen refused to expose themselves at oar or pole in the flash of Ree guns as the horses went down all along the shore, running against picket ropes, struggling in the darkness, the stranded men fighting from behind the carcasses as well as they could. Daylight and sunup came. With those lucky enough to get away drawn into the boats, Ashley ordered the moorings cut, letting the keels drift slowly away on the swerving current, the Indians running along the bank, keeping out of gun range, shouting. In the end fourteen of Ashley's men were dead, with nine wounded but to recover.

Jedediah Smith volunteered to carry word of the attack past the Rees to Henry, up at the Yellowstone. Ashley sent a swift pirogue down the river for help and started one of his keelboats back with the wounded and those afraid to stay with him, which included all but five of his voyageurs.

Colonel Leavenworth, commanding Fort Atkinson, received the news June 18 and realized that he must strike swiftly if the fever of this new arrogance, this new illusion of power against the Americans, was not to spread like a prairie fire over all the Indian country. He had not heard of the Blackfeet attacks but he or someone close to him sensed the mood. Without waiting for orders he moved out the 22nd of June with his three keelboats, two six-pound cannons, several small swivels, and all the men he dared take from the post—with women and children there—220 men, including a company of sharpshooters. He marched part of the force overland safely but lost some men July 3 when one of his boats went down with seventy muskets and other important supplies.

Plainly the Rees had to be punished or the Missouri would be frozen over to trade. At the urging of the Indian agent, Pilcher went to reinforce Leavenworth with two boats, a howitzer from Atkinson and about forty men. These, added to Ashley's and the eighty Henry brought, gave the colonel almost 350, not much of a force against over seven, eight hundred warriors, with who could say how many other tribes ready to join the Rees. A couple hundred Sioux attached themselves to Pilcher, happy to strike their Ree enemies under the protection of white-man cannons. There was an elaborate plan of attack but the Sioux raced ahead for a little wild fighting, and then, when the white onslaught hesitated and wavered, they went to raid the cornfields and withdrew into the hills to feast and see how the fight would go. Leavenworth, furious, said he wouldn't be surprised to find them on the Ree side in the morning.

The attack included lobbing balls from a knoll into the earth-house village. One killed the chief. Whether Leavenworth understood the effect of this is difficult to say, but plainly the heart was gone from the Ree fighters after that, and gradually the defense became a protracted parleying. The traders wanted the troublesome tribe annihilated, cleared out of their way forever, and were furious that Leavenworth discussed peace at all. When only part of Ashley's goods taken from the shore party were returned, the trader protested angrily, demanding an immediate attack for the rest. But Leavenworth knew the weakness of his motley force, his limited ammunition, and realized that he did not dare unite all the western tribes against the Americans by the destruction of the Rees, even if he had had the power and the appetite for the wholesale slaughter. There was some preparation for shelling the palisaded village but the Rees were deserting their homes, slipping away in darkness and light. Thousands of them scattered over the prairie and vanished like quail in the grass, beyond any army's reach, so Leavenworth withdrew. Behind him the village blazed up, set on fire, he was convinced, by Pilcher, but the Sioux still believed, years later, that the fires were from the shelling.

By August the expedition was back at Fort Atkinson, with recriminations and abuse for Leavenworth. It was an unfortunate time for the visit of Prince Paul of Württemberg, this summer of 1823. In the midst of the tumult he wrote of the agricultural progress at Atkinson. There would be better years for titled visitors to the Missouri country but Paul had another purpose besides romantic adventure: he was seeking a new homeland for some of his impoverished Württembergers.

There was considerable whooping for war against England, assumed to be the real culprit behind the Blackfeet and Ree attacks, with diplomatic protests from the state department to the British government. The charges were denied, but it was admitted once more that stolen beaver had been purchased, this time the furs of Immell and Jones, purchased from the Blackfeet. With the admission came offers of restitution—for the hides.

By now fur brigades seemed to overrun the west, scattered everywhere, following the smell of beaver gold as the wolverine sniffed for castoreum. Missouri Fur Company men were out and an invasion of Astor traders, in addition to a motley of hunters and traders from newer outfits, the Ashley-Henry brigades and a growing number of free traders. In addition the Bay men and their North Westers were penetrating not only the Missouri country to the Platte and the upper Arkansas but were trapping the ponds and streams west of the Divide to the last kit to discourage American invasion and eventual settlement.

After the fight with the Rees, Ashley had divided the supplies in his keelboat between two parties. Henry, out first, with too few horses even for the packs, started his party afoot to the mouth of the Yellowstone. On the way he lost Hugh Glass temporarily to a bout with a grizzly, and fought off Indians, with a couple of his men killed, and then at his post discovered that the horse herd had been raided. But fall was upon him and so Henry dispatched a party southwestward and hurried with the rest up the Yellowstone, stopping at that most occupied spot—the mouth of the Bighorn. In the meantime Ashley had sent a small party including Jedediah Smith, Fitzpatrick, Clyman, Rose and Bill Sublette westward past the Black Hills. They, too, ran into incredible hardship, altogether enough perhaps to discourage even Ashley back in St. Louis if he had known, perhaps enough to have changed the whole history of the later beaver trade. But Ashley had other matters on his mind anyway. After Henry's experiences with the Blackfeet and now the obvious difficulty of getting goods to the far Missouri posts, the partners gave up the idea of building trading houses for the Blackfeet as high up as the Marias, near where the ancient trail from the Saskatchewan crossed the Missouri and bore southward to the Yellowstone and the upper Platte. Instead they were planning what had attracted traders as far back as Champlain —a summer trapper and trader rendezvous in the heart of the current beaver regions. This decision, with the news that the Green River country was still as rich in fur as McKenzie of the North West reported it back in 1818, convinced Ashley that he should strike out overland. But now Henry wanted to retire. Although the winter of 1824 was coming close, Ashley waited some time, hoping that he would relent, and finally had to go on without him, up the Platte and the South Fork, taking what the Indians called a wagon gun along, the first wheels to turn on the final, and greatest, highway of the New World.

Ashley managed to get his first rendezvous together in 1825, a small but profitable beginning. It was at Henry's Fork of the Green River, draining to the Colorado. Perhaps Ashley knew there would be troops up the Missouri; he took his furs to the Bighorn and down the Yellowstone, approximately 8900 pounds of beaver, worth an estimated forty to fifty thousand dollars in St. Louis. He was disturbed by the success of the British traders, saying that he saw one party with $200,000 worth of furs. Altogether, there seemed to be about 1000 employees of the British in the upper Missouri country, costing the United States around $1,000,000 in fur and robes a year, in addition to the animosity they stirred up among the Indians.

At the mouth of the Yellowstone Ashley met Atkinson's expedition holding treaty conferences with the upriver tribes, the roving Sioux, Cheyennes and some Blackfeet. The general, in his report that was presented to Congress, mentioned the immense amount of furs that Ashley had brought down, and the possibilities, from the trader's experiences, that South Pass could be traversed by wagons. It was a momentous year, this 1825, with the publicity suggesting a passage to the Pacific, but by wagon, even though no peace had been made with the Blackfeet.

For many years after Auguste Chouteau closed St. Louis to Astor, the trader and his fur company hung like a cloud of prairie locusts on the horizon, sometimes nearer, sometimes far off, but always a present humming in the ears. It had seemed close when Hunt supplied his party out of St. Louis but the war stopped whatever Astor planned for that city. He made up his Astorian losses from the government's need for cash before the war was over. Astor and two Philadelphia financiers rescued the treasury by purchasing a large block of loan bonds at eighty and eighty-two cents on the dollar and paying for them with bank notes worth half their face value.

By that time there had been the trouble with Selkirk, although it was not clear if he realized that half the goods his men confiscated from the North West Company at Fort William and Fond du Lac belonged to Astor, who had been wrecked by the North West at the Pacific coast and now robbed by the Bay's Selkirk. Astor demanded that the gov-

ernment send a man-o'-war to protect his installations at the
lakes and was refused, but he probably received his share
from the compensation Selkirk had to pay North West. By
1817 Astor had acquired all the North West posts in the Mississippi valley and the whole South West Company, reorganization of the old Mackinac or Michilimackinac Company, a
sort of subsidiary of the North West, with the trade of the
upper lakes and upper Mississippi and called the "Indian
Devil" the wolverine of the fur outfits, eliminating independent traders, forbidding the Indians to trade with them.

By this time John Jacob Astor's five feet, nine inches
had become stout and blocky, his forehead still high and
square in the broadening face. He sustained an urbane ex-
terior, with his strong German accent, but many claimed
there was only a money-making machine behind the pleasant
façade, a grasping, parsimonious and hard-fisted creditor, an
aggressive and ruthless competitor. By 1818 he was so powerful that his employees, if crossed by government men, felt
free to threaten them with discharge from the service. As the
American Fur Company tightened its monopoly the men
grew more arrogant and lawless. Astor himself showed no
respect for any citizen or for agent or official of the government or for its laws and policies. His employees got the robes
and furs from the Indians by the method he learned among
the New York tribes: a little whisky doubled the profit, a
little more tripled it, quadrupled it. Many considered it bad
luck for a trapper or small trader in the wilderness to accu-
mulate credit slips or due bills on Astor's company. Some
vanished, others were found dead face down, shot from ambush, by Indians or what was made to look like Indians.
Astor froze out small competitors and finally, through Ramsay Crooks' instigation and the help of Governor Cass and
Senator Benton, he turned upon the government factory system that was always a threat to his fur methods, and suddenly
the government was out of the Indian trade.

Although Astor lived in Europe much of the time by
now, the American Fur Company was still outside of St.
Louis, outside of the queen city of the later fur trade, outside

of all the Missouri trade except what was obtained overland. The winter of 1820-21 Crooks went to Europe to see Astor and lay out a four-year plan, including a Western Department for the company. It was set up in 1822, about the time Astor's most vigorous competitor was organized. When the Hudson's Bay and North West companies combined about 900 clerks and other employees were dismissed, among them Kenneth McKenzie and William Laidlaw. With some Canadians and a couple of United States citizens to legalize their activities they formed the Columbia Fur Company, soon active in the Mississippi trade to the lakes. The early struggles overcome, they established posts from the Mandans south to Council Bluffs and gave the American Fur Company stiff competition for furs and particularly robes, the favorite product of the Plains tribes. In addition, with the knowledge of the Bay trade that McKenzie brought, they worked into the confidence of the northern Indians who had favored Bay men, especially the Blackfeet, finally breaking the wall against American traders.

By then Astor's managers saw the value, and the danger, in those Indian connections and offered to supply the Columbia with trade goods. In 1827 the company was absorbed by American Fur and through its field subsidiary, the Upper Missouri Company, Astor put himself into direct competition with Smith, Jackson and Sublette who took over when Ashley retired in 1826. They were superior to Astor's employees, both as trappers and traders, but their losses to the Indians were heavy and the beaver growing far between. In 1830 the loose organization sold out to Fitzpatrick, Milton Sublette, Bridger and others, who became the Rocky Mountain Fur Company.

The Yellowstone Expedition was long forgotten and with it why Fort Atkinson happened to be built. Now, with the river traffic usually equipped to protect itself against such Indian attacks as seemed probable, and the overland brigades turning off along the Platte, well below Atkinson, the post was condemned the fall of 1826 on the charge that the soldiers were farmers and graziers instead of martial men.

So the troops embarked with their families; the Indian women took their mixed-blood children desolately to their people, and the Fighting Sixth departed the Elysian Fields.*

It was also a time of other changes. In 1831 McKenzie obtained a treaty of peace between the Assiniboins and the Blackfeet and sent a trading party to winter up in the Marias country with the Piegans, the beaver men of the Blackfeet, and brought the usual cutthroat competition from the Hudson's Bay Company, the elimination of his fort hastened by an attack from the Bloods.

With the long hauls from St. Louis, McKenzie suggested a steamboat to his company. In this he got cooperation at St. Louis. The winter of 1826-27 Astor had also taken over Bernard Pratte and Company, finally getting a Chouteau or so, including Pierre, son of the one who dominated so much of the early St. Louis trade. Some said publicly that this was just about twenty years late.

Much of the upper Missouri business with the horse Indians was buffalo robes, tanned soft as heavy velvet, a few of the finest worked with paint and quills or beads. To move such bulky freight Chouteau considered steam the answer but not the floating huts Johnson built, or even like the *Western Engineer,* with its smoke-spouting serpent head and advertised for portage over the Rockies. The result of the McKenzie and Chouteau requests was the *Yellowstone,* a sidewheeler and although called a cracker box with two tall smokestacks set on a platter, she moved up the river rather easily. Once more Indians whipped their horses in to watch but 1831 was a dry year and above the clear waters of the Niobrara twisting through the muddy drag of the Missouri, the boat stuck in the shallows, the paddles thrashing mud and air.

Pierre Chouteau, Jr., sent a fast pirogue up to the post for lighters, and went to a high bluff where bighorn sheep once aired their heads against the sky. From there he watched for boats, for the overdue May rise or a cloudburst. The men arrived first and got the *Yellowstone* into floating

* As described by Lt. Philip St. George Cooke in 1831.

depth and on to Fort Tecumseh. In a few weeks she was back
loaded with furs, buffalo robes and 10,000 smoked buffalo
tongues. The next year the steamboat climbed past the Yellowstone, getting more goodwill from the Blackfeet and ini-
tiating a new era in Missouri trade, as well as starting a cycle
of visiting painters, from George Catlin on. Unfortunately
a serious rival appeared on the river, not a rival combine but
a former upriver employee of the company, Narcisse Leclerc.
He was efficient, knew the trade and had a good following.
With his small savings and those of some others, he was so
successful in 1831 that it was plain to Chouteau and the rest
that he must be stopped before he reached the upper country again, but stopped without endangering the company
license. Apparently the problem was turned over to Cabanné,
long-time Astor man at Bellevue, near old Fort Atkinson.
There were rumors he would offer Leclerc a cash payment
not to go as far up as the Sioux. Perhaps Leclerc viewed
such an overture as a sign of weakness, perhaps Cabanné
didn't want this competition down in his region either.

Washington had put a more stringent ban on liquor
into the Indian country, effective the summer of 1832, the
inspection no longer by Indian agents—traders themselves
—but by officers at Fort Leavenworth. Clark, still Superintendent of Indian Affairs, authorized Leclerc to take 250 gallons of alcohol up the river and when Chouteau protested,
Clark claimed he had no official notice of the new prohibi-
tion. Some said he had an interest in Leclerc's venture, others that he was naturally sympathetic to the whisky trade,
when so much of his fortune and the great wealth of his
nephews and some other relatives came from liquor in the
Missouri country. When the *Yellowstone* returned from the
early trip of 1832, the captain was warned at Leavenworth
that no more alcohol would be passed. Chouteau was furious
and finally Clark gave him permission to send 1,400 gallons
of liquor out on the next company boat, but this would probably not be before next spring. Leclerc would reach the trade
grounds in the fall, and skim the profits from the winter's
harvest. The 250 gallons of alcohol turned into frontier

whisky,* with Leclerc's monopoly, would make him a fortune in one season and win over the more influential of the
alcoholic river chiefs for years. There were many of these
now, men who twenty, even fifteen years ago refused to allow *une boisson,* a drinking match at the beginning of a
trading time and now were as pathetically sodden as any of
the chiefs at the Montreal fur fairs, as any around the St.
Lawrence posts. No whisky, no trade.

Chouteau turned the *Yellowstone* right back up the
river with his 1400 gallons, only to have the lot confiscated at
Leavenworth, as promised. Now only Cabanné's ingenuity
could save the season's trade, and influence far beyond the
season. He left St. Louis after Leclerc but, determined, he
traveled light and fast to beat the trader to Bellevue. On the
way Leclerc hired three deserters from Cabanné's post, giving the Frenchman an opportunity to demand them as his
property and, at Bellevue, to seize them, force them to admit
what was already known, and been passed at Leavenworth,
that there was alcohol on the boat. Without legal power to do
more than report this, he sent Sarpy with a party and a cannon to force Leclerc's surrender of all his goods, to be carried
to the American Fur Company warehouse.

Furious, Narcisse Leclerc hurried to St. Louis to sue
the company and institute criminal proceedings against Cabanné. There was much publicity and some loud demands
that Astor's whole outfit be thrown out of the Indian country.

---

*The recipes varied some, actually and in tall tales. A Montana blend:

1 qt. alcohol	1 handful red pepper
1 lb. rank black chewing tobacco	1 qt. molasses, black
1 bottle Jamaica ginger	Missouri water as required.

The pepper and tobacco were boiled together. When cool other in-
gredients were added and stirred. As the Indian became drunk, more water
was added.

An upper Platte recipe:

1 gal. alcohol	1 handful red Spanish peppers
1 lb. plug or black twist tobacco	10 gal. river water (in flood)
1 lb. black sugar or molasses	2 rattlesnake heads per barrel

Variations in flavor might be a "brush" of *vermout,* wormwood of the
Plains or, for an occasional real beaver man, a castoreum, for the musky per-
fumish odor.

W. B. Astor, son of old John Jacob, wrote to Chouteau that it seemed, in case of defeat, he would appeal to the Supreme Court. But someone was more sensitive to the changing times, and compromised. Leclerc was paid $9,200, apparently chargeable to the Upper Missouri division of the company.

In 1832 Bill Sublette, at last in control of the Rocky Mountain Fur Company, with Campbell and the support of Ashley in Congress, and with, it was said, practically unlimited credit, undertook to challenge Astor on the Missouri, force him to buy out the company as he had Columbia and Pratte. In the spring Sublette moved up the river with the steamboat *Otto*, leaving parties to establish posts near practically every American Fur installation, eventually even near Fort Union, the very throne of McKenzie, King of the River. In retaliation McKenzie stirred up the wilder young warriors to raiding and horse-stealing, and ordered his clerks to pay the Indians any price, but get the furs, starve all these newcomers out. At the Mandan post beaver jumped to twelve dollars a skin, four times the usual price. Soon there were overtures to sell to him, which he ignored, but the home office was frightened, at least by the losses, and came to terms with Sublette and Campbell for one year, meaning permanently.

Angry, McKenzie tried to plan a more prosperous future. Liquor he must have against the Hudson's Bay traders, and to hold the Indians against any other newcomers. His supply was confiscated in 1833 but he had anticipated this and carried a still up the river, with all the grain he could buy around Bellevue. At Union he set up the still and although Mandan corn was limited in supply, it made a fine, sweet liquor, which fed no hungry women and children but piled up profit for Astor's company, as long as the distilling lasted.

In a way McKenzie's vanity hastened the end. The idea of this natural man, the American Indian, captured the imagination of the Romantics of English literature, fitting into the 18th-century dream of an ideal society. The travel accounts of life in the wilderness became a kind of enchantment for adventuresome young men of means, heightened by the romances of James Fenimore Cooper and his presence in London. By the early 1830's, many were turning their faces toward the trans-Missouri west, as Prince Paul did some years before, but with the promise of less hardship now that there were steamboats to this wilderness, and deep into her heart.

Americans too, were attracted, particularly the artist George Catlin, in fringed buckskin portraying Indians, many of them the important and pushing government-made chief-tains, and handling them with something of the aplomb he had learned painting portraits of prominent eastern politicians. He sent back letters, published in the New York *Commercial Advertiser,* publicizing the *Yellowstone*'s unique journey and the Missouri country and the remarkable people he pictured remarkably, stirring up an interest greatly to be shunned in fatter beaver times.

In 1833 Maximilian, Prince of Wied-Neuwied, whose scientific interests had already carried him into the Brazilian jungles, came to America with a young Swiss artist, Karl Bodmer, to study the American west and its inhabitants, particularly the Indian. Hurrying before the sweep of cholera in the east he went to St. Louis, planning to join one of the annual fur caravans to the Rockies. Clark, from whom he had to obtain a passport into the Indian country, and others, pointed out that the fur men avoided contact with Indian life, and that transporting his planned collections of flora and fauna would be difficult. They advised a visit to the American Fur Company posts of the Missouri by way of the annual steamboat.

Maximilian went up the river with McKenzie, spent two months on the Marias and a winter with the Hidatsas and Mandans, where he was later remembered for his faded velvet jacket and his exceedingly greasy buckskin pants, a pipe clamped between his toothless jaws, the young Bodmer, his pants smeared with paint, dapper beside him. Apparently no one listened to Maximilian's complaints.

"It is incredible how much the original American race is hated and neglected by the foreign usurpers," he wrote.

It must have given John Jacob Astor considerable pleasure, this hosting the Prince of Wied-Neuwied, his homeland, where his brother had been a farmer. He must have glowed under Maximilian's expressed gratitude, this poor butcher's son from Waldorf.

It was welcoming these velvet and buckskin visitors to Fort Union that pleased McKenzie so much. He extended himself for them and for a dozen others, and high-up company officials—entertaining here as he had seen it done with the Canadian companies. He couldn't resist showing off his post and his special pride, his distillery. There were protests, chiefly from competing traders, usually to Chouteau who pretended ignorance and talked vaguely of some experiments—testing wild pears and berries for wine, which he understood was not forbidden. He was certainly aware that distilled wine is not wine, and that the great vats contained corn.

McKenzie tried to save himself and the company by pretending he had merely transported the still for a friend up in the Red River colony and that he was experimenting a bit in the meantime with the native fruits. But news of his activities had reached Washington and the enemies of Astor. This, on top of the Leclerc and other instances of company lawlessness, endangered the trading licenses. Senator Benton interceded to save the American Fur Company but McKenzie had to be fired. He came down to St. Louis like any river pole man out of a job and went to Europe.

McKenzie may have been the King of the Missouri but since his appointment as governor of the Hudson's Bay Company in 1826, George Simpson had gradually become the "little emperor" of the fur trade and, through the extra-governmental powers of the company charter, the dictator of the Canadian northwest. He didn't make the wolverine policies against competition; those were long established against the Montreal traders and the North Westers, but he brought a new zest, a new ruthlessness to them as he turned his defense against the Americans. Every fur-bearer was to be hunted down, no seed left anywhere, the opposition undersold, driven out, with whisky wherever it was demanded. When one of Simpson's factors wanted to modify the policy a little he got a lecture from the governor. Opposition must be wiped out. For a while Simpson worked on a new plan—recruiting twenty-five Red River breeds for "voyaging, hunting and as required," but they were not too interested, and besides they might turn the same tactics against traders in their own region.

Even without the breeds, Simpson carried on his vigorous campaign, although Oregon was supposedly under joint administration with the United States. Any Americans who settled near a Bay fort were to be opposed by every resource, but there must be no violence attributable to Bay men. That would bring Washington protection for its traders, stir interest in the Oregon country. Indian raids were something else, and the Americans lost fur and men.

Simpson was increasingly cynical, with a low opinion of politicians, whose price might be anything from a few buffalo tongues to the promise of $100,000, but a price. American politicians all had their tag, he was convinced, and usually low. This opinion was probably not improved by Pilcher's offer, as a citizen of the United States, and an in-and-out Indian agent, to trade in the Missouri country for the Hudson's Bay Company.

Simpson had even less respect for Mexican officials or territory, but his men found little beaver there. It was true that the Americans carried on an active and profitable trade with Santa Fe but outside of the fur obtained along the route, from the Arkansas, say, beaver was not an important item. On October 24, 1834, the Missouri *Republican* reported that the company of traders to Santa Fe had returned. The party of 140 men with forty wagons left Santa Fe September 1, stopped at the rendezvous on the Red and arrived at St. Louis with, as nearly as could be ascertained, $40,000 in gold; $140,000 in specie; $15,000 in beaver; fifty packs of buffalo robes; 1200 pounds of wool and 300 mules valued at $10,000.

The report was probably salted a little with frontier hope but it showed the trend of the Santa Fe trade, a trade in money, with beaver and robes minor items.

The west was being trapped out rapidly now, and those men drawn to the beaver hunt went as to an aging coquette, often naive, or old-timers who clung to the memory of the glorious days as recently as Ashley's first rendezvous, less than ten years in time.

CHAPTER VII

"GONE" RENDEZVOUS, AND FOPPISH SILK

B Y THE end of 1832 Hudson's Bay officials considered the region between the mouth of the Snake and the Rockies a fur desert. Their harvest proved it, dropping from 2,099 large beaver or the equivalent in 1826 to 788 in 1832 and going down to 220 in 1835. Not that much of the whole Oregon country had ever been rich in fur, even before it was scurried over by Americans following a varied number of French and British—Bay, Montreal or North West— searching like hungry ants, smelling out the least cut or canyon for live water.

"We're goners, gone beavers—" some of the Americans said, men who had grown old in ten, twenty years, plodding over the country from the Kootenai to the Gila with little but broken dams now where water flowed at all.

With or without George Simpson, the end had been inevitable long before the turning of those first wheels up the Platte in 1824, even though only on a cannon. In 1830 Smith, Jackson and Sublette took ten heavily loaded wagons with five mules each to within fifty miles of the waters that flowed to the Pacific. Two years later Bonneville's wagons crossed South Pass to the Green. But the first settlers headed toward Oregon were not beaver men who suddenly found the steel jaws of their traps empty or traders with no furs but a party of greenhorn homeseekers escorted by Nathaniel Wyeth. Inspired by Hall J. Kelley, who had dreamed of an American Oregon since 1815 with all the intensity of the 17th-century searcher for the route to the western sea, Wyeth sent a ship around the Horn in 1832 and led his twenty-four hale young men overland westward. He planned to raise funds by some hunting and trapping on the way, to provide a cargo of furs for the vessel's return. At St. Louis he was surprised to discover the vast operations already carried on west of the mountains, operations growing all the twenty-two years since Henry planted his little post at the fork of the Snake.

Undaunted, Wyeth attached his tenderfeet to the Rocky Mountain Fur caravan carrying goods to the annual trader rendezvous. By the time they reached Pierre's Hole and had gone through a Blackfeet attack near there, the majority of his men were discouraged by the dangers still ahead and, turning back, lost seven, killed. With a handful of followers Wyeth went on to the Pacific, to find that his vessel had been wrecked on a reef, his cargo lost, and was graciously taken in by the Hudson's Bay men.

By 1834 Wyeth was back in Boston with big plans for fur posts, a salmon fishery and a solid colony. He started another vessel to Oregon and with a contract from Milton Sublette and Thomas Fitzpatrick to carry their goods of the Rocky Mountain outfit to the annual rendezvous, he returned to St. Louis. With him were two naturalists, Thomas Nuttall, who had been over much of the wilderness, and John K. Townsend, a newcomer, who, on Wyeth's advice, bought several pairs of buckskin pants, an enormous green blanket overcoat and a hard-crowned, wide-brimmed white wool hat to protect the skull and shade the eyes. Together the naturalists started out some days ahead of the party, to walk the first hundred miles or so, enjoying the river valley, pleased with flocks of the handsome green and red parrots (paroquets), going perhaps as far as the tower in the forest that, according to the Iowa legend, was formed by the dung of an ancient and gigantic race of buffaloes.

Wyeth's party also included the missionaries for the Nez Perces and Flatheads, the Indians hoping, with the white man's magic, to produce the guns, powder and other good things that the Iroquois hunters of the North West Company said were made by the power that came from the rituals in the white man's Book. But the magic of Jason and Daniel Lee and their helpers could not make the cows they drove walk fast, and Milton Sublette was in a hurry to get his goods to the rendezvous. There would be at least four other large caravans in the politically open region of Ham's Fork, in dually controlled Oregon: another for the Rocky Mountain Fur Company under Milton's brother Bill, and surely the American Fur, Hudson's Bay, Bonneville and who could tell what others, besides perhaps one from Santa Fe.

April 28 Wyeth and Sublette headed out on the trail, the seventy men, including twenty old-timers, in double file behind them, each rider leading two horses that carried two eighty-pound packs apiece, the missionaries with their cattle driving the flanks. The camp was divided into messes of eight men each, with a tent and a daily ration of flour, and other essentials in addition to pork until fresh meat came in. Evenings the packs were arranged in a sort of fortification—a large hollow square, the horses picketed inside to graze, with a walking guard of six or eight men outside.

Unfortunately Milton Sublette's diseased * leg grew worse from the saddle and he had to return to St. Louis, but urging speed on Wyeth to keep ahead of Bill with the other Rocky Mountain goods. The missionary cows set the pace and so late one evening Wyeth was passed, with only a fresh trail in the morning to show that Bill Sublette was now in the lead. The delay, aggravated by the thought of generally officious preachers, angered the brigaders but Jason Lee, large-bodied and calm-faced driver of cows, managed to avoid open clashes with the rough, and rough-tongued, fur

---

* From an old injury. After an amputation or two Milton Sublette accompanied the 1836 caravan west in a cart drawn by two mules, and died in pain at Fort Laramie in December.

men except when he protested against Sunday travel. The two Lees were the first emigrants to stop at the post Bill Sublette's men were building as a trading house on a fork of the North Platte, to become Fort Laramie, the great center on the busy emigrant path to Oregon.

There must have been many things that the naturalist, Townsend, had never seen before: the dry-land whirlwinds, zigzagging here and there, tossing up dead leaves and grass; heat dances; mirages of snowy mountains that rose beyond shimmering lakes where there were only dusty plains; thunderheads in magnificent mushrooms of white to deepest black climbing toward the zenith, flickering in pinkish lightning or breaking into blinding bolts that shook the earth, the thunder crashing and rolling. And between there would be the burning sun and stinging dust, black sometimes, or gray-white in blistering alkali, the clouds of buffalo gnats, fine as dust, itching and swelling the eyes. Townsend found much to record on the trip, everything from swallows and sagehens, which were remarkably tame, but bitter roasted, to antelope, elk, buffalo and bear, and rattlesnakes, but there seems to have been little sign of beaver on all that long river route most of the way to Ham's Fork in 1834. It was an ominous portent.

The first sight of the rendezvous was the usual shadowing of horse herds on the ridges on both sides of the hidden river valley and off toward the hazed and barren mountains beyond. Strings of meat hunters were coming in off the plains and on the left another trader caravan drew near, jackasses braying, while half a dozen small parties gathered, trappers with packhorses, the men perhaps afoot, an occasional glint of sun on a gun ready across the arm. Thin layerings of smoke clung to the brush and timber along the bluffs, rising from clusters of tents and tipis out along the grassy bottoms and among the scattered brush and cottonwoods. These were groups of traders and trappers, company and freemen, and the various and often more orderly Indian camps. Horsebackers tore this way and that along the river, guns boomed with the slow flowering of powder smoke in the still afternoon air, punctuating the faint sound of whoops and yells. Plainly alcohol had already arrived.

It was not a happy arrival for Nathaniel Wyeth. The loss of Milton Sublette had seemed sad enough. Now, without him for protection, Bill Sublette had managed to pressure or bribe Fitzpatrick into repudiating the contract for the goods Wyeth brought, leaving him not only with an unpaid freight bill but with a whole trading stock on his hands and no connections, trapper or Indians, but having to compete with all the powerful organizations left in the western fur business.

One of Milton's experienced hands had selected a camp ground. Here the packs were dropped, the horses turned loose to roll ease into their sore and sweaty backs, and then start off to water, the herders following. And while tents and tipis went up in a row and the bales were piled for counters and sitting space, Wyeth and some of his men rode out along the other camps, the leader probably trying to get a reconsideration from Bill Sublette, who was moving over from the Green River, or to make a deal elsewhere.

The rendezvous gathered swiftly now: Fitzpatrick in, but evasive with Wyeth; Cerré bringing Bonneville's goods; the Hudson's Bay outfit; and the American Fur too, but with a surprisingly small stock, drawing guarded looks from some, knowing and uneasy looks. There were Indians everywhere, fifteen hundred, Anderson, a tenderfoot with Bill Sublette, wrote later, but perhaps his enchanted eyes and the constant shifting, the coming and going, led him into exaggeration. Large parties of Bannocks, Shoshonis, Nez Perces and Flatheads were there, and Crows, Sioux and smaller groups from other tribes, even several Hidatsas from the Missouri with products to trade to far Indians, but mostly to lure some back there for the corn, and the feasts of squash and melons now that they no longer came to the big fair with beaver and horses to trade for white-man goods. It was a disturbing time for the Hidatsas, and back home a medicine man was fasting on a hill overlooking the Old Crossing of the Missouri, a place still sacred to them.

The trappers and mountain men were a tangle-bearded lot—some Americans, more French-Canadians and breeds, with a scattering of Kanakas, all in soiled and greasy buckskin pants, most of them looking like any Indian except that an Indian would be smooth-faced, his hair usually neat. Certainly many were more earth-footed than their constant associates in one tribe or another, perhaps through the curious accommodations demanded of the outsider by wilderness life. Some even carried medicine bags for their mystical powers as they carried the little bags of castoreum for its power over the beaver.

After more than two hundred years the fur fair, the rendezvous, was little changed from that of the Richelieu or Montreal. There was no gray of Recollets or black of Jesuits here, the two Lees dressed much like any trader's followers, and certainly nobody in the satin small clothes or silver buckles of the governors. The nearest to this was Capt. William Drummond Stewart, Scotsman like many others here, but no canny trader. He was a romantic sightseer at his second rendezvous and to become Sir William some day. Otherwise there was little change since 1623 beyond better guns, perhaps, and less fur.

The Indians went from camp to camp for the welcoming treat, not a drinking match, *une boisson,* but a burning cup. Slow-paced, dignified old chiefs with their blankets about them had come first, followed by their powerful war leaders and painted braves. But as they moved on and on, the dignity melted, moccasins began to stumble, the wearers to whoop and fight and finally fall in sickness and stupor. There were still a few more responsible leaders, refusing all alcohol, and many women with small ones on their backs out to see what else was offered. Youths ran here and there, but some of the pretty young girls still kept modestly to the moccasin heels of the old women as they went from booth to tent to tipi. Excited, they spoke softly among themselves, considering the goods offered: powder, lead and bales of tobacco; boxes of hatchets, knives and awls; bolts of calico, red and yellow and black; strouding, flannel and silks in reds and blues; all displayed to the brilliant sunlight of day or the evening candles of buffalo tallow often stuck into bull horns hung point down from tent and tipi poles. There were boxes of paint and vermilion too, and hanks of beads, great clumps of necklaces of every color; clusters of bracelets, brass armbands and hawkbells; bolts of ribbon and even some lace, not much, but a little for the special favorite of some mountain man who still carried the memory of a woman in laces, far away.

There were foods too, coffee, with tea for those from the British trade regions; hard brown lumps of sugar and perhaps raisins dried on the stem.

But always there was the whisky, frontier whisky made from alcohol and water, first usually a gift round to make good will and rekindle the craving, particularly at Sublette's camp, and more for the chiefs in conferences. Later, when paid for by the Indians, there was often tallow in the bottom of the cup, to make it less, and more and more water from Ham's Fork. Sold in quantity it was often $3 a pint and more. Tobacco, very rough and inferior, brought $2 a pound, these and all other things usually to be paid for by the counters the Indians received for furs and robes still in the old unit of made-beaver.

The missionaries and some of the visitors in fringed buckskin were astonished and horrified by what Jason Lee called the sins that kill, the infidelity and gambling, drunkenness and fornication, with none to protect or to police the region. He had the urge to preach a sermon to the hundreds of white men but knew that none would listen. Once, for a few moments, he was pleased to hear the Indians sing what sounded faintly like a hymn, but then they built a fire and began a war dance, in which white men joined. He was probably mistaken; all Indian dances seem war dances to the tenderfoot, the greenhorn in Indian country. He might have caught sight of a scalp dance for some Indian killed on the way to the Fork, or there, but what he saw was probably one of the dozens of show-offs and social dances of the tribes. There was, however, a great deal of trade in women and maidens for goods, particularly whisky. Townsend was at least impressed by the "available loveliness of the Nez Perce maidens," and so was Anderson, but he seems to have been more startled to see them sit their horses astride. This was not side-saddle country, or a side-saddle time.

There was horse racing, with high bets, as usual, and other gambling, particularly the hand game among the Indians, and buffalo chases over the sun-burnt prairie, horse trading, and pasture changing, as well as formal camp moves. One day a grizzly bear charged through the rendezvous, probably as alarmed as all the people who fled until a Flathead ran out and killed him. Another time a Nez Perce brought a buffalo bull charging through Bill Sublette's camp. He had promised to entertain Bill's guests and this was his attempt—whooping, everybody running out to see, and help fill the bull full of arrows and lead, the body left to wash down the river.

There was much drunkenness among the white men and breeds, and as much fighting and other violence by them as by all the Indians together. The more sober might be cursing the Blackfeet, who had attacked parties around the rendezvous of 1832 up at Pierre's Hole, in what they considered the fringes of their country. Men were killed there and since, good men, who knew the west. Even Bill Sublette had stopped an arrow with his shoulder, and others had dropped their bones in quiet, remote places since, to bleach among the weathered remains of the beaver. The wary and experienced Jedediah Smith was gone too, caught stooping to drink from a hole dug in the bed of the dry Cimarron. Comanche arrows succeeded where a hundred others had failed.

Although the skies were clear and high over Ham's Fork, with noise and boisterousness up and down the stream, there was caution among the traders. Some of their lesser men, particularly the mixed-bloods, were sent out to visit with the trappers and Indians at their fires, acting lonesome for companions, looking, estimating, coming back, perhaps shaking their heads, particularly those from the Indian camps. The bales of furs seemed small, very small.

As the trappers and Indians traded out their harvest, the competition grew, not only for beaver and otter, marten and mink, but lesser hides. Even robes became desirable, bulky as they were to move the far distance overland to St. Louis, and deer and elk—anything, practically. Gradually even the newcomers suspected that the rendezvous was not to be as great as they had expected. Plainly Bill Sublette had pushed Fitzpatrick to refuse the goods he had ordered through Wyeth because they were not needed, would be surplus. Yes, the high, prosperous days of 1832 and 1833 were done, the fabulous ones of the 1820's only a legend—those days when Ashley's men, without a rival at the gatherings, roared and swaggered across beaver land.

Outside rumors thickened the gloom. Some had heard of the elegant French duke, who, it was said, had lost his beaver hat in China and, unable to have it replaced, had a similar one made of silk. The first sight of the hat on his return to Paris sent the fops into cries of envy. Immediately they began to discard their beavers and ordered hats of silk. The usual great train of little imitators, the sheep of fashion, followed. The fad reached London, Montreal, New York and Canton. No more beavers.

To this the rendezvous added another rumor, one proved truer, at least in source. Ever since the difficulties of the American Fur Company with the government over Leclerc, and then McKenzie's still, bolstered by the decrease in beaver, both supply and demand, Astor was moving to unload, to sell out. The name, American Fur Company, went with the Western Department to Pratte, Chouteau and Company, the Great Lakes region to Ramsay Crooks and associates. From now on John Jacob Astor, as banker for the new owners, would take a safe profit, free from blame or loss.

But not all the disasters reached the rendezvous from far off. The campaign begun by Astor's McKenzie and Chouteau against the Opposition, the Rocky Mountain Fur Company, ended here. The price-cutting, ruthless trade practices, incitement of Indians, subsidization of upstart rivals, bribery, piracy and general corruption, as well as suspicion of murder, most of which the Rocky Mountain outfit also attempted, but with limited resources and experience, had succeeded against them. The company went under there around Ham's Fork, only a real whooping distance from Ashley's great rendezvous nine years ago on the Green. True, Fitzpatrick and Bridger, counting Milton Sublette in, made an attempt to carry on as a company because there was nothing else for them. Somehow most of the money they would make would flow to Bill Sublette and his partner, Robert Campbell, both finally rich men. Wyeth, not without bitterness, wrote Milton Sublette: "You will be kept as you have been, a mere slave to catch beaver for others."

The new company lasted only a short time and then Fitzpatrick and Bridger, better men than any that Astor or Chouteau ever developed, finally became company hired hands.

But there at Ham's Fork Wyeth had had the satisfaction of seeing some of the men who cut his throat bleed as deeply. When the rendezvous began to break up, he headed for the west coast, taking the goods left on his hands over toward the Snake where he started Fort Hall as a trading post to dispose of them. Townsend wrote of the going, of Stewart's departure westward, to the "lower country from which he may probably take passage to England by sea," and of the missionaries in the same party. Jason Lee, who had come to bring the white man's Book to the Nez Perces and Flatheads, didn't even visit the camp of the tribes at the rendezvous. Instead the Lees became colonizers in the Willamette valley. There, more interested in agricultural development than in missions, they helped start the Oregon fever.

As the dust settled on Ham's Fork, the wolves and magpies picked the last bones of the camp grounds and finally the grass thrust exploratory spears through the worn earth. Some memories of things done there were less easily healed. A few people had died, of violence and sickness and age, as happens. The Flatheads, instead of obtaining a missionary with a new vision for the new times, lost their oldest man there, a man said to be almost a hundred years of age. Bissonette, one of the Pratte and Cabanné young men sent to feel out the amount of fur in the Indian camps, had evidently sat with him a while. Too ancient to ride a saddle, he had been dragged there in the skin travois of the crippled and the feeble. But he could still move his long bony fingers in sign talk.

"When I was a boy it was a good time," the old Flathead said. "Then the white man came like no wild creature comes—straight into the village, to eat the beaver, all the game, with his iron teeth. Now my grandchildren and their grandchildren are hungry."

The man stopped a long time, his hands down, his eyes closed in the gray and wrinkled face, like an old piece of stained and weathered rawhide lost among the rocks. Then his arms lifted, and he began to talk again. "If the lion or the grizzly come so into the village, he go down under arrow and spear—"

Now the old man was dead, as so many other things died there at the rendezvous. The creature most desperately involved in the developments of that year knew nothing of them, knew nothing of the curious and far distant luck that was to save him from extinction. True, the beaver would still be pursued, still have to flee the steel trap in his waters, the gun among the breaking ice of spring, but never again from men with the hunger of gold seekers burning within them. Now he was no longer the prey, and the pay, of the beaver men and their empire-hungry rulers as he had been for 225 years, from the mouth of the St. Lawrence, from Hudson's River and Bay, westward to the Pacific and back to the remote pockets of the mountain country.

Not that the spread of empire was done. It moved on over the path the beaver men had already worn up the

Platte River and along the west-flowing streams, aimed, like a spear, into the flank of the Oregon country. Thousands, tens and many hundreds of thousands would follow its direction, driven less by an appetite for gold, glittering or soft, than a hunger—the ancient and universal hunger for a home.

NOTES

(Only significant new material and some sidelights on controversial points are mentioned here)

BOOK ONE

Chapter I, *Bearded Men and Summer Fairs*—page 3

Every tribe of American Indians seems to have had stories of pre-Columbian visits from white men, generally unnamed, as were many who came later. Apparently the first to the upper Plains in the 17th century from the east were roaming coureurs de bois, the very first probably the two men called Long Beard and Little Beard. My father obtained their story the summer of 1884 from the Indians who were his friends because he repaired their old guns, made powder and lead available, spoke French and wore a beard. In my childhood I heard about those two men who came to the early Minitari, the Hidatsas from the descendants of French-Indian traders and from aged Sioux like Bad Arm and White Eye. In 1931 I checked on the stories, particularly through the ninety-year-old He Dog, brother of Bad Heart Bull, the Oglala Sioux historian. He Dog was the brother-chieftain of Crazy Horse and fled to Sitting Bull in Canada until 1881.

From Sandoz interview with He Dog at Oglala, S. Dak., June 30, 1931; John Colhoff, interpreter:

"Have you heard of the People of the Beards?"

"Yes, there is a story told of the Village of the Bearded Men . . . in the time of my grandfathers . . . perhaps 300 years ago. . . . Before we crossed the Missouri we hunted that far for buffalo. (In Buffalo Shield's time.) Two . . . from our band were visiting the Missouri village when a runner came. . . . A great thing that they had heard about for years had happened. Two men with beards . . . carrying thundersticks . . . were in the village above. . . . A big party went up to a feast to meet these bearded men and our men went too . . . and saw them, one short, the other about the size of the Indians. They shot off [the thundersticks] to show how the sound was made."

313

He Dog said he talked over the Village of the Bearded Men with an old Mandan captive among the Sioux who recalled the story of the Bearded Ones coming to the Hidatsas, the tribe up the Missouri above the Mandans. The white men had remained; one died in a storm, but his grandson became an early trader for the Hudson's Bay Company and was known as Young Beard to the Indians. Because the white-man names of these early French among the Hidatsas have been forgotten, if ever told, their identification has been impossible even through the 1630-1650 records of Three Rivers and Montreal available in the Dominion Archives at Ottawa.

For Etienne Brule: Consider Le Jeune, Champlain and Cranston. The latter suggests there had been some Jesuit editing of Champlain's *Voyages* to heighten the condemnation of Brule, that the explorer-trader probably did not care if his employee neglected fast days and took up with Indian women. The Dominion Archives offered no definite material on the end of Brule. Charlevoix apparently thought the *Jesuit Relations* could be followed in too close detail. Certainly the purpose of any report or relation is pertinent consideration for the researcher.

Chapter III, *Paddle and Portage*—page 45

For possible Spanish penetration of the upper Plains see Bandelier's three volumes of *Documents,* as well as Bolton and Morfi. This is worth long study. Bancroft doubted any Spanish expeditions into Wyoming before 1650, but there seems more to be said now.

BOOK TWO

Chapter II, *The Romantic Explorations*—page 103

Henry E. Haxo, considered expert in 18th-century French, says that Brymner's translation of Verendrye's journal is faulty. Burpee is apparently based on Brymner. David Thompson reported that the Hidatsas had lived at the Rapids of the Saskatchewan, northward of Eagle Hills. In 1797 he found their upper village on the Missouri at 47° 25′ 11″. The Chippewas mentioned an ancient Hidatsa village site at the mouth of North Antler Creek and another in the Turtle Mountain region. The Indians that Verendrye called Mantannes must have been the Hidatsas above Old Crossing of the Missouri, near 48°, on a point washed away before 1800. Haxo and Libby place them there, as well as the early Cheyenne and Sioux accounts. See He Dog, Notes, Book One, Chapt. I.

Chapter III, *Gentlemen Adventurers*—page 129

For traders west of the Rockies in the 18th century: Material gathered by Thomas Fitzpatrick, mountain man and Indian agent, to establish early tribal territorial claims for the Indian peace treaty of 1851, included an interview with a man variously called Sassaway, Salsaway and Salaway, born 1780 in a Nez Perce village of an Indian woman and a French trader living there—a bear hunter later mauled by a grizzly. Grown, the son had married into the northern Oglala Sioux and knew much of late 18th-century Indian occupancy in the mountains at the head of the Missouri and the upper Yellowstone. (From a tape-tied sheaf of Fitzpatrick interview notes, 1848-1850, in AGO Records, 21st and Virginia Avenue, Washington, D. C., 1937-38.)

See also account of Frank Salaway, Allen, S. Dak., born 1828 in Idaho, of a mixed-blood mother. Her father, a Frenchman, was a noted bear hunter mauled by a grizzly.—Ricker Interviews, Nebraska State Historical Society, Tablet 48, page 1.

Chapter IV, *A Daring Race of Scots*—page 146

H. Bedford Jones questions the complete veracity of Alexander Henry, the Elder, as historian.—Michigan Historical Society *Collections* XL.

BOOK THREE

(Much throughout this section comes from Sandoz Sioux and Cheyenne interviews covering the 19th century on the Plains.)

Chapter III, *The Winter of the Explorers*—page 217

Meriwether Lewis—possible Indian descendants: Son—Turkey Head or Zombie.—*Annals of Wyoming*, XXII; grandson—Waneta, also called Martin Charger. Some thought this was the grandson of Reuben Lewis, brother of Meriwether. Charger played an important part in 1862 in the rescue of women and children captured by the Santee Sioux at Shetek Lake, Minn.—Doane Robinson, *History of South Dakota*, Vol. 1, p. 210. (Letters from possible relatives of Charger are exceeded in number only by those I receive from inquirers about George Armstrong Custer's Cheyenne son. MS.)

William Clark—supposed Indian son: "Capt." Clark, aged, sandy-haired half-breed, is in the Nez Perce camp in Indian Territory.—New York *Times*, Nov. 8, 1878.

Chapter VII, *"Gone" Rendezvous and Foppish Silk*—page 301

For ancient Flathead chief who died at the rendezvous of 1834: Bissonnette, trader, said he accompanied Atkinson's expedition in 1825, worked for Pratte, Cabanne & Co., married into Smoke's Oglala Sioux, and was at the 1834 rendezvous where he visited with the old Flathead who died there.—Ricker Interviews, Nebraska State Historical Society, Tablet 2, loose pages in the back.

SELECTED BIBLIOGRAPHY

General Works

Bailey, Vernon. "Beaver Habits, Beaver Control and Possibilities of Beaver Farming." U. S. Dept. of Agric. *Bulletin* 1078.

Bancroft, Hubert Howe. *The Works of . . .* (Western History, Alaska to Patagonia) 38 vols. (San Francisco, 1883-90).

Bureau of American Ethnology *Reports* and *Bulletins*. Washington, D. C.

Burpee, Lawrence J. *An Historical Atlas of Canada.* (Toronto, 1927).

Martin, Horace T. *Castorologia; or the History and Traditions of the Canadian Beaver.* (Montreal, 1892).

Morgan, Lewis H. *The American Beaver and His Works.* (Philadelphia, 1868).

Parkman, Francis. *France and England in North America.* 7 vols. (Boston, 1874-92).

Thwaites, Reuben Gold, (ed.). *The Jesuit Relations and Allied Documents, 1610-1791.* 73 vols. (Cleveland, 1896-1901).

————. *Early Western Travels, 1748-1846.* 32 vols. (Cleveland, 1904-07).

Warren, Edward Royal. "The Beaver, Its Works and Its Ways." *Monograph*, Am. Soc. of Mammalogists, No. 2. (Baltimore, 1927).

BOOK ONE—SOFT GOLD

Atherton, Wm. Henry. *Under French Régime, 1535-1760.* 3 vols. (Montreal, 1914).

Bancroft, Hubert Howe. *History of Nevada, Colorado and Wyoming 1540-1888.* 1890.

Barbeau, C. Marius. *Huron and Wyandot Mythology.* Anthrop. Ser., Canada, XI, 1915.

Beltrami, G. C. *A Pilgrimage in Europe and America . . . Discovery of Mississippi. . . .* 2 vols. (London, 1828).

Champlain, Samuel de. *The Works of . . . 1604-16.* H. P. Biggar (ed.). 6 vols. (Toronto, Champlain Society, 1922-36).

Charlevoix, Pierre F. X. de. *History and . . . Description of New France.* 6 vols. (New York, 1866-72).

316

Chesnel, Paul. *History of Cavelier de LaSalle, 1643-1687*. (New York-London, 1932).

Cluny, Alexander. *Hudson's Bay Company*. (London, 1769).

Colby, Chas. W. *Canadian Types of the Old Régime, 1608-1698*. (New York, 1908).

Cooper, John M. "Snares, Deadfalls and Other Traps of the Northern Algonquin and Northern Athapascans." Catholic University of America, *Anthrop. Ser.* V.

Cranston, J. T. *Etienne Brule: Immortal Scoundrel*. (Toronto, 1949).

Delanglez, Jean. *Some LaSalle Journeys*. (Chicago, Inst. Jesuit History, 1938).

Dollier, François de Casson. *A History of Montreal, 1640-1672*. R. Flenley (trans. and ed.). (London-Toronto, 1928).

Fisher, Raymond H. *The Russian Fur Trade, 1550-1700*. (Berkeley-Los Angeles, 1943).

Freytas, Father Nicholas de. *The Expedition of Don Diego Dionisio de Peñalosa . . . 1662*. J. G. Shea. (New York, 1882).

Hackett, Charles W. "New Light on . . . Peñalosa. . . ." *Miss. Valley Hist. Review*. VI-3.

Haley, J. Evetts. "L'Archeveque, the Outlaw." *The Shamrock*, Fall 1958.

Hunter, Martin. "Indian Mode of Hunting." *Forest and Stream*, July 30, 1898.

LaSalle, Cavelier de. *. . . Discoveries and Voyages . . . 1679 to 1681*. Melville B. Anderson (trans.). (Chicago, The Caxton Club, 1901).

LeBeau, C. *Avantures du Sr. C. LeBeau . . les Sauvages del l'Amerique Septentrionale*. 2 vols. (Amsterdam, 1783).

Le Jeune, Father Paul. ". . . Relations." *Jesuit Relations*. V-VIII, X.

Lescarbot, Marc. *A History of New France*. H. P. Biggar (ed.). 3 vols. (Toronto, Champlain Society, 1907-14).

Margry, Pierre, *Découvertes et éstablissements des Francais dans l'ouest . . . l'Amerique . . . 1614-1754*. 6 vols. (Paris, 1876-86).

Montanus, Arnoldus. *Die Unbekante Neue Welt. . . .* (Amsterdam, 1673).

Parkman, Francis. *The Old Régime in Canada*. IV (Boston, 1874).

———. *Count Frontenac and New France under Louis XIV*. V. 1877.

Pepper, Geo. H. and Gilbert L. Wilson. "A Hidatsa Shrine. . . ." *Memoirs*, Am. Anthrop. Assoc. II, 1907-15.

Phillips, Paul Chrisler, *The Fur Trade*, 2 vols. (Norman, 1961).

Potherie, Bacqueville de la. *Historie de l'Amerique Septentrionale*. 4 vols. (Paris, 1722).

Radisson, Pierre E. *. . . Peter Esprit Radisson . . . Travels and Experiences . . . 1652-1684*. (Boston, Prince Society, 1885).

Read, John M., Jr. *. . . Inquiry concerning Henry Hudson . . .* (Albany, 1856).

Rich, E. E. (ed.). *Minutes of the Hudson's Bay Company, 1671-1674.*
    Hudson's Bay Co., Ser. V. (Toronto, Champlain Society, 1942).

Rutledge, John Lester. *Century of Conflict . . . between the French
    and the British in Colonial America.* (Garden City, 1956).

Shea, John G. "The Bursting of Pierre Margry's LaSalle Bubble." U. S.
    Catholic Hist. *Magazine,* 1892-93, IV.

Steck, Francis Borgia. *Marquette Legends.* (New York, 1960).

Strong, W. D. "From History to Prehistory in the Northern Great
    Plains." Smithsonian Misc. *Collections,* Vol. 100.

Thwaites, Reuben Gold. "The French Régime in Wisconsin, 1634
    through 1784." State Hist. Soc. of Wisc. *Collections,* XVI-XVIII.

Upham, Warren. "Groseilliers and Radisson, the First White Men in
    Minnesota, 1655-56 and 1659-60." Minn. Hist. Soc. *Collections,* X.

Wheat, Carl I. "The Spanish Entrada to the Louisiana Purchase, 1540-
    1804." *Mapping the Transmississippi West,* I. (San Francisco,
    Inst. of Hist. Cartography, 1957).

Will, Geo. F. and Thad C. Hecker. "The Upper Missouri . . . Abori-
    nal Culture . . ." N. Dak. Hist. *Quarterly,* II-1, 2.

BOOK TWO—THE RISE OF THE COMPANY

Bell, Chas. N. "The Earliest Fur Traders on the Upper Red River . . .
    1738-1810." Hist. and Sci. Soc. of Manitoba, *Transactions.* n.s.I.

——. "The Journal of Henry Kelsey, 1691-1692. IV.

Bryce, Geo. "Life of John Tanner." Hist. and Sci. Soc. of Manitoba.
    Transactions. XXX, 1887-88.

——. "Souris (Mouse River) Country . . ." XXIV.

——. *The Remarkable History of the Hudson's Bay Company . . .
    The French Traders of North-Western Canada and of the North-
    West, XY and Astor Fur Companies.* (London, 1900).

Cocking, Matthew. "An Adventurer from Hudson's Bay; Journal . . .
    1772-1773." L. J. Burpee (ed.). Royal Society of Canada, *Proceed-
    ings* and *Transactions,* Ser. 3, II, Sec. 2, 1909.

DeLand, Chas. E. "The Aborigines of South Dakota." S. Dak. Hist. *Col-
    lections,* III-IV.

Dugas, Geo. *The Canadian West: Its Discovery by . . . Verendrye.
    . . . Development of the Fur-Trading Companies . . . to 1822.*
    (Montreal 1905).

Dunn, Wm. E. "Spanish Reaction against French Advance . . . 1717-
    1727." Miss. Valley Hist. *Review,* II-3.

Ellis, Geo. E. "The Hudson's Bay Company," 1-80. *Narrative and
    Critical History of America.* Justin Winsor (ed.). VIII. (Boston,
    1889).

Haxo, Henry E. "The Journal of La Verendrye, 1738-39." N. Dak. Hist.
    Quarterly, VIII-4.

Hearne, Samuel. *A Journey . . . by Order of Hudson's Bay Company for the Discovery of Copper Mines, a Northwest Passage, etc. . . . 1769 . . . 1772.* (London, 1795).

Hendry, Anthony. "York Factory to the Blackfeet Country: the Journal of . . . 1754-55." L. J. Burpee (ed.). Royal Society of Canada, *Proceedings* and *Transactions*, Ser. 3, I, Sec. 2, 1907.

Henry, Alexander (the Elder). *Travels and Adventures in Canada and the Indian Territories . . . 1760 and 1776.* (New York, 1809).

Houck, Louis. *The Spanish Régime in Missouri.* 2 vols. (Chicago, 1909).

Hudson's Bay Company. *The Governor and Company of Adventurers of England Trading into Hudson's Bay . . . 1670-1920.* (no author). (London, The Hudson's Bay Co., 1920).

James, Thomas. *Three Years among the Indians. . . .* M. M. Quaife (ed.). (Chicago, 1953).

Jay, John. *The Peace Negotiations of 1782 and 1783.* N. Y. Hist. Soc. 1884.

Kellogg, Louise Phelps. Summary, U. S. Factory System for Trade with Indians, Introduction. Wisc. Hist. *Collections*, XX.

Kelsey, Henry. *The . . . Papers.* Intro. by Arthur C. Doughty and Chester Martin. (Ottawa, 1929).

Lahontan, Louis Armande de Lom d'Arce. *New Voyages to North America.* 2 vols. R. C. Thwaites (ed.). (Chicago, 1905).

La Verendrye, see Verendrye.

Libby, O. G. "Some Verendrye Enigmas." Miss. Valley Hist. *Review*, III-2.

Lowie, Robert H. ". . . Social Organizations and Customs of the Mandan, Hidatsa and Crow Indians." Anthrop. *Papers*, part 1, Am. Mus. of Nat. Hist., 1917.

Masson, L. R. *. . . Journals, Narratives, Letters . . . North West Company.* 2 vols. (New York, 1960).

Mooney, James. "Calendar History of the Kiowas." Bu. of Am. Ethno. *17th Report,* part 1.

The Museum Review. State Hist. Soc. of N. Dak. 1946-47.

Nasatir, A. P. *Before Lewis and Clark, Documents . . . of Missouri, 1785-1804,* 2 vols. St. Louis Hist. Docs. Foundation, 1925.

Oliver, Edmund H. (ed.). "The Canadian Northwest" (Documents) 2 vols. *Publications* of the Canadian Archives, No. 9.

Pond, Peter. "Journal, 1740-1775." Wis. Hist. Soc. *Collections*, XVIII.

Rich, E. E. *The History of the Hudson's Bay Company, 1763-1870.* II. (London, Hudson's Bay Record Society, XXII, 1959).

Rogers, Robert. *Journal of Major. . . .* Frank B. Hough (ed.). (Albany, 1883).

Schoolcraft, Henry R. *. . . Expedition through the Upper Mississippi. . . .* (New York, 1834).

Spinden, H. J. "The Nez Perce Indians." Am. Anthrop. Assoc. *Memoirs,* II.

Sturgis, William. "The Northwest Fur Trade and the Indians of Oregon Country, 1788-1830." *Old South Leaflets,* gen. ser. IX-219.

Tabeau, Pierre-Antoine. *Tabeau's Narrative of Loisel's Expedition to the Upper Missouri.* A. H. Abel (ed.). (Norman, 1939).

Thomas, A. B. (trans. and ed.). *After Coronado: Spanish Exploration Northeast of New Mexico, 1696-1727.* Documents, Archives of Spain and Mexico. (Norman, 1935).

———. "The Massacre of the Villasur Expedition. . . ." *Nebraska History,* VII, 1924.

Thompson, David. *Narrative of His Explorations . . . 1784-1812.* J. B. Tyrrell (ed.). (Toronto, Champlain Society, 1916).

Verendrye, Pierre Gaultier de Varennes de la. *Journals and Letters of . . . and His Sons.* L. J. Burpee (ed.). (Toronto, Champlain Society, 1927).

Wallace, Joseph, *The History of Illinois and Louisiana under the French Rule. . . .* (Cincinnati, 1893).

Wallace, W. S. "The Pedlars from Quebec." Can. Hist. *Review.* XIII-4, 1932.

Wedel, Waldo R. "Cultural Sequence in the Central Great Plains." Smithsonian Misc. *Collections.* Vol. 100, 1940.

BOOK THREE—THE FIERCER RIVALRIES

Barker, Burt Brown. *The McLoughlin Empire. . . .* (Glendale, 1959).

Bell, Chas. N. "Journal of Alexander Henry (the Nephew) to . . . the Pacific, 1799 to 1811 . . ." Hist. and Sci. Soc. of Manitoba, *Transactions,* XXXI.

Brackenridge, Henry Marie. "Journal . . . up the . . . Missouri. . . . 1811." Thwaites . . . *Travels,* VI.

Bradbury, John. "Travels in the Interior of America . . . 1809-12." Thwaites. . . . *Travels,* V.

Catlin, George. *The North American Indians.* 2 vols. (London, 1851).

Chittenden, H. M. *The American Fur Trade. . . .* 2 vols. (Stanford, 1954).

Clark, William. . . . *Journals of the Lewis and Clark Expedition, 1804-1806.* 8 vols. R. G. Thwaites (ed.). (New York, 1904).

Clarke, Chas. G. "The Roster of the Expedition of Lewis and Clark." Ore. Hist. *Quarterly,* XLV, 4.

Franchère, Gabriel. *Narrative of a Voyage to the Northwest. . . .* 1811-14. M. M. Quaife (ed.). (Chicago, 1954).

Galbraith, John S. *The Hudson's Bay Company as an Imperial Factor, 1821-1869.* (Berkeley-Los Angeles, 1957).

Gass, Patrick. *Gass' Journal of the Lewis and Clark Expedition* (from 1811 ed.) (Chicago, 1904).

Gregg, Josiah. *Commerce of the Prairies.* . . . (1831-39). (Norman, 1954).

Larocque, François Antoine. "The Journal . . . to the Yellowstone, 1805." Ruth Hazlitt (trans. and ed.). *Sources of Northwest History* XX. Missoula.

Lewis, Capt. Meriwether and Sergt. John Ordway. "The Journals of . . . the Expedition . . . 1803-1806." M. M. Quaife (ed.). Wisc. State Hist. Soc. *Collections,* XXII, 1916.

Mackay, James. "Extracts from Capt. McKay's Journal . . ." (including Evans'). M. M. Quaife (ed.). State Hist. Soc. of Wisc. *Proceedings,* 1915.

Matthews, Washington. "Ethnography and Philology of the Hidatsas . . ." U. S. Geol. and Geog. Survey, Misc. *Publications.* VII, 1877.

Maximilian, Prince of Wied-Neuwied. *Travels in the Interior of North America.* . . . 1832-34. Thwaites. . . . *Travels,* XXII-XXIV.

Newhouse, S. *The Trapper's Guide.* (Wallingford: Ct. 1867).

Pattie, James O. *Personal Narrative.* . . . *From St. Louis . . . to the Pacific.* . . . (1824-30). Thwaites. . . . *Travels,* XVIII.

Payette, B. C. *The Oregon Country under the Union Jack.* (Montreal, 1961).

Porter, Kenneth W. *John Jacob Astor, Business Man.* 2 vols. (Cambridge, 1931).

———. "John Jacob Astor and Lord Selkirk," N. Dak. Hist. *Quarterly,* V, I.

Ross, Alexander. "Adventures of the First Settlers on the . . . Columbia River . . . Pacific Fur Company. . . ." (1810-14). Thwaites . . . . *Travels,* VII.

Russell, Carl P. "The Guns of the Lewis and Clark Expedition." N. Dak. *History,* XXVII, 1.

Sandoz, Mari. *Love Song to the Plains.* (New York, 1961).

Taylor, James. "Lord Selkirk . . ." Hist. and Sci. Soc. of Manitoba, *Transactions.* XXXVI.

Thwaites, R. G. "American Fur Company Employees, 1818-19." State Hist. Soc. of Wisc. *Collections,* II, 1892.

Townsend, John K. "Journey Across the Rocky Mountains to the Columbia River . . . 1834." Thwaites. . . . *Travels,* XXI.

Watkins, Albert (ed.). "Missouri River Fur Trade, 1808-1861" from Missouri *Republican,* etc. Nebr. State Hist. Soc. *Publications,* XX.

Wyeth, Nathaniel J. "The Correspondence and Journals of . . . 1831-36 . . ." *Sources of the History of Oregon,* I. (Eugene, 1899).

INDEX

(Subheads of events arranged chronologically, items alphabetically)

Aguilar, 100, 101

Alcohol, 158, 211, 223; HBC* and NWC, 273; at rendezvous, 305-06
  Brandy, at summer fairs, 18-20; among Montagnais, 36, 49; Indians ask ban, 52; Hurons, 55; outlawed, 58-60; Brandy Parliament, 77-8; at posts, 86; in Fox war, 93 Rogers, 152; on *Beaver,* 267
  Rum, to the west, 150, 152, 157, 267
  Whisky, outlawed, 294-96; recipes, 295

Algonquin monster, see windigo

American flag, 205, 207, 220

American Fur Co., 149, 259, 291, 295, 296-98, 303, 305; sold, 309

American Revolution, 156, 163

Americans, 28, 161-62, 165, 181, 195, 241, 245, 257, 274, 299

Anderson, 305, 308

Anglo-American treaty, 160

Annapolis valley, 21, 23

Archeveque, Juan, 98-100

Arms (early), to upper Missouri, 5; Champlain's, 32; Christianized Indians, 54

Ashley, Wm. H., 285-89, 292, 296, 309-10

Astor, John Jacob, 149, 165, 259-60, 267, 270, 288, 291, 296, 298, 309-10

Astor, W. B., 296

Astoria, 260, 263, 267, 270

Atkinson, Gen. Henry, 278-79, 281-282, 290

Avantures du Sr. C. Le Beau, 26

Barrington, Lord, 151

Basques, 29, 31

Bearded Men, 3, 178, 314

Beauharnois, Viceroy, 112, 114, 117, 125, 137

Beaver, The, 70

Beaver, Astor ship, 267

Beaver Club, 162

Beaver Hall (NWC), 162

Beaver Meadows, 28, 203

Beavers, 4, 67-73, 129-30, 185, 222, 256; castoreum, 47-8, 68, 133; curatives (general), 48-9; dams, 67-9, 71, 73; fat, 49; felting, 27; fur, 16, 27, 46, 67; giants, 25-6, 186, 278; hide, 49, 137; history, 22-3; houses, 69-70, 71, 73; hunting and trapping, XIII, 10-1, 73, 131-36, 276; legends, 22, 23-7; meat, 13, 45-6; pelts, 14, 21; skins, 46, 48, 136 (see also castor)

Beaver trade, 14-5, 16, 47, 49, 52, 57, 61, 67, 95, 108, 114, 137, 148,

* Abbreviations for fur companies.

157, 161-62, 182, 230, 243, 256, 296, 301, 304; glut, 85-6; HBC, 91-2; made-beaver, 137-38, 307; price, 40; Sioux, 90-1 (see also hats)
Bellevue, 294-96
Beltrami, G. C. A., 27
Biddle, James, 279
Biddle, John, 279
Bienville, 89, 95
Big Horn Basin, 88
Blackfeet Wall, 242, 255, 262, 284
Boats, batteaux, 190; canoes, 189-190; *canotes de maitre,* 189; keel-boats, 191; pirogues, 190, 201-02; steamboats, 278-79
Bobé, Father, 106
Bodmer, Karl, 297
Boisson (big drunk), 295, 306
Bonneville, Capt. B. L. E., 301, 305
Bourgmont, Etienne Veniard de, 93, 95, 108
Brackenridge, Henry, 262, 266
Braddock, ambushed, 142
Brandon House, 173
Brandy, see alcohol
Brandy Parliament, 77
Brebeuf, Father, 42, 44, 55-6
Bridger, Jim, 285, 292, 310
British trade, goods, 53; traders, 165, 218, 290
Brule, Etienne, 33, 36, 38, 40-1, 42, 49, 314; rumors of torture and death, 42-3
Buffalo, dance, 225; medicine, 227; tolling, 225-26
Buffaloes, 9, 13, 25, 63, 206, 217, 221-23, 225, 227, 229, 231, 240-41, 302, 308; robes, 293, 300; frost cloud, 221
Burr, Aaron, 243

Cabanné, Jean P., 294-95, 311
Cabots, 29
Cadillac, 79
California, 85, 89, 199
Campbell, Robert, 285, 296, 310
Canada, 60, 66, 76, 86, 95, 104-05, 259, 270, 273, 299; surrender to British, 142; Franklin wants it for U.S.A., 160

Carondelet, Gov.-gen., 165, 167-69, 171, 192
Cartier, 28, 29, 129
Carver, Jonathan, 153, 200
Castor, 22, 45; *castor canadensis,* 129; *castoroides,* 22
Catlin, George, 294, 297
Cerré, 164, 166, 277, 305
Champlain, Samuel de, 30-1, attacks on Iroquois, 32, 34, 38; explorations and trade, 37-8, 44, 49, 50, 56, 75, 79, 81
Charbonneau, Toussaint, 213-14, 223, 228-29, 231-32, 262, 264; descendant of, XIII
Charlevoix, Father, 81, 107
Chauvin, Pierre, 29, 30, 193
Chicory (blue lettuce) 155, 189
China passage, 28, 30, 37, 82, 88, 94, 104, 111, 278
Chouteau, Auguste, 149, 159, 164, 166, 173, 194, 258-59, 274, 290
Chouteau, Pierre, 149, 159, 164, 166, 244, 246-49, 251, 274
Chouteau, Pierre, jr., 293, 298, 309, 310
Clamorgan, Jacques, 164, 166, 169, 171, 173, 193-94
Clark, George Rogers, 199, 200
Clark, William, 200-02, 205, 207-08, 211, 213, 215-16, 221, 223, 225, 228-31, 242, 249, 315; Supt. of Indian Affairs, 279, 282, 294, 297 (see also Lewis and Clark Expedition)
Clarke, John, 267-69
Clyman, James, 285, 289
Cocking, Mathew, 155
Coffee, 155, 189 (see also chicory)
Colbert, Finance Minister, 60, 62, 77-8
Collot, 194, 195
Colonization, 29-31, 37, 39, 41, 50
Colter, John, 70, 244-46, 251-54
Columbia Fur Co., 292, 296
Company of Explorers of the Upper Missouri: see Missouri Co.
Company of Gentlemen Adventurers: see Hudson's Bay Co.
Company of the Habitans, 53, 55, 60

Company of the Indies, 108
Company of New France (Hundred Associates), 41, 50
Company of the West, 60
Cooper, James Fenimore, 297
Corry, Thos., 155
Council Bluffs, 204, 292
Coureurs de bois, see Fur trade
Creeks, see Rivers and creeks
Croghan, George, 151
Crooks, Ramsay, 251, 260-61, 263, 265, 269, 291-92, 309
Cumberland House, 155, 174

D'Abbadie, Dir. Gen. (La.), 149
Darac, Ensign, 89
De Caën brothers, 39-41, 43
D'Eglise, Jacques, 165, 166
Degie, 212
Delassus, Lieut, Gov. (La.), 193, 196-97
De L'Isle, 88
Denonville, Marquis, 80, 90
De Noyan, 88
De Peñalosa, Gov., 63, 64
De Soto, Ferdinand, 82
De Troyes, 80
Dictionary of Chemistry, Watts, 48
Distillery (McKenzie's), 296, 298
Dobbs, Arthur, 138-39, 154
Dog Lodge (or Tipi) Butte, 175-77, 217
Donnes, 59
Dorion, Pierre, 206, 243, 246-47, 260, 266, 268-69
Drake, Sir Francis, 85, 109, 128
Drouillard, Geo. 198, 221, 228, 244, 254
Ducharme, 157
Duluth, Daniel Greysolon, Sieur Du Lhut, 74-76, 78-80, 90
Durantaye, 80
Dutch traders, 28, 34, 37, 39, 44, 52-3
Du Tisne, 95, 96

Eagle Hills, 180
Eagle Pass, 64
El Quartelejo, 63, 98, 101
Embargo Acts, 270

England, 41, 49, 66, 85-7, 89, 96, 104, 140-41, 146, 160, 171
English traders, 28-9, 34, 37, 39, 44, 52, 74, 107 (see also HBC)
Evans, John, 169-74, 192, 215

Factories (fur posts), 257
Father of Beavers (Quahbeet), 25
Feltmakers Co., 138
Ferdinandina, 74
Finlay, François, 154
Finlay, James, 154, 162
Finlay House, 144, 154, 155
Fitzpatrick, Thos. 285, 289, 292, 302, 305, 309, 310
Five Villages (upper Missouri), 168, 171-73, 177-81, 209, 215, 217, 225, 235, 242, 264, 266; earth houses, 3, 204, 224
Folly of the Woods, 113, 186
Forts and posts (trading and military): Albany (N.Y.), 77; Atkinson, 281, 286, 292; Beauharnois, 110; Benton, 284; Blondishes, 150; Cedar Island, 194, 207, 254, 266; Detroit, 93, 157; Frontenac, 79; George, 270; Gibraltar, 272; Green Bay, 151; Hall, 310; Kaministiquia, 113; Laramie, 304; La Reine, 118, 124, 141; Leavenworth, 294-95; Lisa, 245; Mandan, 213, 217; Manuel's, 245; Maurepas, 114-15, 141; Michilimackinac (later Mackinac), 74, 85, 87, 90, 92, 104, 115, 151, 153-154, 157, 159, 161, 164, 173; Mount Royal, 36; Natchitoches, 94; Niagara, 79, 80; Orleans, 108; Prince of Wales, 139; St. Charles, 114-15, 117; St. Louis, 89; St. Pierre, 113; Tecumseh, 294; Union, 296, 298; William, 272, 290; York, 137, 141, 143, 151, 155 (see other fur places under name, and in key to endpaper map)
Fothergill, Charles, 26
France, 23, 49, 61, 66, 79, 85-7, 89, 95, 96, 104, 106, 108, 140, 146, 148, 151, 156, 160, 181, 195-96
Franceway (trader) 144, 155

Franklin, Benjamin, 160, 164
French Indians, 38, 60, 80-1, 87
French Republic, 163, 194
French Revolution, 163
French traders, 28-30, 34, 41, 74, 89, 98, 103, 141; fermiers, 60-1 (for chronological penetration, see Champlain, Brule, Bearded Men, Nicolet, Duluth, LaSalle, Du Tisne, St. Denis, etc.)
Freytas, Father, 64
Frobisher brothers, 155, 161-62
Frontenac, Gov., 76, 78, recalled, 79; returned, 82, 85-6
Fur trade, 15, 20, 50, 53-4, 57, 60, 76-7, 82, 85-6, 92, 106, 140, 156, 163, 193, 205, 221, 229-30, 234, 272; contraband, 59; cordelles, 190; price control, 166; smuggling, 86; *employees:* coureurs de bois and bush lopers, 17, 19, 20, 31, 39, 48-50, 53, 55, 57, 58, 74, 76, 78, 82, 85, 87, 93, 95, 104, 109, 141, 148, 185; engagés, 59; voyageurs, 17, 109, 185, 187-92, 198, 201-02 (see also Beaver trade)

Gage, Gen., 151
Gallut, 94, 95
Galvez, José de, 195
Garraway's Coffeehouse, 92
Garza, Juan de la, 63, 64
Gass, Sgt., 221
Gayoso de Lemos, 192
Georgian Bay, 38, 54
Germany, 23, 66, 92
Glass, Hugh, 289
Gold, 29, 107-08, 154
Gomara, 29
Gonner, Father, 110
Gooseberry, Mr., see Groseilliers
Graham, HBC factor, 141
Grand Banks, 29
Grand Portage, 153, 155, 162, 235
Grant, of NWC, 172, 173, 272
Gratiot, Chas., 164, 166
Graveline, 212, 231
Green Bay, 44, 50, 159
Gregory, John, 154, 162

Greinyea (Grenier), 212
Grenoble (with Brule), 39
Greysolon, Chas. (brother of Duluth), 75
Groseilliers, Medard Chouart, 57-8, 64

Hats, beaver, 49, 62, 85, 92, 163; silk, 309
Hatters' Guild, 27
Hearne, Samuel, 70, 155
Hendry (or Henday), Anthony, 141
Heney, 194
Hennepin, Father, 74-5
Henry IV, France, 29, 111
Henry, Alexander, 149-50, 152, 161-62
Henry, Alexander (younger), 26, 271
Henry, Andrew, 249, 252, 254-55, 262, 263, 284-89
Hippocrates, 47
Hoback, 264, 268
Hochelaga village, 28, 30
Horses, 102, 114, 119, 127, 178, 180, 201, 215, 236, 308 (see also Sioux Winter Counts)
Hudson, Henry, 37
Hudson, Henry, of Muscovy Co., 37
Hudson's Bay, 67, 91-2, 105, 187
Hudson's Bay Co., 64, 67, 75, 82, 91-2, 104, 115, 137-45, 150, 152, 154-57, 161, 167, 172-74, 187, 211, 214, 217-18, 228, 240-41, 243, 251, 257, 270-74, 284-88, 290, 292-93, 298-99, 301-03, 305; challenge to charter, 105; challenge met, 106; Dobbs challenge, 139; Gentleman Adventurers, 129-45
Huguenots, 29, 36
Hundred Associates, 41, 50, 52, 53, 60
Hunt, W. P. (of Astorians), 260-61, 263-67, 269-70, 278, 290
Huronia, 54

Iberville, 87, 89
Illinois, 44, 89, 148
Immell, Michael, 254, 284
India, passage to, 29, 37

Indian calendar: Moon of Cherries Ripening, 240; Moon of the Trading Fair, 233

Indian: *chiefs* (made), 203, 205-07; medals, 210, 220; *council*, 203, 205, 207; *games*, 223; la crosse, 55; ice hockey, 55; *legends*, 23-6 (see also windigo, giant beavers, etc.); *produce*, see items or tribe; *religion*, 25, 32; calumet, 62; medicine bags, 49; bundles, 133; war medicine, 228; *trading fairs*, 63, 74; Hidatsas, 233, 236-239; *war*, against Iroquois, 32, 34, 38; against Hurons, 55, 57; against Lachine, 80-1; *war captives*, cannibalism, 33, 42, 56, 186; torture, 32-3, 35, 42, 56; slavery, 89, 95; *women*, 42, 216, 221, 241, 306-07; Hurons, absolute power over men, 137; Matrilinear system recognized by U.S.A., 272

Indians: Bad Arm, 313; Bad Heart Bull, 313; Big White, 210-11, 243, 246-47, 249; Black Bird, 169, 204; Black Cat, 215; Crazy Horse, XV, 313; Battiste Good, 159; He Dog, 313-14; Horned Weasel, 219; Le Borgne, 231, 236-37, 239-240, 243; Little Raven, 213; Man, Enemy Is Afraid of His Horse, 80; Man, Enemy is Afraid of His Dog, 80; Mitain, 281; Ochagach, 110, 113; Red Calf, 237-38, 240; Red Fish, 240; Sacajawea, 262; Sitting Bull, 313; Tacchigis, 110; White Eye, 313; White Wolf, 220

Indian tribes: Algonquins, 18, 25, 28, 32, 34, 40, 42-4, 46, 49, 52, 57, 59, 126, 181, 187; Apaches, 63, 97-8, 101, 148; Arikaras (Rees), 108-9, 148, 166, 168-9, 171, 209, 214-15, 244, 247, 264, 266, 285-8; Assiniboins, 62, 104-105, 114-16, 119-20, 141, 153, 158-59, 174, 176, 178, 198, 213, 215, 217-18, 227, 230, 237, 244, 293; Athapascans, 18, 126; Bannocks, 234, 305; Beaver People,

25; Blackfeet, 49, 70, 141-42, 147, 155, 178, 220, 234, 237, 242, 245-246, 251, 252-55, 264, 266, 273, 278, 284-85, 293, 302, 308; Bow Indians, 126; Catatouch, 268-69; Cheyennes, 43, 49, 221, 243; Chippewas, 26, 75, 116, 118; Clatsops, 242; Comanches, 63, 95, 108, 147-48, 197; Crees, 75, 104-05, 114-16, 141, 153, 174, 215; Crows, 234, 236, 238-40, 243, 245-46, 305; Fall Indians (see Hidatsas); Flatheads, 234, 245, 303, 305, 308, 310-11; Foxes, 93; Gros Ventres, 180, 254; Hidatsas (Village of Bearded Men), 118, 167, 171, 173, 177-81, 209-10, 213, 215, 219, 222, 228, 235-36, 239-40, 250, 273, 297, 305, 313-14; Horse Indians, 127, 293; Hurons, 14-5, 32, 34, 38-43, 49, 52-9, 81, 104; Illinois, 93, 108; Iowas, 193, 302; Iroquois, 14, 16, 18, 23, 25, 32-5, 38, 40, 44, 49, 52, 54-7, 60, 74-6, 79-81, 85-7, 93, 303; Jumanos, 97, 147; Kansas, 89, 95, 97, 193; Kiowas, 51; Laytanes (nomadic Apaches) 148; Little Cherry, 126; Loup-Pani (see Pani); Mandans, 51, 158, 166-68, 170-71, 178-181, 209-10, 213-15, 218-25, 228, 231, 244, 246, 250, 297; Mantannes, 116, 119-20, 122-25; Metchegamias, 108; Micmacs, 23, 131; Minitari, (see Hidatsas); Missouris, 93, 95, 108; Montagnais, 19, 30, 32-4, 36, 42, 49; Navajos, 96; Nez Perce, 159, 234, 267-8, 305, 308, 310; Nipissings, 181; Omahas, 167, 169-70, 192-193, 281, 202, 204; Onondagas, 38; Osages, 93, 95, 108, 148, 194, 197-98, 258; Otos, 95, 108, 169, 203, 269; Ottawas, 58-9, 62; Ouachipouennes, 114, 116; Padoucas, 95; Panis, 89, 95, 192-93 (Loups, 193); Panis-Noirs, 148; Panis-Piques, 148; Pawnees (Panys) 62-3, 96-101, 165-66, 193, 203; Piegans, 174, 178, 293; Poncas, 167, 193; Senecas, 80, 90;

Serpents, 126; Shoshonis (see Snakes); Sioux, 7, 18, 43, 46, 57, 62-3, 67, 75-6, 80, 90-1, 105, 107, 110, 114-16, 120, 126, 141, 152, 166, 168-71, 173, 176, 178, 205, 207-08, 215, 218-19, 221, 244, 246, 251, 266, 287, 305; Sioux of the West, Plains Sioux, Tetons, 166; Underground Sioux, see Mantannes; Snakes, 126, 205, 214, 229-30, 232, 234, 236, 243, 252, 305; Taos, 63; Utes, 205; Wattassoons, 171; Weepers (Assiniboins), 118; "Welsh Indians," 170; Wichitas, 148; Winnebagos, 43, 51

International ambition, XIV, 66-7, 88-9, 91, 104, 107-08, 140-43, 149, 299

Iroquois Confederation, 38

Irving, Washington, 260

Jackson, David, 285, 292, 301

James II, 80, 146

James, Thomas, 250-53

James Bay, 137

Jay, John, 160

Jefferson, Thomas, 181, 196, 199, 200, 210, 219, 232, 243, 258-59, 282

Jemeraye, 112-15

Jesuit Relations, 42, 129

Jesuits, 20, 41, 56, 59, 67, 76-7, 79, 82, 93, 107, 306; dissolved, 151

Jolliet, Louis, 59, 74, 77, 82, 105

Joques, Father, 52

Jusseaume, Rene, 167, 171-72, 174, 178, 202, 212-13, 215, 221, 223, 229, 246-48

Kanakas, 306

Kaskaskians, 198

Kelley, Hall J., 302

Kelsey, Henry, 105, 139-40, 141

Kertk (Kirk) brothers, 41

Kuhl, 129

Labbadies, 164

Labaddie, Sylvester, 249

La Barre, Lefevre de 79, 80

Lachine, 78, 80-2, 149, 190

Laclede, Pierre, 149, 164

LaFrance, 217, 220, 223

Lahontan, Baron de, 88, 106

Laidlaw, William, 292

Lakes: Big Stone, 76; Cedar, 155; Champlain, 32, 159; Devils, 118; 122, 180; Erie, 93; Great Lakes, 16, 156-57, 159, 160; Huron, 25, 93; Little Slave, 67; Michigan, 23; Nipigon, 110; Okoboji, 74; Ontario, 38, 80; Rainy, 106, 113; Superior, 23, 26, 39, 52, 58, 67, 72, 88, 107, 110, 113, 150, 162; Winnipeg, 88, 104, 106, 114; Lake of the Woods, 114

L'Allemant, Father, 56

La Marque, 117-18, 122-23

LaMothe-Cadillac, 93

Langlade, Chas., 127, 142, 159

La Novë (or Nouë) 106, 111, 113

Laroque, François, 217-18, 220, 230, 235-42

LaSalle, Cavelier de, 74-5, 77, 79, 82, 87, 89, 96, 98, 100

La Salle, Nicolas de, 89

Laval, Bishop, 76, 78

Leavenworth, Col. Henry, 286-88

Le Beau, C., 26-7, 68, 129

Leclerc, Giles, 268

Leclerc, Narcisse, 294-96, 298

Lee, Jason and Daniel, 303, 304, 306, 307, 310

Le Jeune, Father, 42-3, 50, 52, 60, 129

Leland, Charles, 25

Léon (captured Archeveque), 100

Le Page, 212

LeSueur, Pierre, 90

Lewis, Fielding, 200

Lewis, Meriwether, 196-97, 200, 205, 210, 212, 218-20, 225, 228-31, 242, 249, 259, 315

Lewis, Reuben, 249-51

Lewis and Clark Expedition, 196-197, 198-232, 235-36, 242-43, 246, 259, 264

Lewis and Clark Pass, 242

Liquor, see Alcohol

Lisa, Manuel, 193-94, 244-47, 249-255, 260, 270, 281-82, 284-85; overtaking Hunt, 262-65

Little Beard, 12, 151
Loisel, Regis, 194, 196, 207
Long Beard, 7, 8, 11-12, 14, 150
Long, Stephen H., 279-81, 283
Louis XIII, 41, 111
Louis XIV, 64, 77, 80, 82, 93, 111
Louis XV, 94, 106, 108, 111-12, 125
Louis XVI, 163, 166
Louisiana, French, 79, 87, 89, 95, 104-05; Spanish, 143, 147, 152, 163-64, 171; French, 181, 191-92, 195; American, 196, 199, 258, 282
Lucius III, Pope, 23
Lugtenberg, 88
Luther, Martin, 28

McClellan, Robert, 251, 160-61, 263, 265, 269
McCracken, Hugh, 174, 178, 209, 212, 218
McDonald, Crooked Arm, 241
McDonnell, 173
McDougall, Duncan, 260, 269
McGill, of Todd and McGill, 144
McGillivray, 161
McKee, Alex, 260
McKenzie, Duncan, 260, 267-69
McKenzie, Kenneth, 289, 292-93, 296, 297-98, 309
McKenzie, Roderic, 185
McLeod, Alex, 154, 162
McTavish, Simon, 161, 162

Macarty, 148
MacDonell, Miles, 272
Mackay, James, 167-71, 192
Mackenzie, Alexander, 128, 154, 162
Mackenzie, Chas., 217-20, 222, 230, 237, 260
Mackinac (or Michilimackinac) Co., 291
Madison, James, 200
Maisonneuve, founded Montreal, 52
Mandan dancing women, 180
Marest, Father, 89
Marquette, Father, 74, 82, 105
Maurepas, Minister of France, 111, 117
Maxent, Laclede and Co., 149

Maximilian, Prince, 51, 297, 298
Menard, 167, 177, 235
Menard, Father, 59
Menard, Pierre, 244, 247, 251-54
Menoah, 177 (see Menard)
Mexico, 28, 64, 96-7, 108, 197, 284
Michaux, Andre, 181, 199
Mines, 107; copper, 90; gold, 154; lead, 90, 159; silver, 94, 109
Minguez, Father Juan, 98, 100
Missionaries, 20, 37, 39, 41-2, 51, 54-6, 66, 77, 303
Missouri Co., 166-68, 170-72, 192-193, 249, 254, 262
Missouri Fur Co., 284, 285, 288
Missouri *Gazette,* 251, 278
Missouri *Republican,* 285, 299
Missouri Territorial Militia, 249
Mitche Amicks (giant beaver), 26
Monopoly trade rights, 108, 166, 193, 259
Montana, 154
Montanus, Arnoldus, 27
Montreal, 15, 20-1, 44, 52, 57, 60, 76, 80-2, 86, 114, 144, 146, 155, 156, 159, 161-62, 187, 195, 234, 270, 306
Moro, 194
Morrison, William, 244, 272
Mountains: Alleghenies, 151, Big Horns, 63, 241; Black Hills, 108, 196; Killdeer, 69; Rocky, 72, 108, 154, 167, 205, 227; Turtle, 118, 175-76; Wind River, 266
Mount Royal, 15, 28, 30-1, 36
Muscoy Co., 37

Nantes, Edict of, 29
Napoleon, 163, 181, 192, 199, 270
Naranjo, José, 98, 99
Navigation Acts, 156
Netherlands, 92
New France, 15, 29, 32, 37-8, 48-9, 53-4, 57, 59, 76-7, 85, 151, 165; capture and restoration, 41
New Mexico, 63-4, 89, 94-6, 196-97
New Orleans, 108, 147, 157, 163
New Spain, 63, 64, 94
New York *Commercial Advertiser,* 297
Nicolet, Jean, 42, 44, 49, 50

Nonintercourse Acts, 270
North West Co., 140, 145, 161-62,
    167, 168, 172, 174, 181, 209, 210,
    212, 217-18, 228-29, 232, 235,
    240-42, 257, 260, 267, 269-74, 284,
    288, 290-92, 299, 301, 303
Northwest Passage, 104, 139-40, 152
Northwest Treasury, 162
Nutria, 270

O'Fallon, Benjamin, 279, 285
Old Crossing (of Missouri), 13, 43,
    69, 122, 131, 167, 178-79, 222,
    234, 305
Old French House, 144
Ordway, Sgt., 207, 216
Oregon, 64, 299, 301-03, 304, 310
Otto (steamboat), 296
Overland Trails, 190; first wheels,
    289

Pacific Fur Co., 260, 269-70
Pacific Ocean, 85, 88-9, 110, 168,
    170, 196-97, 199, 200, 218, 242
Pangman, Peter, 162
Papins, 164
Parral, 97
Parilla, Capt. 148
Paul, Prince, 274, 288, 297
Peale, Titian, 279, 280
Pedlars from Quebec, 143, 155
Perraults, 164
Perrot, Nicholas, 79, 80, 82
Pierre's Hole, 302, 308
Pilcher, Joshua, 284, 287-89
Plains Indians, 25, 99, 203, 292
Pliny, 47
Poland, 23, 108
Pond, Peter, 156, 162
Portage of the Prairie, 118
Potts, 252
Prairie du Chien, 159, 193
Prairie fire, 210, 217.
Pratte, Bernard and Co., 293, 296
Pratte, Chouteau and Co., 309, 311
Pratz, Le Page du, 93
Primo (Primeau), Louis, 143
Provost, Etienne, 285
Pryor, Nathaniel, 246-48, 263

Quahbeet, 25
Quebec, 17, 19, 31, 33, 41, 57, 61,
    62, 76, 88, 90, 105, 156, 195
Quivera, 28, 63, 96

Radisson, Pierre, 57-8, 64, 91-2, 273
Raimbault, Father, 52
Recollect friars, 37, 42, 66, 74, 306
Reed, John, 268
Regnaut, Christophe, 56
Religious freedom, 29
Rendezvous of the Rockies: Ash-
    ley, 289; Pierre's Hole, 302, 308;
    Ham's Fork, 304-11 (see also
    Trader fairs)
Rezner, 264, 268
Richelieu, Cardinal, 41, 53
Rivers and creeks: Arkansas, 62,
    74, 87, 97-8, 148, 170; Assini-
    boine, 117, 181, 212, 271; Atha-
    basca, 191; Belle Fourche, 64;
    Bighorn, 64, 245, 289; Blackfoot,
    242; Boise, 268; Colorado, 64,
    85, 170; Columbia, 242-43, 260;
    Gallatin, 245; Garcitas, 89, 96,
    100; Gila, 301; Grand, 264, 266;
    Green, 301, 305, 310; Ham's
    Fork, 302-10; Henry's Fork of
    Snake, 254, 264, 266, 302; Horse,
    74; Hudson, 37; James, 205; Jef-
    ferson, 69, 252-54; Kaskaskia, 74,
    89; Knife, 212, 240; Kootenai,
    301; Little Missouri, 125, 212,
    228, 230, 240, 266; Little Powder,
    266; Long, 88; Lost, 70; Madi-
    son, 253; Marias, 242, 297; Min-
    nesota, 63-4, 90; Mississippi, 57,
    74, 79, 82, 87-9, 103, 157, 198-99;
    Missouri, 14-5, 79, 87-9, 94, 104,
    227, 229, 252, 279; Missouri nav-
    igation, 198, 201-03, 283; Mis-
    souri, Upper, 63, 95, 155, 205,
    209, 213, 233, 249 (see also Old
    Crossing); Moose, 137; Mouse
    (Souris), 118, 122, 175-77, 180;
    Niobrara, 62, 88, 148, 170, 206;
    North Platte, 74, 99, 304; Notta-
    way, 143; Ohio, 87, 198; Ottawa,
    16, 23, 38, 44, 52, 57, 112, 190;
    Pigeon, 113; Platte, 64, 98, 101,
    108, 148, 165, 169, 193-94, 203-04,

269; Portage, 236; Powder, 241; Rapid (see Niobrara); Red (of North), 103, 115, 117, 271-72; Red (of South), 87, 94, 300; Richelieu, 15, 32, 40, 306; Rio Brava (Rio Grande), 63-4; "River Michipi" 64; of Gros Ventres, 180; of Mantannes, 122; of West, 114; of Western Sea, 128; Running Water (see Niobrara); Saskatchewan, 124, 143-144, 154-55, 159, 162, 234; Saskatchewan (North), 174, 176; Saskatchewan Rapids, 180; Saskatchewan (South), 141; Smoky Earth, 194; Snake, 254, 264, 267; Souris (see Mouse); South Platte, 97-8; Spokane, 267-68; St. Lawrence, 12, 15, 19, 28-9, 37, 39, 41, 44, 51, 62, 87, 95, 107, 116, 144, 154, 156; Sweetwater, 269; Tongue, 241; White Earth, 10; Yellowstone, 63, 67, 125, 159, 191, 227, 242, 245

Rivet, François, 209, 220, 224

Robidoux, 164, 166

Robinson, 264, 268

Robson, Joseph, 139, 140

Rocky Mt. Fur Co., 285, 292, 296, 302-03, 309

Rocky Mt. Indians, 230, 234, 238

Rogers, Robert, 151-54, 161

Rogers' Rangers, 142, 151

Rose, Edward, 288-89

Rouville, Hertel de, 110

Russia, 37, 260

Russian Fur Co., 267

Russian settlements, 170, 244

Russo-American Co., 260

Sagard, Brother, 42

St. Barbe mines, 95

St. Charles, 262

St. Denis, 94, 96

St. Louis, 145, 149, 157, 164-66, 187, 192, 197, 211, 243, 300

St. Louis *Enquirer,* 280

St. Louis Missouri Fur Co., 249-50

Salaway, Frank, 315

Santa Fe, 63, 88, 96, 98, 100, 165, 197, 299-300, 303

Sarpys, 164, 193, 295

Saswaw (Saswee), 144

Schneider and Co., 164

Scots of Montreal, 146, 149

Selkirk, Lord, 271-74, 290-91

Semple, Gov., 272

Senex, John, 107-08

Serna, Capt., 99, 100

Seven Oaks, 272

Seymour, Samuel, 279

Silver sage tea, 229

Simpson, George, HBC, 298-99

Sioux Winter Counts, 207-08, 253; "Brought-Home-Assiniboin-Horses-Winter," 1709-10, 119; "Smallpox-Used-Them-Up-Winter," 1779-80, 159; "Winter-the-Black-Man-Froze-His-Man-Part" 1804-05, 223

Sirdaw, Francis, 144

Smallpox, 44, 55, 158, 193, 204, 214, 223

Smith, Jedediah, 285-86, 289, 292, 301, 308

Soft gold, 3, 28, 155

Solomon, 48

Songs, "The Black-eyed Marie whose Skirts Fly up," 192; "Old Joe with the Wart on His Nose," 192; "Three Little Ducks," 192; 261; Windigo, 186

South Sea passage, 165, 166, 195

South West Co., 291

Spain, 66, 87, 92, 96, 104, 108, 151, 160, 162, 164-65, 170-71, 181, 195-96, 199, 260

Spaniards, 28-9, 31, 63-4, 74, 85, 89, 93-4; penetration, 107-08, 148, 241

Spiesmachus (Spiesmacher), Capt., 153

Star Mound, 118, 180

Stewart, Wm. Drummond, 306, 310

Stuart, David, 260, 267

Stuart, Robert, 260, 267, 269

Sublette, Milton, 285, 292, 302-03, 305, 310

Sublette, William, 285, 289, 292, 296, 303-05, 307-10

Sulpicians, 20, 77

Sutherland, 173

Tadoussac, 29, 30
Taffe (tafia), 221, 224
Talleyrand, 194
Tall tales of the new world, 26-7, 278
Talon, Intendant, 61, 62
Tax on beaver, 53, 86, 164
Tea, 189
Texas, 63, 74, 82, 100, 284
Thomas, Dr., 250, 251
Thompson, David, 174-181, 260, 314
Three Forks, 69, 242, 245, 252-54, 284
Three Rivers, 38, 109, 110
Tobacco, 189, 205, 307
Todd, 144, 155
Tonquin (ship), 270
Tonty, 79, 80, 87, 93
Townsend, John K., 302, 304, 308, 310
Trading fairs, 215, 229, 236-38, 273, 289, 300; Richelieu, 15, 40; Montreal, 15, 18, 21, 234; Grand Portage, 153, 162, 235 (See also Rendezvous)
Trudeau, 165, 167
Truteau, 166, 167

Ulibarri, 89, 100
Ulloa, 85
Unicorn, 27, 187, 278
United States, 75, 160, 161, 199, 230; Army, 281; factory system, 257-258; Great Father, 203, 206, 211, 213, 249; Joint occupation of Oregon, 279
United States Expedition, 196
Upper Missouri Fur Co., 292
Utrecht, Treaty of, 103

Vallé, 254
Valverde, 96-8, 101, 108
Vandreuil, 106
Vasquez, Benito, 164, 166, 192-93

Verendrye, François, 125, 127
Verendrye, Jean, 113-16
Verendrye, Louis-Joseph, 122, 125, 127
Verendrye, Pierre, 114, 117
Verendrye, Pierre, Gaultier de Varennes, sieur de La, 109-27, 140, 141, 177, 213, 314
"Vermillion" sea, 85, 88, 102, 107
Vignau, 37
Vilemont, Louis, 195
Village of the Bearded Men, 14, 15, 18, 20, 26, 43, 51, 53, 69, 106, 234
Villasur, Pedro de, expedition, 98-101, 108, 165

Wars: Thirty Years, 53, 66; Queen Anne's, 92; French and Indian, 141; of 1812, 269, 270
Warfington, Sgt., 232
Western Engineer (steamboat), 278-81, 283, 293
Western Sea, search for, 88, 109-10, 167, 168, 198, 232
Whisky, 202, 258, 291; frontier recipes, 295
William III, 75, 92, 138
Wilkinson, Anne Biddle, 279
Wilkinson, Benjamin, 249
Wilkinson, James, 199, 243, 258, 279
Willamette valley, 310
Windigo (monster), 186-87, 192, 278
Winnipeg, 107
Wisconsin region, 103
Woolens, 27, 270
Wyeth, Nathaniel, 302-05, 309-10

XY, fur co., 242, 243, 260

Yellowstone (steamboat), 293-95, 297
Yellowstone Expedition, 292
York (servant of Wm. Clark), 200, 223, 225, 229

Key to numerals on map on pages ii–iii

BEAVER HARVEST OF NORTH AMERICA

◯ *FRENCH of New France and Louisiana, to 1760-63:*

1 1608 Quebec established as a fur post by Champlain.
2 1609 Champlain thrust his guns into an Indian attack on the Iroquois.
3 1610 Brule discovered L. Huron.
4 1611 Champlain built a fur post at Montreal.
5 1622-23 Brule reached L. Superior, some think the west end.
6 1630-40 Two Frenchmen arrived above Old Crossing of the Missouri at the Hidatsa village, thereafter called "The Village of the Bearded Men."
7 1654-61 Radisson and Groseilliers explored southwest of L. Superior and discovered the Mississippi. Groseilliers grew corn on Prairie Island, Radisson wintered with the Sioux.
8 1673 Marquette and Jolliet paddled down the Mississippi to below the Arkansas, where DeSoto had been in 1541.
9 1682 LaSalle reached the mouth of the Mississippi, took possession of the drainage basin for France, called it Louisiana.
10 1685 LaSalle landed at Matagorda Bay, built Ft. St. Louis, probably on Gracitas Creek, was killed 1687, probably near Navasota.
11 1688 De Noyon reached L. of the Woods.
12 1714 St. Denis, French trader, reached the Rio Grande.
13 1714-17 Bourgmont explored the Missouri to the Platte, some think as far as the mouth of the Little Missouri.
14 1720 French traders long among the Pawnees of the upper Platte.
15 1734 Jemeraye established Ft. Maurepas on L. Winnipeg, third of the Verendrye posts (St. Pierre on Rainy reactivated, St. Charles on L. of the Woods).
16 1738-39 Verendryes to Hidatsa, and Mandan, villages of upper Missouri.
17 1739 Mallet brothers and traders reached Santa Fe.
18 1742-43 Verendrye sons probably reached the Big Horns, buried a plate at the Missouri, found 1913 above Bad River.
19 1750, Hidatsa villages, site of ancient trading fair, now with both French and Hudson's Bay representatives present each summer.
20 1751 Ft. La Jonquierre built by Saint-Pierre for Verendryes, at foot of Canadian Rockies.

☐ *HUDSON'S BAY COMPANY, 1670, with trade and governmental jurisdiction over an indefinite territory, including the Bay drainage basin, much of it already posted by the French. They fought off French attacks on the Bay forts and expected the Indians to paddle and portage to them but the ubiquitous French intercepted the furs and finally the company sent out pedlars with their wares:*

1 1669 Ft. Charles at foot of James Bay, became Ft. Rupert.
2 1671-1684 forts at mouths of Bay rivers: Moose 1671; Severn 1680; Albany 1683; York, finally on Hayes.
3 1750's Saskatchewan River region, reached by trade drummers sent out with goods to tempt the Indians to York.
4 1754 Anthony Hendry to upper South Saskatchewan, to Ft. La Jonquierre region with presents and trade goods.
5 1772 Mathew Cocking, to Blackfeet country west of Eagle Hills.
6 1787 David Thompson wintered with Piegans on Bow River.
7 1793 Brandon House established on Assiniboine, outpost for trade south and southwest to Missouri and Yellowstone.
8 1811-12 Selkirk Colony, on 116,000 sq. mi. across North West Company access to western posts.
9 1817-18 Walla Walla (Ft. Nez Perce) on Columbia below mouth of Snake.
10 1834 Ft. Boise, on Snake River.

◻ *MONTREAL—dominated repossession and penetration after French expulsion 1760-63:*

1 1773 Ft. La Traite, on Churchill River, by Frobisher to cut into Hudson's Bay trade.
2 1780 and before. Nez Perce village west of Bitterroots. French trader called Sassaway, Salsway and Salaway, with Indian family.
3 1782 Upper Yellowstone, on old Indian trail along east slope of the mountains, challenging Spanish goods.

◻ *NORTH WEST COMPANY, 1784-1821, organized from the fluid alignments of the French and the later Montreal traders, largely Scots, increasing the pressure on the Hudson's Bay Company:*

1 1784 on, built up Grand Portage as a general summer rendezvous for all companies and free traders, drawing furs from as far as Oregon and the Arctic Circle.
2 1785 strengthened far west trade through such forts as Athabasca and English River.
3 1793 Alexander Mackenzie, first overlander to reach the Pacific north

of the Spaniards, (by Peace Pass, and then withdrew to XY Company 1798-1804).

4 1800 Des Moines River, controlling most of trade to there out of upper Mississippi River posts and Fond du Lac.

5 1807 Upper Kootenay House, built by David Thompson.

6 1813 Astoria, bought from Astor's representatives under pressure of War of 1812.

⬡ UNITED STATES (and the parent colonies of the north, the *trade centered at Ft. Albany, largely through Iroquois middlemen reaching beyond L. Superior by 1670*):

1 1686 Mackinac region, Rooseboom and McGregor opened trade but were seized by the French.

2 1747 Pickawillany. Colonials set up supply houses for wandering traders, supplied 50 in 1752, but sacked by Langlade in June.

3 1804 Santa Fe, La Lande trading party from St. Louis.

4 1805 Ft. Clatsop, built by Lewis and Clark near mouth of Columbia.

5 1810-11 Ft. Henry, by Andrew Henry on fork of Snake.

6 1811 Astoria, by Astor's Pacific Fur Company, sold to North West 1813.

7 1811 Ft. Okanogan by David Stuart, one of the *Tonquin* Astorians.

8 1825 South Pass opened to wheels by Wm. Ashley party, to become great emigrant gap to the west.

9 1825 Henry Fork of Green, first American rendezvous for wandering trapper brigades, by Wm. Ashley.

10 1834 Fort on the Laramie, by Campbell and Sublette, to become great outpost on emigrant trails.

△ SPANIARDS, *fur ventures north and northeast from New Mexico, and 1763-1802, from Louisiana. (Early disappointed gold seekers up along the Rockies and to the Black Hills turned to furs)*:

1 about 1598 Vincente de Zaldivar of Oñate's force camped near present Denver, named South Platte Rio de Chato.

2 1650 Bighorn River region, ancient ruins credited to Spaniards.

3 1720 Villasur's defeat by Pawnees with French guns, Archeveque, reported murderer of La Salle, among dead.

4 1780 Prairie du Chien, Spaniards from New Mexico appeared this far seeking trade and Indian allegiance.